The Dow Jones-Irwin Guide to
MODERN PORTFOLIO THEORY

The Dow Jones-Irwin Guide to
MODERN PORTFOLIO THEORY

ROBERT L. HAGIN

Vice President—Director of Quantitative Research
Kidder, Peabody & Co., Incorporated

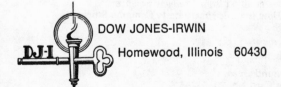

DOW JONES-IRWIN

Homewood, Illinois 60430

Some material in this book is adapted from *The New Science
of Investing* and from *The Dow Jones-Irwin Guide to Common Stocks.*

ISBN 0-256-02379-4 paperbound

ISBN 0-87094-181-X hardbound
Library of Congress Catalog Card No. 79–51785

Printed in the United States of America

3 4 5 6 7 8 9 0 K 6 5 4 3 2 1

To Susie

Preface

Modern portfolio theory (MPT)—which enables investment managers to classify, estimate, and then control the sources of investment *risk and return*—is revolutionizing traditional approaches to investment management. This book explains the evolution, meaning, and practical significance of MPT—sometimes referred to as the "new investment technology" or "modern investment theory."

The goal of the book is to provide a complete, accurate, and *easily understandable* explanation of MPT. The occasionally formidable math has been replaced by verbal explanations and easily understood diagrams. Technical definitions and equations are presented in footnotes for readers interested in such details. For the average reader, however, technical details have been kept to the barest minimum, and no special knowledge or educational level is assumed. The result is an accurate, yet easily understood, presentation of the subject matter of an advanced investments course.

The book is written for two broad groups of people—those who use professional investment management services and those who provide such services. The knowledge of MPT gained here should be helpful to pension plan sponsors, trustees, attorneys, and accountants, who are responsible for the selection and monitoring of professional investment managers. Similarly, the book is intended to give investment professionals a better understanding of the elements of MPT so that they can evaluate its usefulness to their clients.

Part One explains the three forms of the efficient market hypothesis and the theoretical foundation of MPT. Part Two explains additional building blocks: Risk, performance, expected returns, and diversification. Part Three develops the structure of MPT. Part Four describes tests of the theory, as well as the major extensions and applications.

Many people have contributed to the growth, interest, development, and practical use of MPT. Some of these contributors are acknowledged throughout the text, but references to numerous others have been omitted because of space limitations. My thanks to all of those who have shared their thoughts on this exciting subject both publicly through published articles and in personal conversations.

I would like to extend special thanks to Stefanie O'Keefe, who edited the manuscript; to Renee Romagnole, who assisted me with the research and typing; and to Laurel Mehl, who through the resources of the information center at the Girard Bank assisted with the bibliographic material.

Readers wishing to address comments, criticisms, and inquiries to the author are encouraged to do so. Every effort will be made to draft an individual reply to such letters. Correspondence should be addressed to:

Robert L. Hagin
Vice President
Director of Quantitative Research
Kidder, Peabody Co., Incorporated
10 Hanover Square
New York, NY 10005

Contents

PART III: MPT: CONCEPTUAL FOUNDATION

PART IV: MPT: TESTS, EXTENSIONS, AND APPLICATIONS

INTRODUCTION

Chapter 1

The changing investment environment

The investments profession is in the midst of a philosophical revolution. The "battle statistics" in this revolution are startling. Enormous sums of the new, or transferred, pension monies are being given to practitioners who use elements of modern portfolio theory (or, as it is coming to be known, MPT).

In the face of evermore stringent laws governing the deployment of pension funds, it is safe to assume that the decision to employ these MPT practitioners is not made casually. In fact, given the size and resources of the companies which employ pension managers with MPT expertise, it is clear that the decision is being made by some of the investment profession's most astute and well-educated clients. This increased use of MPT raises many questions—both outside and inside the professional investment management community.

Outside the professional investment community, there are hundreds of thousands of people with varying degrees of responsibility for the selection and monitoring of investment managers. These individuals are becoming increasingly aware of MPT and need to answer many questions. Will MPT provide better results? Is it imprudent not to employ an MPT-based approach? Inside the investment profession, in addition to questions regarding the usefulness and prudence of MPT, there is one more: Can firms compete effectively without an MPT-based approach?

The purpose of this book is not only to explain MPT but also to contrast MPT-based investment techniques with other investment philosophies. This comparative examination will answer the above questions as well as equip the reader to distinguish between true and pseudopractitioners, who are attempting merely to relable their old products "MPT."

3

A RAPIDLY CHANGING WORLD

We live in a rapidly changing world. In 1946, Presper Eckert and John Mauchly built ENIAC—the forerunner of today's electronic digital computers. With its 18,000 vacuum tubes, ENIAC weighed 30 tons, occupied 1,500 square feet, and could not operate without large-scale specialized power sources and air conditioning. Today, computer microprocessors are so small that it would take 40 such processors to cover a standard postage stamp. More importantly, when powered by energy cells the size of a shirt button, modern microprocessors possess more computing power than the early room-size computers.

In October 1957, the USSR announced to a stunned world that it had launched an earth-orbiting satellite—Sputnik I. In 1969, Neil Armstrong set foot on the surface of the moon and, after space walks by other members of the crew, returned safely to earth.

In 1952, Harry Markowitz [185][1] published a paper succinctly entitled "Portfolio Selection." This paper was the catalyst in an unbroken stream of ideas—both pre- and post-Markowitz—which have found practical application in what is now called *modern portfolio theory*, or more typically, MPT.

INVESTING: SIMPLE OR COMPLEX?

Investing is at one and the same time both simple and complex. The simplicity of stock market investing was aptly summarized by Andrew Tobias when he wrote,

> . . . there are just two ways a stock can go: up or down. There are just two emotions that tug in those opposite directions: greed and fear. There are just two ways to make money in a stock: dividends and capital gains. And there are just two kinds of investors in the market: the "public," like you and me; and the "institutions," like bank trust departments and mutual funds and insurance companies. It's the amateurs against the professionals, and it's not clear who has the advantage." [267, p. 68]

From this perspective, investing is very simple. Anyone with enough money can purchase a share of common stock. Further, because of the long-term underlying growth of the economy, the odds are good that this share of stock will prove

---

[1] Bracketed numbers refer to bibliography at end of book.

to be a good investment. In fact, research which will be discussed later has shown that roughly three out of four randomly selected investments, held for randomly chosen lengths of time, have been profitable!

Such "success" is often attributed to the "process" used to select the investment. Conversely, if the investment proves to be a poor selection, such "failure" is often attributed to the fact that the "market" was bad. Such investors explain their successes by saying, "XYZ Widget went up because it was a good company," and rationalize their failures by saying, "ABC Devices went down because of the market."

An important but subtle factor is at work in such explanations of investment performance. First, these investors are aware of the distinction between risk and return. Second, they recognize the important distinction between security- and market-related sources of risk and return.

Meaningful explanations of investment performance require explicit statements of risk and return which, in turn, each break down into security- and market-related components. This is the linchpin of MPT—the classification, estimation, and control of the sources of both risk and return.

A useful way to consider investment alternatives is to think of the risk-reward spectrum shown in Figure 1–1. Investing is

FIGURE 1–1: Risk-reward spectrum

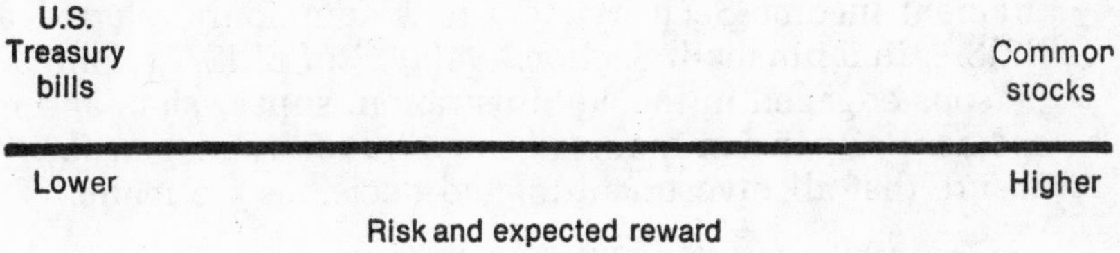

U.S. Treasury bills	Common stocks
Lower	Higher

Risk and expected reward

subjecting a sum with a certain present value to risk, in hopes of obtaining an uncertain future reward. The left-hand end of the spectrum represents the lowest risk investment. Probably the lowest risk instrument available is a short-term interest-bearing obligation of the U.S. Treasury. Here the investment risk (defined as the deviation between the actual and the expected rewards) is very low.

Moving to the right on the risk-reward spectrum increases both risk and expected reward. That is, by selecting any investment other than U.S. Treasury bills, an investor increases the expected return. Concomitantly, however, as is true of common stock investments, higher anticipated rewards go hand in hand with increases in the deviations (risk) between the "expected" and "actual" results.

Thus, when pairs of reasonable investment alternatives are compared across the risk-reward spectrum, greater risks and larger "expected" returns will always go together. In fact, popular terms such as *investing, speculating,* and *gambling* came into use to describe progressively higher levels of both risk and expected (but, by definition, progressively uncertain) reward. Although this important gradation of risk and reward has been built into our everyday vocabulary, traditional forms of investment management are severely deficient in the quantification of the relationship between risk and expected return.

Modern portfolio theory can be thought of as magnifying and refining the relationship between risk and reward which is depicted by the risk-reward spectrum. More specifically, MPT provides the ability to classify, estimate, and hence control, both the types and amounts of risk and expected return.

ERISA

Although elements of modern portfolio theory have been around for a long time, the current revolution was "sparked" in late 1974. In that year, Congress enacted the Employee Retirement Income Security Act—now commonly referred to as ERISA. In a nutshell, Section 404(a)(1) of ERISA requires that persons engaged in the administration, supervision, and management of pension monies have a *fiduciary responsibility* to ensure that all investment-related decisions are made:

1. With the care, skill, prudence and diligence . . . that a prudent man . . . *familiar with such matters* [italics added] would use . . . ,
2. By *diversifying the investments . . . so as to minimize risk* [italics added]. . . .

If this law is extended to all fiduciary and trust relationships under which individuals have responsibility for other people's investments (and, after all, there is nothing unique about a trustee's fiduciary responsibility for a pension account), it is clear that the law now virtually mandates two significant changes in traditional investment practices.

The first deals with the age-old "prudent man" issue. Note that ERISA demands "a prudent man . . . *familiar with such matters.*" Thus, the general interpretation is that ERISA does not require a prudent man but a prudent "expert." While it is admittedly difficult to define an expert and it is clearly within the province of experts to disagree, many people who now manage other people's money could not meet this test. A well-meaning family friend who is a part-time student of investments would likely not qualify as a prudent expert. Similarly, a group of physicians which collectively manage their staff's pension fund would probably be unable to satisfy this criterion. As a result, all of the admittedly sincere, honest, hardworking people who at one time were charged with the management of trust investments now have a *new responsibility—the selection and monitoring of a prudent "expert."*

The second change mandated by ERISA is the requirement that investments must be *diversified* "so as to minimize risk." MPT could be defined as "the control of risk through diversification." Thus, much as the concept of a prudent expert has replaced that of the prudent man, *the notion of a prudent portfolio has replaced the concept of a prudent investment.* Practically speaking, this means that investments must be analyzed—and managed—within the context of an overall risk-controlled portfolio.

From this perspective, it is easy to see why a tidal wave of demand is forming for MPT practitioners. Faced with ever-more stringent legal requirements, persons who are charged with the prudent selection and monitoring of professional investment managers cannot treat this responsibility lightly. Furthermore, the *law now requires* that pension monies be managed by prudent experts who "diversify the investments within portfolios so as to minimize risk." Broadly speaking, this is MPT!

MPT OVERVIEW

Historically, the investment profession has focused on "classical" forms (those that do not quantify risk) of security analysis. It was widely believed that investment selections which were made through a combination of this analysis and hard, honest work would yield handsome rewards. For some 20 years, a generally rising market provided little test of this belief. Further, the generally favorable results obscured the need, until relatively recently, to focus on the relationship between the potential risks, as well as the potential rewards, of investing. In short, conscious efforts to deal explicitly with the dimension of risk did not enter the picture.

The investment results of the last ten years have now shown that information derived from classical security analysis is neither complete nor infallible. In fact, in the face of MPT, "traditional" forms of investment management which do not incorporate the explicit estimation and control of risk stand, along with ENIAC and Sputnik I, as relics of another era.

Concise definitions of MPT are difficult—if not outright dangerous. As used here, MPT is intended to emcompass *all notions of modern investment and portfolio theory.* Hence, terms such as new investment technology (NIT) and modern investment theory (MIT) can be regarded as synonomous with MPT.

Four types of MPT-based applications are shown in Figure 1–2. Starting with the foundation, MPT can be thought of as

FIGURE 1–2: Four types of MPT-based applications

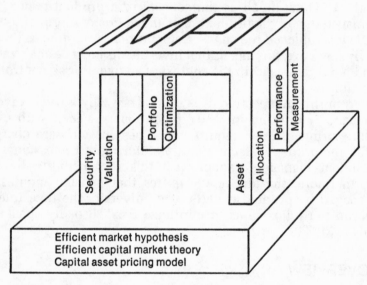

the theoretical constructs that have spawned applications for security valuation, portfolio optimization, asset allocation, and performance measurement. Viewed from this perspective, it is clear that MPT rests on the theoretical foundation of such concepts as the efficient market hypothesis, efficient capital market theory, and the capital asset pricing model. Thus, the first step in evaluating MPT must begin with an essential part of its foundation—the efficient market hypothesis.

PART ONE

THE EFFICIENT MARKET HYPOTHESIS

Chapter 2

Forms of the efficient market hypothesis

An *efficient capital market* is an arena in which many participants, with similar investment objectives and access to the same information, actively compete. The stock market—with numerous profit-motivated professional and private investors continually searching for misvalued securities—certainly provides such a setting. Profit-motivated investors do have strikingly similar objectives. Each prefers a high rate of return to a low one, certainty to uncertainty, low risk to high risk, and so forth. Furthermore, securities law provides that both parties to a transaction must have access to the same material facts.

The efficient market hypothesis asserts that it would be impossible consistently to outperform the market—which reflects the composite judgment of millions of participants—in an environment characterized by many competing investors, each with similar objectives and equal access to the same information. In the context of this hypothesis, "efficient" means that the market is capable of quickly digesting new information on the economy, an industry, or the value of an enterprise and accurately impounding it into securities prices. In such markets participants can expect to earn no more, nor less, than a fair return for the risks undertaken.

In an efficient market, for example, news of an earnings increase would be quickly and accurately assessed by the combined actions of literally millions of investors and immediately reflected in the price of the stock. The purported result of this efficiency is that whether you buy the stock before, during, or after the earnings news, or whether another stock is purchased, only a fair market rate of return can be expected—commensurate with the risk of owning whatever security is bought.

THE FORMS OF THE EFFICIENT
MARKET HYPOTHESIS

The efficient market hypothesis does not by any means deny the profitability of investing. It merely states that the rewards obtainable from investing in highly competitive markets will be fair, on the average, for the risks involved. Importantly, however, the three forms of the efficient market hypothesis hold that acting on publicly available information cannot improve one's performance beyond the market's assessment of a fair rate of return.

The *weak form* of the efficient market hypothesis describes a market in which historical price data are efficiently digested and, therefore, are useless for predicting subsequent stock price changes. This is distinguished from a *semistrong form* under which all publicly available information is assumed to be fully discounted in current securities prices. Finally, the *strong form* describes a market in which not even those with privileged information can obtain superior investment results.

If the stock market efficiently digests all available information, as the progressively stronger forms of the hypothesis imply, there is little justification for seeking extraordinary gains from investing. However, this does not lessen the importance of investing. It merely changes the underlying investment philosophy of a prudent and knowledgeable investor from that of trying to beat the other person to one of seeking a rate of return that is consistent with the level of risk accepted.

Thus, rather than being the all-encompassing specter of gloom which some people assume it to be, the efficient market hypothesis in its various forms provides a useful benchmark. From its perspective, researchers can determine how "efficiently" or "inefficiently" information is processed. It is thus possible to scrutinize the market's ability to impound various kinds of information into securities prices. Most importantly, if research can determine which information is efficiently processed, investors can avoid analyzing this useless, fully discounted information—the first step in the successful and prudent application of MPT techniques!

TWO USEFUL ASSOCIATIONS

The following chapters in Part One review the conclusions of the many tests of the three forms of the efficient market hypothesis (weak, semistrong, and strong). However, before these findings are presented, it should prove useful to discuss the association between two forms of the efficient market hypothesis and two popular (although highly suspect) approaches to investment analysis—fundamental and technical.

Fundamental investment analysts base their predictions of stock price behavior on factors which are "fundamental" or internal to a company, its industry, or the economy (for example, earnings, products, management, competition, consumer spending, and so on). A market fundamentalist might issue a purchase recommendation for a company which has consistently shown year-to-year earnings increases and is in an industry that he or she believes will grow faster than the economy.

Technical analysts, by contrast, hold that all such fundamental factors are reflected in the market behavior of the stock. Thus, to a pure technician, all data of importance are internal to the stock market, and future stock price movements can be predicted from the diligent study of historical stock market information (for example, changes in stock prices and trading volume). A market technician might, therefore, base a buy recommendation on a certain pattern of recent price and volume changes.

Under the weak form of the efficient market hypothesis, information on historical price trends is of no value for the prediction of either the magnitude or direction of subsequent price changes. As such, the weak form is directly opposed to the basic premise of technical analysis. Similarly, the semistrong form of the efficient market hypothesis holds that all publicly available information (as well as forecasts developed from such data) is of no value in the prediction of future prices. Thus, the semistrong form of the hypothesis is diametrically opposed to the concept of fundamental analysis.

Chapters 3 through 5 discuss research findings on the weak form of the hypothesis. Chapters 6 through 11 then examine the value of traditional forms of fundamental analysis within the context of the semistrong form of the efficient market hypothesis. Chapter 12 addresses the subject of inside information and the strong form of the hypothesis. The conclusions reached in Chapters 3 through 12 are summarized in Chapter 13.

Chapter 3

Early research

According to the weak form of the efficient market hypothesis, historical price and volume changes cannot be used to predict either the direction or magnitude of subsequent price changes. Historically known as the *random-walk model* of stock prices, this highly important countertheory to technical analysis has received much attention. Numerous university researchers, investment practitioners, and students of the stock market have devoted countless hours to developing and testing this model.

Remarkably, however, some members of the investment community have failed to assimilate these findings into their decision making. The sad result is that certain segments of the financial community still base investment decisions on analysis for which there is no theoretical or empirical justification!

THE WEAK FORM—DEFINITION AND MEANING

The weak form of the efficient market hypothesis or, as it was referred to for many years, the random-walk model, states that the pattern of recent changes in the price of a stock provides no useful information for predicting the next price movement. In early works, the random-walk model was described by means of an analogy to a "drunkard's walk," the pattern of whose steps cannot be forecast with any accuracy—either in size or direction. Similarly, the random-walk issue boils down to one basic question: Is historical price information on a stock useful in predicting future price movements of that stock? Those who support the random-walk model answer this question with an emphatic no!

It was unfortunate that the word "random" was first used in connection with the description of this model. The *Webster's New Collegiate Dictionary* lists the following synonyms for random: haphazard, casual, and desultory. These words carry the implication of "happening by accident," "at the mercy of chance," "working without intention or purpose," and "ungoverned by a method or system." It should be emphasized that the random-walk model does not imply that changes in stock prices "just happen by accident." Indeed, the forces of supply and demand, most often converging on the floor of the stock exchange, cause price changes. As such, stock price levels are determined by the well-defined economics of a competitive marketplace. This is not a random or chance process.

Many researchers have tested the model by studying the movements of actual stock prices. If such studies are unable to discern repetitive price patterns (which can be used for prediction), the researcher must, by default, accept the weak form of the efficient market hypothesis and conclude that stock price changes cannot be forecast from prior price information.

Before turning to this research, it is important to remember that the random-walk model does not "assume" anything—it is a description of the way prices move. While "efficient" or "competitive" markets might explain what we observe, their existence, or lack thereof, does not alter the assertion of the random-walk model that price changes occur without trends or patterns. Also, the random-walk model does not deny the possibility of "experts" (or lucky dart throwers) being able to achieve higher than average returns. The random-walk model simply states that investors should not try to predict future price movements from historical price information! Now let's examine the work which has been done to test this assertion.

BACHELIER AND SLUTSKY

The random-walk model dates back to one of the first academic studies of speculative price behavior. In 1900, Louis Bachelier [10], a brilliant French mathematics student studying under the distinguished mathematician, H. Poincaré, formulated and tested the random-walk model of stock price behavior in his doctoral dissertation.

Bachelier's dissertation is an amazing document even today. Not only did he discover one of the most significant phenomena of the stock market—over 75 years ago—but his research was filled with other landmark contributions as well. In fact, the equation Bachelier used to describe the random walk was identical to that developed by Albert Einstein, five years later, to describe Brownian motion.[1]

Bachelier's dissertation bears on modern stock market research in two significant ways. First, it provided an explicit statement of the random-walk model. Second, Bachelier's tests of actual security prices corresponded closely to those predicted by the random-walk model. In short, the prices he studied did not move in meaningful trends, waves, or patterns. Thus, Bachelier showed that recent historical price data were useless for predicting future price changes. Either because Bachelier's work ran so counter to intuition or because it took an "Einstein" to understand it, his research findings fell into obscurity until they were rediscovered in 1960.[2]

An important lesson to be learned from Bachelier's work is that a person with an intellect comparable to Einstein's could spend years studying the stock market and could develop a model that was to spark intellectual excitement 60 years later, but could not succeed in changing the investment behavior of his period. Apparently, in 1900, scientists quietly applauded Bachelier's achievements but made little effort to bridge the gap between theory and practice. Hopefully, we have learned an important lesson from the case of Bachelier.

A number of other studies performed early in this century raised doubts over the usefulness of historical price data in predicting price movements. The work of the Russian economist Eugene Slutsky [258] in 1927 is recognized as an independent rebirth of the random-walk model. Slutsky, who was not aware of Bachelier's work, showed that randomly generated price changes resemble actual stock price movements and seem to exhibit cycles and other pattterns. Unfortunately, ten years passed before Slutsky's work was translated into English, and even in 1937, it did not spark the intellectual interest of either academicians or investment practitioners.

---

[1] Named after Robert Brown, the Scottish botanist who first observed the phenomenon, Brownian motion is the name given to the random movement of microscopic particles that are suspended in liquids or gases. This motion is caused by the collision of such particles with surrounding molecules and is of great interest to physicists. In 1905, Albert Einstein presented the renowned paper in which he "discovered" the mathematical equation that describes the phenomenon of Brownian motion. Einstein reportedly regarded this discovery as one of his greatest contributions. Yet, Einstein died not knowing that Bachelier, five years earlier, had discovered the same equation could be used to describe the random behavior of stock prices!

[2] The first modern-day reference to Bachelier's work was published by Alexander [1] in 1961.

THE ERA OF DISREPUTE

Although market technicians proliferated during the boom preceding the 1929 stock market crash, there were no rigorous attempts to establish the validity of technical analysis during this period. Following the 1929 debacle, virtually all enthusiasm for investment advice evaporated during what was known as Wall Street's "era of disrepute." Memories of Black Tuesday, stock manipulation by investment pools, and suicides persisted. Nor could the public forget the corruption exemplified by Richard Whitney, scion of the wealthy Whitney family and former president of the New York Stock Exchange, who was jailed for misusing company funds. Wall Street bore the stigma of these events for almost two decades, and both the general public and qualified researchers had little to do with the market. In fact, only two research studies that made material contributions to the science of investments were reported in the United States between 1930 and 1959.

WORKING AND COWLES—SOLE U.S. CONTRIBUTORS FOR THREE DECADES

In 1934, Holbrook Working [288] of Stanford University demonstrated that even artificially generated series of price changes form apparent trends and patterns. He later offered charts of simulated as well as real price changes and challenged readers to distinguish between the real and the artificial series. [289] Working's studies unfortunately lacked both the mathematical rigor and empirical evidence needed to attract the attention of qualified researchers.

In 1937, two distinguished researchers, Alfred Cowles and Herbert Jones [54] of the Cowles Commission (now Foundation) for Research in Economics, gave authoritative support to the case for technical analysis when they reported that stock prices indeed moved in predictable trends. As it happened, these findings were withdrawn in 1960 after an error in the analysis was discovered. For more than two decades, however, the widespread belief that Cowles had put the random-walk theory to rest deterred would-be U.S. researchers from further examination of the subject. As a result, another 15 years passed until someone again questioned the basic tenet of technical analysis: stock prices move in discernible patterns.

KENDALL—SERIAL CORRELATION

While the seeds sown by early researchers lay dormant in the United States, Maurice Kendall [145] at the London School of Economics made significant advances in the study of the random-walk model. In 1953, Kendall found, to his surprise, that stock price changes behaved almost as if they had been generated by a suitably designed roulette wheel. That is, each outcome was statistically independent of past history.

Using periods of 1, 2, 4, 8, and 16 weeks, Kendall reported that when price changes were observed at fairly close intervals, the random fluctuations from one price to the next were large enough to swamp any systematic patterns or trends which might have existed. He concluded that, ". . . there is no hope of being able to predict movements on the exchange for a week ahead without extraneous [that is, something besides price] information." [145, p. 16]

In contrast to the widely quoted (but later shown to be erroneous) research by Cowles and Jones, Kendall's 1953 work was published in the rather obscure *Journal of the Royal Statistical Society* and received little attention. So, while there was scattered evidence challenging the theory, prior to 1959 no one seriously questioned the doctrine of technical stock market analysis.

ROBERTS AND OSBORNE—THE SEED OF CONTROVERSY

In 1959, a widely read paper by Harry Roberts [220] of the University of Chicago and another study by M. F. M. Osborne [209], and astronomer at the U.S. Naval Research Laboratory in Washington, D.C., plus the discovery of Bachelier's 60-year-old dissertation by Professor Paul Samuelson and others at the Massachusetts Institute of Technology, kindled interest in using computers to study the random-walk model.

After placing the earlier work of Holbrook Working and Maurice Kendall in the context of the random-walk model, Roberts showed that a series of randomly generated price changes would very closely resemble actual stock data. Noting that this chance behavior produced patterns, Roberts was the first modern author to conclude that "probably all the classical patterns of technical analysis can be generated artificially by a suitable roulette wheel or random-number table." [220, p. 10]

Osborne's paper developed the hypothesis that the subjective perception of profit is the same for a price change from $10 to $11 as one from $100 to $110. This means that one should study price changes in logarithmic form, which Osborne showed did conform to the random-walk model. These widely read papers thus planted the seed of the random-walk controversy in the United States!

WORKING AND ALEXANDER—FALSE PRICE CORRELATIONS DETECTED

Additional cornerstone research was reported in 1960 and 1961 by Working [290] and Sidney Alexander [1], respectively. Each author discovered on an independent basis that research employing weekly or monthly stock price averages could show erroneous correlations which would not appear if un-averaged prices were used.

This finding was extremely important because in 1937, Cowles and Jones, both respected researchers, had reported that historical price movements could be used to predict monthly price changes—a study which, as mentioned before, provided weighty empirical support for technical analysis. When Cowles realized that data composed of averages could produce his original results as a statistical artifact, he withdrew his earlier findings (in an article published concurrently with Working's [53]). In the 1960 article Cowles concluded that there was no evidence that historical month-to-month price data could be used to predict the direction of price changes in subsequent months!

Chapter 4

More rigorous tests

Working's 1960 discovery that studies of average prices could show fallacious period-to-period correlation, together with Cowles' admission that his 1937 investigation suffered from this statistical bias, combined to open up new avenues for research. Furthermore, the ever-increasing availability of electronic computers and the introduction of high-level programming languages such as FORTRAN provided the long-needed tools for detailed statistical analysis. A careful research study was now warranted to show whether or not the random-walk model was indeed a tenable representation of price movements in modern capital markets.

THE "DIFFERENCING INTERVAL" ISSUE

The random-walk model states that "any price change is independent of the sequence of previous price changes." It is essential to understand that "price change" implies a period-to-period measurement. For example, one can test the validity of the random-walk model for daily (day-to-day) price changes, monthly (month-to-month) price changes, or any other interval.

This span between price observations is called the *differencing interval*. Daily price quotations in newspapers represent a one-market day differencing interval. Similarly, the quotations in the financial weekly *Barron's* show a one-week differencing interval.

Since the random-walk model is concerned with how prices change from period to period, the differencing interval must be specified when discussing the model. Differencing intervals can vary from the shortest possible interval (consecutive transactions shown on the ticker tape) to extremely long intervals of a year or more. Also, instead of reflecting fixed time periods, differencing intervals can be defined by the occurrence of particular events, such as a new price high, the formation of a certain pattern, and so on.

Thus, the object of research is not simply to test the validity of the random-walk model. Instead, research must ask, "Is the model valid for some particular differencing interval?" That is, is the relationship between day-to-day price changes random? What about the week-to-week and month-to-month comparisons as well?

The early random-walk experiments by Kendall and Osborne were criticized for assuming fixed differencing intervals. Their research had shown that a series of price changes, measured at fixed one-week or one-month intervals, could not be used to predict future price movements. But suppose a prediction scheme relied on certain "events" such as large price swings or specific chart patterns, which can occur at variable time intervals?

Variable-time models seek to reveal complicated patterns of price behavior which fixed-time models will not detect. Myriad variable-time models have been developed, but they all monitor a continuous series of price changes in search of some extraordinary "event." One common variable-time model forms the basis for "point-and-figure" charting. This method of technical analysis is based on recording the "event" of a stock's price moving by some predetermined amount. Chartists employing this technique plot xs and os for stocks which rise or fall, respectively, by a specified amount, often $1 per share.

An exhaustive analysis of the infinite number of possible variable-time models would be an impossible undertaking. Fortunately, a single premise does underlie all technical prediction methods. This premise is that the market repeats itself in patterns and that historical information about price movements is therefore useful for prediction. Consequently, the commonly used techniques of technical analysis—be they fixed- or variable-time models—can be classified and explicitly tested against the random-walk model.

ALEXANDER—TESTING OF FILTER TECHNIQUES

In 1961, Sidney Alexander [1] of M.I.T. reported the first scientific investigation of a variable-time model of stock price behavior. Alexander tested what is known as a "filter technique."[1] He contended that if the filter technique could show above-average profits, this return would be indicative of non-random price movements. Alexander evaluated his filter technique with Kendall's [145] data and reported that it was more successful than a buy-and-hold strategy, although brokerage commissions would have had a significant impact on profitability. Alexander's results are summarized in Table 4–1.

TABLE 4–1: Comparative profitability of the filter technique, 1928–1961

| Filter size | Number of transactions | Terminal capital as multiple of initial capital | | |
		If no commissions	With commissions	Buy and hold
1.0%	1,730	41.3	0.0	5.1
4.0	418	10.7	0.0	5.1
8.2	142	14.8	0.9	5.1
12.5	88	4.0	0.7	5.1
17.0	54	2.1	0.7	5.1
21.7	32	6.4	3.4	5.1
29.5	20	5.3	3.6	5.1
34.6	16	4.8	3.5	5.1
40.0	12	6.2	5.0	5.1
45.6	8	10.6	9.2	5.1

Source: After Alexander [1].

Thus, although Alexander found some "statistical" evidence which contradicted the random-walk model, he concluded his investigation by saying, "I should advise any reader who is interested in practical results . . . and . . . [who] must pay commissions, to turn to some other source for advice on how to beat [the] buy and hold [strategy]." [1, pp. 351–52]

---

[1] Filter techniques are based on the assumption that trends exist in stock prices but that these patterns are obscured by insignificant fluctuations, or market "noise." The filter precept is utilized to justify a procedure whereby all price changes smaller than a specified size are ignored. The remaining data are then examined. A typical filter rule might be: If the stock price advances 5 percent (signaling a breakout), buy and hold the stock until it declines by 5 percent (signaling the start of a reversal). At that time, sell the stock held and sell short an equal amount until the stock again moves up 5 percent. Under such a rule, all moves of less than 5 percent are ignored. Filter techniques seek to discover "significant moves" by studying price changes of a given magnitude, irrespective of the length of time between them. In short, the filter technique substitutes the dimension of the "move" for the dimension of "time." This precept is the basis of the point-and-figure chart technique (cf., Cohen [42] and [43]), the rationale for the so-called Dow theory (cf., Alexander [1]), and many other forms of technical analysis.

It should also be emphasized that while one might find a grain of support for technical analysis in Alexander's results, Paul Cootner [50] has noted a procedural error in Alexander's computations. Another problem is that Alexander did not state his conclusions in terms of statistical confidence. Thus, the likelihood of obtaining similar research results purely by chance, or a "dart board" selection, is not known.

HOUTHAKKER—COMMODITY FUTURES

In another 1961 paper, Harvard economist Hendrik Houthakker [125] similarly reported that a variable-time decision rule yielded superior returns when applied to commodity futures. Houthakker advanced the hypothesis (cf., Darvas [59]) that changes in prices are characterized by long "runs" (that is, a series of price changes in the same direction). If this hypothesis were correct, standing sell orders, called "stop orders," could be used by a speculator to liquidate his or her position when adverse runs were encountered. Conversely, a standing sell order would not be triggered when favorable runs were being experienced.

Thus, if a trader wished to limit losses to, say, 5 percent, a stop order could be placed to sell when the stock's price dropped to 95 percent of the purchase price. If price fluctuations were not random, and if a price drop were likely to lead to a further decline, such a trading policy would reduce losses without affecting upward runs of profits. Hence, average profit would increase. Houthakker's test of his trading rule on wheat and corn futures proved quite successful and led him to say, "I feel that. . . [the results]. . . indicate the existence of patterns of price behavior that would not be present if price changes were random." [125, p. 168]

HAGIN—NO EVIDENCE IN SUPPORT
OF TECHNICAL ANALYSIS

Aside from Houthakker's surprising results with commodity futures, numerous experiments with variable-time decision rules by other researchers have not turned up any evidence in support of technical analysis. This author's (see Hagin [116]) own experiments in the early 1960s tested numerous fixed- and variable-time decision rules against a four-year file of daily data on 790 actively traded stocks. Several hundred tests of decision rules based on moving averages, filters, thresholds, consistently found no *evidence in support of technical analysis!*

COOTNER AND MOORE—ACCELERATION OF THE DEBATE

By 1962, the academic debate on the validity of the random-walk model had picked up momentum, although the issue was still almost unknown on Wall Street. Cootner's research focused attention on a common source of confusion in random-walk research—the differencing interval. The random-walk model, it will be remembered, states that "future" price changes cannot be predicted from "past" price movements. Cootner's research emphasized that there is not one random-walk model, but rather one for every definition of "past" and "future." Thus, when Cootner defined "past" and "future" as "one week," his test of the random-walk model indicated that price changes were random. But when "past" was defined as 14 weeks, the random-walk model was not valid!

Thus, as the debate intensified, it seemed that predictions based upon the more distant past might be useful. But, in the race for "hot new information," it appeared that information on recent price changes is worthless!

Further evidence that studying weekly price changes is futile came from Arnold Moore's 1962 doctoral dissertation at the University of Chicago. Moore's research [196] validated the random-walk model for weekly price changes with a sample of 33 representative stocks listed on the New York Stock Exchange.

THE DEFINITIVE STUDIES OF THE MID-1960s

Eugene Fama's 1965 doctoral dissertation [68] also at the University of Chicago, was regarded as the definitive study of the random walk during the mid-1960s. A number of tests were used to examine the validity of the model; data included daily to 16-day differencing intervals for the 30 stocks in the Dow Jones Industrial Average—spanning periods from five to seven years. The results of one of these tests is shown in Table 4–2. Following his exhaustive study, Fama found no evidence of trends in stock prices for any differencing interval he tested.

TABLE 4–2: Runs of consecutive price changes in same direction: Actual versus expected for each Dow Jones industrial company

Stock	Daily changes		4-Day changes		9-Day changes		16-Day changes	
	Ac-tual	Ex-pected	Ac-tual	Ex-pected	Ac-tual	Ex-pected	Ac-tual	Ex-pected
Allied Chemical	683	713	160	162	71	71	39	39
Alcoa	601	671	151	154	61	67	41	39
American Can	730	756	169	172	71	73	48	44
AT&T	657	688	165	156	66	70	34	37
American Tobacco . .	700	747	178	173	69	73	41	41
Anaconda	635	680	166	160	68	66	36	38
Bethlehem Steel	709	720	163	159	80	72	41	42
Chrysler	927	932	223	222	100	97	54	54
DuPont	672	695	160	162	78	72	43	39
Eastman Kodak	678	679	154	160	70	70	43	40
General Electric	918	956	225	225	101	97	51	52
General Foods	799	825	185	191	81	76	43	41
General Motors	832	868	202	205	83	86	44	47
Goodyear	681	672	151	158	60	65	36	36
Int'l. Harvester	720	713	159	164	84	73	40	38
Int'l. Nickel	704	713	163	164	68	71	34	38
Int'l. Paper	762	826	190	194	80	83	51	47
Johns Manville	685	699	173	160	64	69	39	40
Owens Illinois	713	743	171	169	69	73	36	39
Procter & Gamble . . .	826	859	180	191	66	81	40	43
Sears	700	748	167	173	66	71	40	35
Standard Oil (Cal.) . .	972	979	237	228	97	99	59	54
Standard Oil (N.J.) . .	688	704	159	159	69	69	29	37
Swift & Co.	878	878	209	197	85	84	50	48
Texaco	600	654	143	155	57	63	29	36
Union Carbide	595	621	142	151	67	67	36	35
United Aircraft	661	699	172	161	77	68	45	40
U.S. Steel	651	662	162	158	65	70	37	41
Westinghouse	829	826	198	193	87	84	41	46
Woolworth	847	868	193	199	78	81	48	48
Averages	735	760	176	176	75	75	42	42

Source: After Fama [77].

The conclusion: Information on stock price changes over any or all days of a given 16-day period is useless!

Subsequently, Fama and Marshall Blume [76] conducted a thorough analysis of the filter technique. They employed a variety of filter sizes in an effort to determine the "best" size. Their conclusion was that none of the approaches tested would have been more profitable (after commissions) than a buy-and-hold strategy. On another front, James Van Horne and George G. C. Parker [277] studied "breakouts" from moving averages. Again, in no case was the profitability (after commissions) of a buy-and-hold strategy surpassed.

LEVY—AN IMPORTANT DISTINCTION

In 1966, Robert Levy's doctoral dissertation at the American University in Washington, D.C., was described by *Fortune* magazine as a "decisive refutation of the random walk." [293, p. 160] This characterization was erroneous, however, as two facts had been overlooked. First, there are any number of random-walk models—each with an explicit definition of what is "past." Second, research dating back to Cowles [54] in the 1930s, and to Cootner [48] in the early 1960s, has correctly shown that when stock price changes are studied over long differencing intervals, discernible trends do appear.

Levy [160] reported that stocks exhibiting higher than average price changes in any six-month period also tended to show higher than average price changes during the next six months. Random price behavior should have resulted in only average movements for the second six-month period. This phenomenon has been called *relative strength*, or *relative strength continuation*.

Thus, Levy reported that stocks with relatively above- (or below-) average price performance in the "past" six months tended to maintain above- (or below-) average performance in the "next" six months. This phenomenon is not new, however, nor does it refute the random-walk model. Levy's findings were perfectly consistent with other research. As long ago as 1937, Cowles reported that, "taking one year as the unit of measurement . . . the tendency is very pronounced for stocks which have exceeded the median in one year to exceed it also in the year following." [54, p. 285][2]

Furthermore, a careful study of Levy's work by Michael Jensen [131] revealed that Levy had overstated the returns earned from his relative strength trading rules (see [161] and [162]). When correct rate of return calculations are used, none of Levy's "profitable" trading rules showed greater returns, after transaction costs, than those available from the correct buy-and-hold returns. The conclusion: Levy found evidence of a well-known, subtle form of long-term, nonrandom behavior

---

[2] It should be noted that while Cowles' article had a statistical error (referred to earlier) which invalidated the apparent predictability of monthly prices, the error did not invalidate his conclusions with regard to one-year relative strength.

which, nonetheless, cannot be used to beat average market returns!

To verify this conclusion, Jensen and George Benington [137] tested two of Levy's "better" decision rules on 200 individual securities over successive five-year time intervals from 1931 to 1965. Jensen and Benington concluded that after allowance for transaction costs, Levy's trading rules, on the average, were not significantly more profitable than the buy-and-hold policy.

NIEDERHOFFER AND OSBORNE—THE OTHER END OF THE DIFFERENCING INTERVAL

Victor Niederhoffer, individually [203, 204] and with Osborne [206], studied the other end of the differencing interval time spectrum—successive transactions on the ticker tape. Research on this smallest possible differencing interval provides striking evidence of dependence between successive stock transactions.

Niederhoffer and Osborne reported that successive transactions display several nonrandom properties:

1. There is a general tendency for prices to reverse between trades.
2. Following two changes in the same direction, the chances of continuing in that direction are greater than after changes in opposite directions.
3. Price reversals occur more frequently just above and below integers. [206, p. 194]

Unfortunately, these short-term and small-percentage dependencies, although consistent, are eclipsed by transaction costs and consequently provide no basis for successful trading strategies.

SUMMARY

The preceding two chapters have examined historical milestones in the development of the weak form of the efficient market hypothesis. This research illustrates how the renaissance of investing knowledge has been accompanied by progressively more rigorous, and more probing, computer-based investigations. In addition, the conclusion reaffirmed by each investigation is that no research yet discussed has refuted the random-walk model, given a differencing interval of between 1 and 16 days.

Chapter 5

Definitive tests: Weak form

By the mid-1960s, the body of evidence in support of the random-walk model was growing but still rested on possibly incomplete tests and limited test data. It might be argued, for example, that the statistical tools (serial correlation, run tests, and so on) used to study stock price behavior were inadequate to detect the complicated patterns (for example, head and shoulders) which, according to some chartists (cf., Jiler [139]), serve as predictors.

Similarly, test data tended to be confined to only a few stocks. Fama's [68] data base, for example, consisted of daily prices for only the 30 stocks of the Dow Jones Industrial Average. Furthermore, although early research on the random-walk model neglected trading volume, many technicians contended that volume was a necessary adjunct to historical price data.

Also, early studies of the random-walk model searched almost exclusively for patterns that were present throughout the data. It was quite possible, however, that a test which looked at all price data might indicate randomness, while a test examining only a portion of the price changes (for example, "large changes") would show predictable patterns.

As a result, during the mid-1960s it was not known whether the findings obtained from these limited tests on limited empirical data could be substantiated for a much larger sample of stocks, studied over various intervals. It was unknown, for example, whether or not a systematic investigation of chart patterns would reveal a potential tool for forecasting that went undetected by traditional statistical analysis. Further, it was not known whether industry or price-range differences might invalidate the random-walk description of stock price behavior.

By the mid-1960s, then, the early shortcomings of the research on the random-walk model could be summarized as
follows:

1. The random-walk model had not been tested on enough
    stocks over a long enough period of time.
2. Research on the random-walk model was incomplete be-
    cause it did not include trading volume information,
    which was seen by some as a necessary adjunct to histori-
    cal price data.
3. Random-walk research was too limited because it was de-
    signed almost exclusively to detect patterns present
    throughout the entire time period.
4. The statistical techniques used to confirm the random-
    walk model might be unable to detect the complicated
    visual or graphic relationships discovered by chartists.

ALL ACTIVELY TRADED STOCKS

To overcome the foregoing limitations, this author (see
Hagin [116]) studied the daily prices and volume for 790 actively traded stocks on the New York and American Stock
Exchanges over several three-year periods. The first research
question was: Does the random-walk model hold for all actively traded stocks? A large variety of computer programs
and statistical tests yielded quite conclusive findings: There
was no systematic behavior in stock prices that could be used
for profitable prediction when the data were studied with differencing intervals of between 1 and 16 days. Further, there
were no systematic differences that would allow profitable
prediction when the findings were cross-tabulated by stock
price range, stock exchange, or industry.

In summary, this author's research, based on an exhaustive
investigation of fixed-time stock price dependencies utilizing
traditional statistical tools, found no evidence that profitable
prediction schemes can be developed from recent historical
price data. In other words, knowledge of a stock's price behavior during any 16-day period provides no useful information for
predicting the direction of future price changes.

PRICES AND VOLUME?

Is it true, as many technicians contend, that the combination
of price *and* trading volume data is what provides useful pre-

dictive information? To answer this question, this author (see Hagin [116]) studied the possibility that price changes can be predicted from the simultaneous interaction of preceding price and volume changes. The study employed a computer-readable file of prices and volumes on 790 stocks, and while the details of the research are beyond the scope of this book (they are available in [116]), the results are significant for anyone who invests: Knowledge of preceding volume changes,[1] even coupled with information on preceding price changes, does not improve one's ability to predict the direction of the next price change.

In sum, these results reaffirm previous findings that short-term (defined as less than 40 days in this study) stock price changes exhibit random, and hence unpredictable, patterns. Further, the introduction of the preceding period's trading volume data does not provide even a slight improvement in the ability to predict the direction of future period-to-period stock price changes.

BREAKOUTS?

There is conclusive evidence that data on the direction of short-term (within 40 days) price and volume changes cannot be used to predict the direction of subsequent price changes. This conclusion was reached by studying historical market data over fixed-time intervals. Most stock market technicians do not purport to predict price changes solely from fixed-time models, however. They contend that situations occasionally arise which foreshadow certain kinds of predictable price behavior. Thus, technicians typically characterize the stock market by a variable-time or event-triggered model. This author (see Hagin [116]) has conducted exhaustive tests of the premises underlying such variable-time models. For example, do relatively large daily price changes precede predictable events?

There are several conflicting viewpoints on how stock prices behave after large price changes. On the one hand, some investors contend that steep advances or declines are typically followed by reversals—brought about either by profit taking at the high price or by bargain hunters attracted to the lower

---

[1] It should be noted that "information" concerning various relative and absolute volume levels was also tested and that none of these schemes invalidated the above conclusions.

price. On the other hand, there are investors who believe that large price increases signal "breakouts" which are apt to continue. If both kinds of investors participate in the market, one group's actions would tend to offset those of the other group. Large price changes, then, might be followed by movements which are typical of those generated by a random process.

Benoit Mandelbrot [182] suggested yet another model. He submitted that any large price change might tend to be followed by further large changes, either up or down. Fama has provided the following rationale for this model:

> . . . this type of dependence hinges on the nature of the information process in a world of uncertainty . . . when important, new information comes into the market, it cannot always be evaluated precisely. Sometimes the immediate price change caused by the new information will be too large, which will set in motion forces to produce a reaction. In other cases the immediate price change will not fully discount the information, and impetus will be created to move the price again in the same direction. [68, p. 85]

Fama tested this hypothesis on ten stocks and found only slight evidence of large changes being followed by further large changes. Furthermore, such successive price changes were unpredictable in direction. The same results have been substantiated by this author (Hagin) in a study of 790 stocks over a four-year period. That is, there is some evidence that "large" price changes occur in succession, but the direction of the change is random. This result interests economists but is of little value to investors, who are obviously interested in the direction of the subsequent price movement.

In addition, numerous other hypotheses have been formulated by this author to test the usefulness of coupling trading volume information, such as "volume shocks," with data on large price changes. In summary, there was no evidence that the occurrence of any special price or volume situation over the short run (less than 40 days) has any predictive value.

CHART PATTERNS?

There are two kinds of chartists: bar chartists (cf., Edwards and Magee [62] and Jiler [139]) and point-and-figure chartists (cf., Cohen [42], [43]). Bar charting is a fixed-time model, while point-and-figure charting is a variable-time model. Both types plot price on the vertical scale. On bar charts, the horizontal scale is uniformly divided into fixed-time periods. One point-and-figure charts, the units on the horizontal scale indicate reversals in the direction of stock prices and occur at variable-time intervals.

Once the stock's historical record has been charted, the technical analyst visually studies the configuration for predictive signals. While it is unlikely, it must be conceded that chartists might be able to pick out extremely complex patterns that the traditional statistical tests used by researchers are unable to isolate.

The validity of basing predictions of stock price movements on chart patterns can, however, be tested rigorously by an unconventional use of a computer. Such investigation is possible because all charting theories rest on a single premise: They assume that visually detectable price patterns have repeating characteristics. This premise has also been rigorously tested by this author (Hagin). It is again beyond the scope of this book to discuss such research on chart patterns in detail.[2] Rather, a brief summary of the two methodological approaches and the general findings should be sufficient.

The first research approach was to simulate a chartist's vision. Chartists look for specific kinds of patterns, such as head and shoulders, saucer bottoms, and triple tops. During the first phase of this research, a computer was used to search the price history of each of 790 stocks for specified patterns that are purported by chartists to serve as predictors.

The computer was instructed to "look for" the computerized equivalent of what a chartist hopes to find visually. Next, the occurrence of any of these patterns was recorded, and the stock's succeeding price behavior was noted. Finally, a statistical analysis was conducted to determine whether these patterns indeed preceded certain kinds of price performance. The investigation was unable to detect any evidence that the commonly used chart patterns were forerunners of certain price changes.

Under the second research approach, the computer attempted to derive original predictive patterns from the data. The computer was first instructed to group charts on the basis of the price behavior following the chart. For example, one classification consisted of all chart patterns which appeared before dramatic price increases. Then each group of patterns

---

[2] Some of this author's early work on computerized detection and classification of chart patterns is reported in [116].

was studied for similarities. Again, this research offered no evidence that predictable stock price movements follow visually detectable chart patterns.

DOESN'T TECHNICAL ANALYSIS WORK SOMETIMES?

For some readers, the evidence presented here may seem to contradict their personal experience. Such people "know" that technical schemes which are based on historical price and volume work. But do they? The answer is quite clear. There is absolutely no evidence that information on the price and volume movements of a stock over the recent past will aid in predicting the future price behavior of that stock.

Yet, many practitioners persist in using this kind of technical analysis. They must occasionally consider themselves successful; otherwise, they would abandon the technique. Success in the stock market, however, must be gauged against a realistic benchmark. One could expect a certain level of performance even if technical analysis is indeed useless. Stated another way, the benchmark for comparing investment performance should be the rate of return one would expect from unskilled stock selection.

Suppose that instead of basing investment decisions on the results of elaborate technical analysis, an investor selected stocks by throwing darts at the financial page of a newspaper. Further, suppose transaction dates were chosen by throwing darts at a calendar. What investment returns would be achieved from such random selection processes?

The work of Lawrence Fisher and James Lorie [91] has revealed that the median rate of return from random investment in common stocks was 9.8 percent compounded annually during the period from 1926 to 1960. Also, using random holding periods averaging several years, they found that 78 percent of such transactions were profitable.

These findings become especially interesting when you consider that technicians generally claim to be accurate only some of the time. For example, Edmund W. Tabell, regarded as the dean of chartists until his death in 1965, said that he was right only about 70 percent of the time. Admittedly, the longer a position is held, the more likely it is to become profitable, and Tabell made no statement as to how long or short a period it took for him to be "right." Also, the total annual rate of return is usually more important than the percentage of individual purchases with profitable outcomes.

Nevertheless, until proven otherwise, it must be concluded that people who credit their success to technical analysis have not, in fact, benefited from it in any way. They have merely obtained normal results, as could be achieved from random investment.

SO WHERE DO WE STAND?

Academic research, which has no vested interest in the matter, is in overwhelming agreement—technical market prediction schemes based on price and volume movements over the preceding 40 days appear to be useless. Some market practitioners will react to this statement by asserting that they use such technical analysis only occasionally. This is ridiculous! The evidence is overwhelming that such analysis should never be employed.

Why, then, does this kind of technical analysis persist? Why does the investing public support advisory services which rely on charts? Isn't it strange that hospital patients who will trust their lives to a computer's ability to read their electrocardiograms will not listen when told that the same pattern detection techniques cannot discern any useful patterns in historical stock price data?

In spite of this research, "technical" jargon remains an integral part of Wall Street's vocabulary. Financial pages make frequent references to events such as a "technical correction," even though few commentators agree on its definition or occurrence. Unfortunately, most of this gobbledygook appears to serve the purpose of the psychiatrist's inkblot—to project meaning into nothing.

Yet, in spite of its thoroughness, the research summarized here is subject to several provisos. First, it should be emphasized that technical analysis, as discussed here, refers to the study of recent (within 40 days) price and/or volume information. Second, direct investigative comparisons against the actual work of technicians are difficult because these practitioners usually interpret basic price data with the help of "necessarily secret" formulas to calculate relative strengths, moving and geometric averages (see James [130]), ratio lines, trend forecasts, and the like. Third, prediction schemes under the rubric of "technical analysis" are by no means limited to the study of price and volume information. Hence, our analysis of the technical point of view will not be complete until we examine the usefulness of such nonprice technical indicators as splits and odd-lot transactions in Chapters 10 and 11.

In spite of these provisos, several definitive statements can be made about technical analysis. William Sharpe has said that "many regard technicians as the lunatic fringe of the investment world. Descriptions of their activities are felt to be a suitable subject for anthropologists, but inappropriate in a book intended for a serious investor." [252, p. 489] The evidence clearly supports this view. It is doubtful that the tea leaves left behind by today's stock market can foretell tomorrow's tracings. For now, an important "don't" of prudent investing is: Do not use technical analysis based on recent historical price or volume information.

This does not mean, of course, that practitioners who use 'elements" of technical analysis have disappeared from the investment scene. Unfortunately, while it is virtually impossible to find either theoretical or empirical evidence in support of technical analysis, the technical gobbledygook of "trends, resistence, strength, and patterns" has obvious marketing appeal to naive investors. Thus, a situation exists in which a stock selection technique that has been so thoroughly researched—and debunked—that it would no longer be a fitting subject for an investments seminar at any leading business school can nonetheless form the basis for an investment management approach just a few blocks away. Unquestionably, employing such analysis is *illogical*. What constitutes *imprudence* is a matter which, in the final analysis, must be decided by the courts.

Chapter 6

Usefulness of information

The semistrong form of the efficient market hypothesis focuses on how rapidly and how efficiently market prices adjust to new publicly available information. We have seen that the weak form of the hypothesis (that is, the random-walk model) has been the subject of inquiry for many years. In fact, given the duration of the controversy over the weak form and the wealth of evidence in its support, it is fair to say that its validity is now generally recognized by both academic researchers and astute professional investors.

This chapter moves from the weak form of the efficient market hypothesis (which focuses on the usefulness of historical price and volume information) to the semistrong form of the hypothesis (which deals with the usefulness of all publicly available information). Since the semistrong version of the hypothesis is a relatively new concept (compared with the old weak-form random-walk model), the subject has, to date, received far less attention in the financial literature.

Basically, the semistrong form of the hypothesis states that if the market is truly efficient in both disseminating and processing publicly available information, any value that this information might have to a recipient is destroyed by the competitive forces of the market. Thus, to achieve consistently above-average risk-adjusted investment performance, an investor must know: (1) that certain kinds of *information* (2) will, with known *probabilities*, (3) influence certain investment *instruments* (4) in certain investment *markets*, (5) in known *directions*, (6) by approximate *magnitudes*, and he or she must (7) *act on the information before other investors*.

If this cannot be done, and the semistrong form of the efficient market hypothesis is a valid description of the stock market, investment analysis becomes an expensive exercise in wishful

37

thinking! The fact that more than 100,000 professional security analysts, brokers, and portfolio managers—plus approximately 25 million U.S. residents who directly own shares of common stock—are all trying to do the same thing makes this a very competitive endeavor.

KINDS OF INFORMATION

Several kinds of information can precipitate price movements of various instruments in various markets. Three broad categories of such data are:

1. *Economy-related information.* General economic news typically affects the market as a whole. On days when several hundred stocks reach new lows while only a few achieve new highs, it is clear that even the stocks of well-managed companies in growing industries cannot withstand a bear (downward) market.
2. *Industry-related information.* Instead of affecting the general economy, news sometimes only has an impact on a single industry. For example, news that dry breakfast cereals contained little or no nutritional value had an adverse effect on all breakfast cereal manufacturers; publicity over the potential health hazards of cyclamates and saccharine have affected only users of those products; an industrywide strike would affect only the firms in that or related industries, and so on.
3. *Company-related information.* Announcements regarding a company's earnings, dividends, forthcoming stock splits, patents, merger offers, new discoveries, and so forth—with little or no bearing on an entire industry or the general economy—can still prompt a change in the price of a firm's stock.

If one is going to attempt to predict price movements, a logical first step is to determine the relative importance of each of these three basic kinds of information before turning to the question of how efficient the market is at impounding the various kinds of information into the price of a stock. For example, if the relative importance of information related to a company, an industry, and the economy is about equal (and the market is equally inefficient across each information category), it might behoove analysts to allocate their research efforts to these three areas equally. Similarly, if 80 percent of the fluctuations of a stock's price are associated with market and industry factors, it would be inappropriate for an analyst to concentrate on company-related information. In such a situation, the relative importance of company-related information would be swamped by the effect of market swings.

WHAT CAUSES PRICE CHANGES?

Benjamin King [149], in his doctoral dissertation at the University of Chicago, sought to determine the relative importance of these underlying causes of price movements: the market, the basic industry (such as metals), the industry subgroup (such as nonferrous metals), and the company. After studying 403 consecutive months of data (1927–60) for 63 NYSE stocks, King reported that:

1. There is a strong tendency for stocks to move with the overall market.
2. Stock price comovements correspond closely to industry classifications.
3. Only a minor proportion of overall price movements can be attributed to company-related factors.

King's research is startling in its consistency. First, his findings parallel earlier but less comprehensive results reported by Granger and Morgenstern [111] and by Godfrey, Granger, and Morgenstern [108]. Second, King's market and industry comovements were remarkably consistent, especially after consideration of the industry changes which doubtless occurred over the more than 33 years spanned by his study. In the most recent period he examined (1952–60), King showed that, on the average, price changes were attributable to the investing public's reaction to four discernible components in the following proportions:

1. The market as a whole 31%
2. The basic industry 12%
3. The industry subgroup (or other common factors) . 37%
4. The particular company 20%

On the average, 31 percent of a stock's price movement was ascribable to general economic factors influencing the market as a whole. About half of the movement was traceable to the influence of a firm's basic industry and its industry subgroup—12 percent and 37 percent, respectively. After these market and industry comovements were accounted for, only a scant 20 percent of the total price movement could be attributed to individual-company developments!

These aggregate figures do not present the entire picture which King developed. There were some interesting differences within the composite averages. These are summarized in Table 6–1 using King's most recent data.

TABLE 6–1: Classification of price comovements by industry membership

Industry membership	Percentage movement explained by:			
	Overall market	Basic industry	Industry subgroup	Individual company
Railroads	47	8	26	19
Metals	46	8	31	15
Petroleum	37	20	28	15
Utilities	23	14	41	22
Retail stores	23	8	42	27
Tobacco	9	17	49	25
Average	31	12	37	20

Source: Derived from data in King [149].

These data show that the shares of railroads, metal companies, and petroleum firms rank highest in overall market dependence, with the stocks of tobacco firms being relatively insensitive to overall market swings. The industry columns confirm King's statement that the "general adherence to the pattern of industry comovement is ineluctable . . . the strongest industry effects are those for petroleums, utilities, and tobaccos—the weakest for metals, [retail] stores, and rails." [149, pp. 203–4]

King's research is important for three reasons. First, he showed that, on the average, roughly one third of a stock's movement can be traced to general market swings. Second, and very important, there are clear industry differences. In the tobacco industry, for example, King could attribute only 9 percent of stock price variations to general market swings. Third, this relationship between stock swings and market swings appears to be consistent over time.

King's research was expanded and updated in 1968 by Marshall Blume [28] in his doctoral dissertation at the University of Chicago. Blume, who studied 251 securities, confirmed that certain stocks had a tendency to move with the market and that this relationship persisted over time.

INFORMATION HIERARCHY

The semistrong form of the efficient market hypothesis encompasses all publicly available information. A more useful classification of "all" information can be distilled by:

1. Specifying the investment "instrument" (for example, common stock).
2. Defining the "market" (for example, the NYSE).
3. Tabulating the kinds of "information" that might affect the value of this instrument at each of the four levels of the information hierarchy.

This procedure is illustrated in Figure 6–1.

FIGURE 6–1: The investment analysis function

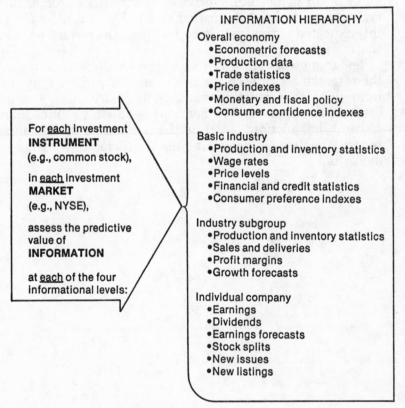

For each investment
INSTRUMENT
(e.g., common stock),

in each investment
MARKET
(e.g., NYSE),

assess the predictive value of
INFORMATION

at each of the four informational levels:

INFORMATION HIERARCHY

Overall economy
- Econometric forecasts
- Production data
- Trade statistics
- Price indexes
- Monetary and fiscal policy
- Consumer confidence indexes

Basic industry
- Production and inventory statistics
- Wage rates
- Price levels
- Financial and credit statistics
- Consumer preference indexes

Industry subgroup
- Production and inventory statistics
- Sales and deliveries
- Profit margins
- Growth forecasts

Individual company
- Earnings
- Dividends
- Earnings forecasts
- Stock splits
- New issues
- New listings

When possibly useful information is placed in the perspective of Figure 6–1 for specific investment vehicles in specific markets, one can assess how efficiently information is processed at each hierarchical level. If the news is quickly and accurately impounded into the security's price, the market would be deemed economically "efficient" in terms of the impact of that information on that instrument. But, if for some reason the market does not fully react to a certain kind of news, or reacts slowly, the discovery of this economic "inefficiency" will permit one to profit in excess of a fair rate of return.

It should be reiterated, however, that one does not have to discover market inefficiencies to profit from investments. An efficient market is one in which everyone can expect a "fair return" for assuming risk. If such a market is efficient at digesting earnings information, for instance, investors acting on such information could not increase their expected profits beyond a fair-game return or reap "abnormal" profits. Importantly, and unlike the situation in Las Vegas or Atlantic City, this expected normal return is positive—the reward for assuming market risk.

The framework shown in Figure 6–1 will be used to explain the research bearing on the usefulness of various types of information for predicting market-, industry-, and company-caused price changes. The first topic—on which much modern research has focused—will be the usefulness of fundamental security analysis to determine the comparative worth of common stocks.

Chapter 7

Fundamental security analysis

Investing is to forego present spending in exchange for expected future benefits. Since today's stock price is a known quantity, investing entails a certain sacrifice for an uncertain future benefit. These uncertain future returns depend on a firm's earning power, which will determine the extent of its future divided distributions and, to varying degrees, the future selling price of the company's stock.

A wealth of evidence shows that stock prices tend to move together, reflecting investor expectations about the overall economy or various industry segments. However, in spite of these comovements, companies are fundamentally different. Clearly, profit expectations differ among firms, as do the risks associated with these various profit expectations.

Recognizing these obvious differences, thousands of security analysts study publicly available information in an effort to discover over- and undervalued companies. On the other hand, the semistrong form of the efficient market hypothesis holds that such analysis cannot accurately discern over- or undervalued securities. Specifically, this form of the hypothesis maintains that any and all publicly available information is efficiently reflected in the price of the underlying stock.

If this is true, the use of such information for fundamental security analysis is a rather expensive waste of time. To examine this important controversy, we will first describe the process of fundamental security analysis.

FUNDAMENTAL SECURITY ANALYSIS

When buying common stock, an investor acquires the legal right to share in the company's future earnings through dividends. A cornerstone of fundamental security analysis is that a share of common stock is worth the present value of the future income its owner will receive. Since the income from dividends will be received in the future, the discounted present value[1] of this stream of income can reflect both rates of return and risk.

A popular, and much simpler, way to think about the price of a share of stock is in terms of its price-earnings ratio. A P/E, as it is generally called, is simply the ratio of a stock's current price to its annual earnings. Thus, by using the price-earnings ratio, a stock can be described as selling at five times earnings, ten times earnings, and so on.

The analyst faced with the task of assigning some measure of value to a security thus has two alternatives. The first is to calculate the present value of the security from estimates of the future stream of income that the owner will receive. This, in turn, requires an estimate of an appropriate discount rate, which in turn is derived from estimates of required future risk-adjusted rates of return. In view of the theoretical, as well as practical, complexity of this estimation procedure (which MPT has now minimized), analysts have traditionally opted for the much simpler second alternative—valuation based on price-earnings ratios.

PRICE-EARNINGS RATIOS

Fundamental analysis based on price-earnings ratios is conceptually very simple. It calls for

1. Estimating a stock's earnings per share for the next year or so.
2. Estimating the price-earnings ratio that is expected to prevail when the estimated earnings are reported.
3. Multiplying the estimated future earnings per share by the estimated price-earnings ratio to obtain the estimated future price.

To examine the usefulness of this approach, we must determine

1. The degree to which security prices are related to differences in price-earnings ratios.
2. The degree to which security prices are related to earnings.

---

[1] The concept of present value is explained in Chapter 30.

THE RELATIONSHIP OF PRICES TO MARKET-LEVEL FACTORS

The average price-earnings ratios for the Dow Jones Industrials over the 1961–78 period are shown in Figure 7–1. As illustrated, since 1961, the P/E for the Dow Jones Industrials

FIGURE 7–1: Price-earnings ratios for the Dow Jones 30 industrials, 1961–1978

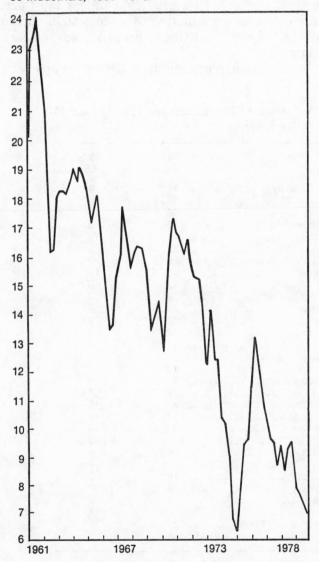

has averaged about 14 and has ranged from less than 7 to over 24 times.

To provide a real-world forecasting exercise, cover the right-hand portion of Figure 7–1 so that only the P/E ratio for the first part of 1961 is visible. Then slowly uncover the P/Es for the succeeding years—while trying to guess both the direction and magnitude of each year-to-year change. This exercise clearly demonstrates that even if *earnings* for the Dow Jones Industrials could be forecast with complete accuracy, the future price level could not be predicted unless the "perfect" earnings forecast was combined with a "reasonably accurate" estimate of the P/E ratio that would prevail when the earnings were announced.

Table 7–1 shows a representative list of company price-

TABLE 7–1: P/E ratios for 30 large companies on February 6, 1973 and January 8, 1979

Company	1973 P/E ratios	1979 P/E ratios
Aetna Life & Casualty	11	4
AT&T	11	8
Avon Products	60	14
Chase Manhattan	12	6
Coca-Cola	45	15
Delta Airlines	22	6
duPont	20	9
Eastman Kodak	46	13
Exxon	13	9
Ford	8	3
General Electric	24	9
General Foods	12	8
General Motors	10	5
Gulf Oil	11	7
IBM	39	16
IT&T	13	7
McDonnell Douglas	10	9
Mobil Oil	12	7
Philip Morris	27	11
Polaroid	78	16
Procter & Gamble	31	14
Safeway	11	9
Sears, Roebuck	29	8
Tenneco	11	7
Texaco	12	9
Texas Utilities	16	7
Union Carbide	13	6
U.S. Steel	10	13
Weyerhaeuser	21	9
Xerox	48	10

Sources: *The Wall Street Journal*, February 5, 1973 and January 5, 1979.

earnings ratios as of February 6, 1973 (the market's most recent high) and January 8, 1979. Note that the 1973 P/Es range from a high of 78 for Polaroid to a low of 8 for the Ford Motor Company. This means that in early 1973 the market valuation of earnings for Polaroid was almost *ten times* the multiple of Ford Motor Company stock.

The variations in P/Es reflect investors' assessments of the prospects for growth and/or certainty in the earnings and dividends of the market as a whole as well as individual companies. Notice that in early 1973 the outlook for oil companies was remarkably consistent across the groups as represented by the P/Es for Exxon (13), Gulf Oil (11), Mobil Oil (12), and Texaco (12). By early 1979, the overall level of the market had fallen (as reflected by generally lower P/Es). Yet, in spite of the broad decline in stock multiples, the *relationships* between P/Es—such as those of the oil companies Exxon (9), Gulf Oil (7), Mobil Oil (7), and Texaco (9)—remained relatively stable. When relative shifts in P/Es do occur, it is because investors anticipate differing growth rates and/or degrees of uncertainty in forecasted dividends and earnings of individual stocks.

THE RELATIONSHIP OF STOCK PRICE TO EARNINGS FACTORS

One of the first widely read studies of earnings growth rates and P/E ratios was published in 1963 by Volkert Whitbeck and Manown Kisor at the Bank of New York. After examining historical growth rates, Whitbeck and Kisor concluded that, "as investors, we buy common stocks not simply for records prior to purchase, but, more fundamentally, for what we anticipate from them after our commitment." [285, p. 337]

The conclusion reached by Whitbeck and Kisor was that differences in expected growth rates explain about 60 percent of the differences in normal P/E ratios. Similarly, John Cragg, of the University of British Columbia, reported that anticipated growth in earnings explained, on the average, 67 percent of the differences in P/E ratios (see [55, p. 79]).

Richard Crowell [56], in his doctoral dissertation at M.I.T., studied the relationship between expected earnings and P/E ratios in different industries. Of the 12 industries analyzed, Crowell demonstrated that at one extreme, 69 percent of the differences in P/E ratios for bank stocks could be explained by differences in anticipated growth rates; at the other extreme, only 5 percent of the differences in the P/E ratios accorded steel stocks could be traced to expected growth differences.

Further research relating earnings to stock prices was reported by Philip Brown and Ray Ball.[38] Stock price changes of selected companies were adjusted to eliminate the movements attributable to swings in the general market. These "nonmarket" stock price changes were then analyzed for 12 months before, and 6 months after, the date of each company's earnings announcement. They found that where actual earnings exceeded the forecast amounts, the price of the stock had typically risen during the preceding 12-month period, with the rise faltering in the 6-month period after the actual earnings announcement. This tendency is depicted in Figure 7–2, where 0 on the horizontal scale denotes the official earnings announcement date.

FIGURE 7–2: Average price movement during months preceding and succeeding the earnings announcement of stocks of companies producing unexpectedly good earnings

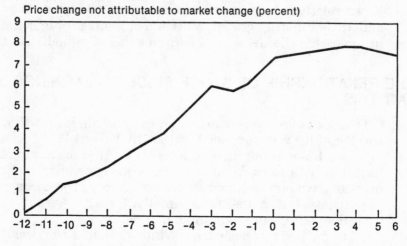

Price change not attributable to market change (percent)

Month relative to preliminary report

Source: After Brown and Ball [38].

Brown and Ball also reported that price movements during the months both preceding and following unexpectedly poor earnings announcements showed declines. Figure 7–3 traces the average price movement when actual earnings were below the forecast level.

The information portrayed in Figures 7–2 and 7–3, which show what typically happens to a stock's price in the months that precede and follow an unexpected earnings performance,

FIGURE 7–3: Average price movement during months preceding and succeeding the earnings announcement of stocks of companies producing unexpectedly bad earnings

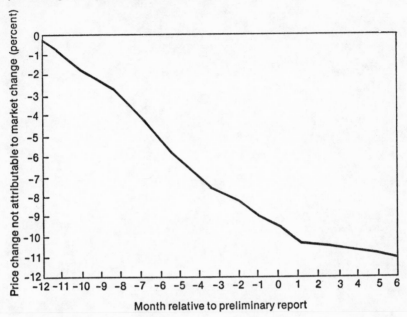

Source: After Brown and Ball [38].

is very revealing. *Note that by the time earnings were announced, the market had almost fully anticipated the contents of the report.*

This research indicates that on the average, stock prices react well in advance, and over time, to the reported annual earnings of companies. Further, the process by which the market anticipates this future earnings stream is both continuous and accurate. The market action, derived from the aggregate decisions of millions of investors, is remarkably efficient at anticipating published earnings announcements.

Chapter 8

Earnings forecasts

There is a strong, albeit not perfect, relationship between stock prices and earnings. The research of Whitbeck and Kisor, Cragg, and Crowell has shown that differences in P/E ratios are only partially explained by differences in anticipated earnings growth. Brown and Ball have shown that on the average, the price change in response to an earnings change is gradual and extends over many months while the actual earnings are being realized. These studies can be capsulized by saying that *there is a partial relationship between stock prices and earnings.*

The question remains: If an investor had the ability to forecast earnings with complete accuracy, could such information be used to predict stock price changes? Henry Latané and Donald Tuttle, at the University of North Carolina, answered this question by comparing changes in earnings with changes in the corresponding stock's price for 48 companies over a 14-year period. They found large year-to-year differences in the proportion of price changes that could be explained by changes in earnings, ranging from 64.5 percent to 0.8 percent. *The correlations were all positive,* however. That is, stock price gains were generally associated with increases in company earnings. Likewise, price declines were, on the whole, accompanied by decreases in company earnings.

In some years, this tendency was almost eliminated by market factors, while in others the influence of earnings on prices was quite strong. Over the entire 14-year period studied, Latané and Tuttle reported that only 17.4 percent of all price variations could be explained by earnings changes. This is a surprisingly small proportion. Nonetheless, Latané and Tuttle concluded that "perfect knowledge of future earnings would be of great value in selecting stocks." [156, p. 347]

Richard Brealey has expanded the work of Latané and Tuttle to determine just how much benefit could be realized if one had perfect knowledge of future earnings. Commenting on their research, Brealey states that "the average annual price appreciation of the 48 stocks was 12.2 percent. If, however, at the beginning of each year, an investor had been able to select from this group, stocks of those 8 companies (out of the 48 studied) that were to show the greatest proportion of earnings increase, his average annual profit would have been 30.4 percent." [34, p. 85]

Thus, two conclusions are well supported in the research literature. First, P/E ratios reflect, to some degree, the anticipated growth in company earnings. Second, if one could accurately estimate future earnings, an investment strategy that would provide above-average returns could most certainly be devised. The term one, however, is more than literary impartiality. Indeed, if many individuals could predict future earnings accurately, one's profitable strategy would succumb to an efficient capital market.

If accurate earnings forecasts can provide investors with above-average performance, the important question becomes, "Can changes in earnings be predicted?"

CAN CHANGES IN EARNINGS BE PREDICTED?

There is good reason to expect companies with consistently strong earnings records to continue to be capable of producing good earnings in the future. Similarly, companies with low profitability in the past intuitively seem likely to have similar difficulties in the future. Some of the super-growth stocks of the past, such as Avon Products, IBM, Polaroid, and Xerox, enjoyed a certain monopolistic advantage in rapidly expanding markets, enabling them to post consistently good results. It therefore seems reasonable that companies with satisfied customers and large, successful investments in product development, personnel, and plant and equipment should have a competitive advantage that is likely to persist.

It is important to remember, however, that if a company continues to outgrow the economy, it will eventually become the economy! The old adage that "trees do not grow to the sky" is apt. It is reasonable to expect that as companies become progressively larger, their growth rates will approach that of the overall economy. Therefore, the "model" for a growth stock should assume that growth will be above average for a number of years and thereafter will approximately parallel that of the economy.

Nonetheless, is there any evidence that over the short run, say year to year, earnings records persist? Richard Brealey [34] sought to answer this question by studying the earnings changes of approximately 700 industrial companies over a 14-year period. Contrary to what intuition would suggest, Brealey found that year-to-year earnings changes do not tend to be in the same direction! Based on separate classifications for 62 different industries, Brealey could not find any evidence that period-to-period earnings changes occur with discernible patterns or trends.

Similar findings have been reported by Joseph Murphy, Jr., who studied the earnings of 344 companies in 12 industries over 38 different time periods. Murphy, who conducted his research at the University of Minnesota, reported that "there appears to be little significant correlation between relative rates of growth of earnings per share in one period and relative growth in earnings per share in the next period." [199, p. 73]

Thus, a company which has achieved a consistent pattern of earnings growth does not have a better than average chance to sustain such growth into the future. In the context of investment theory, this means that *period-to-period earnings changes behave in accordance with a random-walk model.*

Intelligent discussion of the random-walk model, when applied to either price or earnings changes, must include the time span over which one attempts to make predictions. Random-walk research on price movements has shown, for example, that recent price and volume changes do not provide predictive information. Conversely, however, we have seen that long-term price movements are not random.

To determine whether or not changes in earnings can be described by the random-walk model, two questions must be answered. First, are long-term earnings changes, such as long-term price changes, predictable from past results? Second, can earnings be forecast from information other than historical performance?

LONG-TERM TRENDS IN EARNINGS?

John Lintner and Robert Glauber [171] of Harvard have studied the earnings of 323 companies over varying periods of time (up to five years) in an attempt to discern predictive patterns. Somewhat surprisingly, while there is evidence of long-term patterns in price movements, Lintner and Glauber were unable to detect consistent patterns in long-run earnings which could be used to produce above-average investment results.

Manown Kisor and Van Messner [151] studied earnings changes over six-month intervals. They first showed that if they could calculate the direction of earnings changes six months into the future, irrespective of the magnitude of the change, they could outperform the market. But based on a sample of 813 industrial companies, they found only one pattern that could be used to predict the direction of subsequent earnings changes. The pattern, which they called "increased momentum in relative earnings," is characterized by acceleration in the rate of change in a company's earnings relative to the earnings performance of the general market.

Thus, Kisor and Messner showed that when the momentum of a company's relative earnings accelerates, the likelihood of some increase in earnings for that company over the subsequent six months is significantly better than it is for the universe of companies whose shares make up the market as a whole. Consequently, there is evidence that a company whose earnings gains substantially outpace those of the market in one six-month period will continue to show positive earnings growth in the succeeding six months.

The Kisor-Messner findings tend to parallel Levy's [160] and this author's [116] evidence that stocks which advance in price substantially faster than the market in any six-month period tend to show slightly above-average price appreciation in the following six-month period. However, with the exception of a six-month pattern characterized by accelerated earnings growth, *there is overwhelming evidence that future earnings changes cannot be forecast from past movements.*

The research summarized here concludes that apart from the possible exception which has been noted, neither the direction nor magnitude of earnings changes can be predicted from historical patterns. But does anyone really *try* to predict earnings from historical patterns? The answer is a resounding yes!

There is considerable evidence that individual investors, as well as Wall Street professionals, rely heavily on historical results to predict future earnings. John Cragg and Burton Malkiel [55] have studied earnings estimates made by professionals who specialize in bank trust management, investment banking, mutual fund management, general brokerage, and the investment advisory business. The remarkable conclusion of the Cragg-Malkiel study was that when these experts were asked to forecast earnings, the overwhelming tendency of the group was to base their predictions on recent changes in historical earnings.

Even more startling was the fact that the predictions of the top analysts were ". . . no better than the simplest strategy of the naïve investor—who simply believes the company growth will parallel changes in gross national product." [256, p. 43] Thus, many people base earnings projections on apparently useless historical earnings data—in the face of evidence which shows that (with one minor exception) *the study of changing patterns of earnings is worthless!*

This research, it should be emphasized, does not mean that earnings cannot be predicted from information other than past earnings. Thus, a vital question is, "Can earnings be forecast from such things as balance sheet items, sales estimates, computerized cash-flow simulations, and so forth?" To answer this question, we must first define what is meant by "earnings."

EARNINGS

The concept of corporate earnings would seem to be simple enough. Since the securities legislation of 1933, certified public accounting (CPA) firms have been required to attest to the authenticity of earnings reported by publicly owned companies. These accounting statements have traditionally been prepared within the broad guidelines of so-called generally accepted accounting principles (popularly referred to as GAAP, pronounced gap).

But because of the accounting profession's belief that its rules should not impinge on management's flexibility, some latitude is allowed within the realm of "accepted" principles. As a result, companies which appear to be similar based on size, common products, and so forth, can, from an operating point of view, elect to manage their assets quite differently.

The accounting for these differences can cause substantial variations in reported earnings among different companies. More important, however, is the fact that under the "generally accepted" guidelines, even identical operating decisions can be accounted for differently. One airline, for example, might depreciate its airplanes over 12 years, while another might employ an 18-year schedule.

This flexibility has given rise to the allegation that companies will take advantage of this flexibility to "smooth" reported period-to-period earnings comparisons. Evidence from Barry Cushing's [57] doctoral dissertation at Michigan State

University supports this belief. But there is also substantial evidence that for all the confusion such accounting variations generate among the public and for all the grief they cause corporate officers and their CPAs, *the market is remarkably efficient at properly reflecting the true worth of a company.*

Robert Kaplan and Richard Roll [142], who studied the impact on securities prices of elective changes in investment credit or depreciation accounting, had difficulty discerning any statistical significant price effects. Their research is evidence of the market's efficiency at incorporating all publicly available information into the price of a stock.

EARNINGS AND THE ECONOMY

The sensitivity of corporate earnings to the economic climate of particular industries has been studied by both Richard Brealey [35] and Brown and Ball [38]. Brealey found that in some industries less than half of a particular firm's earnings changes were attributable to differences between it and competitor companies. Industries which exhibited a strong tendency to parallel the economy included the auto, department store, nonferrous metal, paper, rubber, and clothing segments. Overall, Brealey found that the impact of the general economy on the earnings of a firm is not only significant but also fairly consistent. He concluded that an understanding of the implications of major economic events should be of considerable value to those attempting to forecast earnings changes.

THE DEFICIENCY OF FUNDAMENTAL ANALYSIS

The most popular approach to valuation entails (a) estimating a stock's future earnings per share, (b) estimating the future price-earnings ratio, and (c) multiplying the two numbers to obtain the expected future value of the stock. While the technique is appealing in its simplicity, its application has several shortcomings. First, large percentages of corporate earnings reflect the state of the economy and the health of a company's industry. Conversely, the expertise of the individual company accounts for a minor portion of its earnings and the price performance of its stock. Thus, while it is conceivable that information on economy-, industry-, and company-related factors could be combined to develop reliable earnings estimates, the methodology is not well suited for the comparative valuation of a universe of securities.

Second, even if this type of analysis is used to develop a probabilistic range of earnings estimates, the methodology does not lend itself to explicit estimates of risk—the crux of MPT. Third, an investor who could forecast future P/E ratios would realize superior rates of return on that basis alone. Thus, linking unreliable estimates of the second variable in the forecasting equation—the future P/E ratio—to even reliable earnings estimates is comparable to using a rubber band to measure distance.

In spite of the case against the traditional forms of fundamental analysis, it will always have its disciples. These people generally recognize the late Benjamin Graham—who (with David Dodd and Sidney Cottle) wrote the classic book *Security Analysis* [109]—as the father of fundamental security analysis. This author (Hagin) had the pleasure of knowing Benjamin Graham, first as a graduate student and later on as a friend. For those who blindly use these techniques, the following quotation stands as a solemn memorial to the professional stature and intellectual integrity of a truly great man.

> . . . I am no longer an advocate of elaborate techniques of security analysis in order to find superior value opportunities. This was a rewarding activity, say, 40 years ago, when *Graham and Dodd* was first published; but the situation has changed . . . [today] I doubt whether such extensive efforts will generate sufficiently superior selections to justify their cost. . . . I'm on the side of the "efficient market" school of thought. . . .
>
> Benjamin Graham, 1976 [292, p. 20].

Chapter 9

Dividends

The rate of return on an investment depends on two factors: capital appreciation and dividend income. To many investors, however, dividend income is something for widows or orphans. But as Richard Brealey has emphasized, "if in 1926 a tax-exempt investor had purchased an equal amount of all New York Stock Exchange equities, and if he had reinvested all subsequent dividends he would have found that by the end of 40 years his capital had multiplied 35 times" (after Fisher and Lorie [91]). Without dividends, "the value of his portfolio would have increased by a factor of only six." [34, p. 4] This would hardly seem to be an advantage sought only by widows and orphans.

While an investor can elect to buy either a high- or a low-dividend payout stock, dividend decisions are made by company management. Basically, a company can do two things with its aftertax earnings. They can be distributed to stockholders as dividends, or they can be retained and reinvested, or plowed back, into the company. It is important to remember, however, that dividends received by a shareholder are included in the shareholder's taxable income. Retained earnings, by contrast, represent an automatic plow back of earnings which, if distributed to stockholders, would be taxed *before* being reinvested. Further, after earnings are distributed to stockholders, and then taxed, they generally cannot be reinvested without an underwriting or brokerage commission.

DIVIDEND-REINVESTMENT PROGRAMS

One way to reinvest dividends without incurring brokerage commissions is to utilize one of the automatic *dividend-reinvestment programs* now offered by over 600 major corporations. AT&T, the largest publicly held U.S. company, instituted a dividend-reinvestment program in 1973. While it should be emphasized that AT&T is an extremely public-minded company, individual investors' overwhelming response to the program is, in the words of Warren Buffett, "out of *Alice in Wonderland*." [40, p. 266]

In 1978, AT&T paid out more than $3.0 billion in cash dividends to the nearly 3 million owners of its common stock. By the end of the year, almost one out of every four stockholders had reinvested a total of $786 million in additional shares supplied directly by the company. This means that AT&T got back 26.7 percent of the money it paid out in dividends by means of what analysts call *disguised payouts*.

Generally speaking, an investor seeking dividend reinvestment has three alternatives. An investor might purchase very low- or zero-dividend payout stocks; reinvestment is truly automatic, and the investor avoids the twin burdens of dividend taxation and reinvestment transaction charges. Alternatively, an investor can participate in an automatic dividend-reinvestment program. With this plan, the investor avoids reinvestment transaction charges and can frequently purchase new stock at a 5 percent discount, although income taxes must be paid on the amount of the dividend. Under the third alternative, an investor can reinvest dividends merely by purchasing additional shares in the open market. In this situation, reinvestment expenses and taxes must be paid.

The real "price" of the automatic dividend-reinvestment alternative for tax-paying investors can be best appreciated by comparing two admittedly extreme situations. In the first case, suppose that in 1978 AT&T, instead of declaring a dividend, merely reinvested the $3.0 billion. In the second situation, suppose that AT&T declared a $3.0 billion dividend and every shareholder signed up for the dividend reinvestment plan.

Under the second program, AT&T would notify each stockholder, as well as the IRS, that the "dividend" had been paid, and the company would supply each investor with the equivalent dollar value of shares of AT&T stock. Shareholders would be required to pay income taxes on the portion of the retained earnings which management had declared as "dividends." If shareholders tax rates averaged 30 percent and the "dividends" totaled $3.0 billion, the IRS would collect $900 million from reinvesting shareholders.

In each situation the company ends up in the same cash position and each investor retains the same proportionate interest in the company. In the latter case, however, the investors end up paying $900 million to the IRS. In this situation, again quoting Warren Buffett, "imagine the joy of shareholders in such circumstances, if the directors were then to double the dividend." [40, p. 267] Such action would double the shareholder's tax bill while all other consequences would remain the same.

DIVIDEND INFORMATION

Research on dividend information has focused on two important decision-making areas:

1. Should you buy a high- or a low-dividend stock?
2. Can news of dividend changes be used to select stocks with above-average returns?

High- versus low-payout stocks. The percentage of a company's total earnings that is distributed as dividends is called the "dividend payout ratio." Typically, a rapidly growing company will retain all or most of its earnings to finance expansion. Similarly, companies with sufficient plant and equipment to meet the demand of their customers have modest expansion needs and can distribute a large fraction of their profits as dividends.

The importance of the dividend payout ratio lies in the fact that the timing and rates of taxes on dividends differ from those on capital gains. Dividends are taxed currently as part of income, while long-term capital gains (assets held more than one year) are subject to taxation only upon sale of the appreciated asset and at rates which are generally half those on income. As a result, for the average investor, *after taxes, a dollar of dividends is worth significantly less than a dollar of capital gains.*

We could therefore reasonably assume that low-dividend payout stocks are relatively more attractive for any investor subject to taxes. It follows, then, that in an efficient market made up only of tax-paying investors, the price of a low-dividend stock would include a premium for this advantage. This conclusion, that *low-dividend stocks are worth more to* tax-paying investors, is counter to one of the age-old tenets of fundamental security analysis. Authors such as Graham, Dodd, and Cottle [109] have long held that the market's pricing mechanisms overwhelmingly favor liberal dividends.

Clearly, however, if the prices of low-dividend stocks were

bid up by tax-paying investors, tax-exempt investors would capitalize on this "temporary" inefficiency and, through their actions, restore the market to an "efficient," fairly priced, state. Not surprisingly, therefore, the actual evidence indicates that there are no substantial differences between the values placed by the market on dividends and those accorded capital gains (see Brealey [35, pp. 4–21]).

While certain kinds of valuation models (discussed in Chapter 28) add the yield "dimension" to a stock's other characteristics, on the average, the market seems to have struck a balance between the traditional belief that liberal dividends are overpriced and the logic that because of differential taxation, cash payouts should receive a lower valuation.

This means that on the average, the investor pays roughly the same price for a dollar of future dividends that is paid for a dollar of future capital gains. But since dividends are taxed at a higher rate, they are worth proportionately less. Hence, for tax-paying investors, there appears to be a slight unadjusted *penalty for owning high-dividend stocks.*

Dividend announcements. Several researchers have examined the rationale which underlies how a firm decides on the percentage of earnings to distribute as dividends versus the amount to be retained by the company. For a variety of reasons, this research shows that the most significant factor in the decision is the amount of earnings which management feels "should" be distributed. To the astonishment of many people, it appears that notions of an "appropriate," or "target," dividend tend to dominate this decision process.

In turn, it appears that the target dividend level is guided by management's desire to establish a pattern of stable dividend growth. This reluctance to change the level applies to both dividend increases and decreases. Dividend reductions are typically viewed as a last resort, while the hesitancy to increase a dividend is attributed to the fear that a higher dividend implies a commitment to continue at that level. Paul Darling [58] has supported this conclusion by showing that the levels of dividends paid between 1930 and 1955 could not be explained by variations in earnings, but instead corresponded to management's optimism about the future.

Here, then, is an important point to consider in examining the usefulness of dividend announcements. Studies that have relied on interviews with corporate management [165], and others which have studied dividend histories [75], conclude that firms do not make dividend changes without thorough assessment of the future. Decreases take place largely because firms have little choice other than to cut the payout. Increases, in addition to reflecting high current earnings, reflect management's optimism that the new dividend level can be sustained. It follows, then, that if dividend changes reflect management's opinion about the future, and if managers can correctly assess the future, dividend changes should serve as barometers of a firm's future prosperity.

This possibility raises two questions. The first, and most obvious, is whether or not dividend changes portend future changes in earnings. If they do, the next question is whether or not the stock's price reflects the fact that prosperity or difficulty lies ahead, by the time the news of the dividend change is available.

To answer the first question, whether or not dividend changes portend future changes in earnings, Joseph Murphy [200] studied the relationship between dividend changes and the subsequent earnings of 244 companies between 1950 and 1965. While the association between dividend changes and subsequent earnings was not as strong as one would like, Murphy was able to conclude that dividend changes tend to reflect the usually accurate assessment by management of future earnings.

Another study of the relationship between dividend announcements and subsequent changes in both earnings and stock prices was made by Richardson Pettit [212] at the Wharton School of Finance and Commerce. Pettit studied the impact of dividend announcements on the subsequent earnings and price performance of 625 companies over four and one-half years. He found that dividend announcements were closely associated with subsequent price performance and that the effect was generally proportionate to the magnitude of the dividend change.

In terms of the market's efficiency, Pettit concluded that the "market's judgment concerning the information implicit in the [dividend] announcement is reflected almost completely as of the end of the announcement month." [212, p. 38] It can be concluded, therefore, that *news of a dividend change contains useful information that is not immediately reflected in the price of the stock*—evidence that the semistrong form of the efficient market hypothesis is not a valid description of the market in this regard.

SUMMARY

Two conclusions can be made regarding dividends. First, contrary to the thinking of many seasoned market professionals, as well as noted authors such as Benjamin Graham, there is evidence that high-dividend payout stocks provide the tax-paying investor with a somewhat lower rate of return than low-payout stocks of comparable risk. Second, presumably because corporations do not alter their dividends casually, dividend changes do mirror management's largely correct assessment of a firm's future earnings trends.

Chapter 10

Company information

The semistrong form of the efficient market hypothesis holds that all publicly available information—not just historical price and volume data—is already reflected in the prices of various investment vehicles. A definitive test of this hypothesis would require the study of all kinds of information, bearing on all types of investment instruments, in every capital market. Fortunately, however, the most popular investment vehicles are those stocks listed on the New York Stock Exchange (NYSE) and the American Stock Exchange (AMEX).

Further, of the four main kinds of information—that is, on the overall economy, a basic industry, an industry subgroup, and a company—many analysts concentrate on company-related data. These people claim that the specificity of company-related information makes this the most predictable level in the information hierarchy. But those who support the efficient market hypothesis argue that the constant scrutiny of company-related information by millions of investors destroys its value to any individual.

This chapter summarizes the research on three kinds of company-related information—stock splits, new listings, and professional opinions.

STOCK SPLITS

The average investor has more misconceptions about stock splits than any other event. A stock split is a decision by the management of a firm to increase (often double) the number of shares of stock outstanding. Many people fail to understand that even though the company has decided to issue more shares, everything else about the company remains unchanged. For instance, following a two-for-one stock split, the

65

price of each new share should be exactly one half the price of an old share and earnings per share, exactly one half their original level.

After a split, each shareholder has exactly enough additional shares to compensate for the lower price. The total worth of each person's holdings, and of the firm's securities, is unchanged. An investor's pieces of paper represent precisely the same proportion of ownership as before the split. In the classic words of A. Wilfred May, one of Wall Street's elder statesmen, "a pie does not grow through its slicing!" [187, p. 5]

Some people contend that the lower price per share brought about by a stock split will "broaden the market" for the company's shares and that the lower price will, in turn, stimulate investment demand. There is no merit to this contention, however, unless one is referring to those investors who could not afford to buy a *single* share at the former price. But, the argument runs, a split lowers the price of 100 share purchase, and investors prefer to buy stock in round lots because they carry lower commission rates. The problem with this reasoning is that while commissions on some trades are lower after a split, the increased volumes of trading at the lower share prices that result from stock splits typically generate higher commissions for the same dollar amount of business.

A final reason some people might give for interpreting splits favorably hinges on the so-called self-fulfilling prophecy. In the stock market, if enough people believe something will happen, their actions will make it happen—despite the fact that the logic underlying their belief is defective. Thus, even though there is no theoretical reason to expect the value of one's holdings to increase because of a stock split, if splits are seen as expressions of progress or management optimism, they might become self-fulfilling predictions.

The first widely read articles on splits were published by C. Austin Barker in the *Harvard Business Review* in 1956. In his first article, Barker concluded that "contrary to the general belief, stock splits do not automatically produce a lasting price gain." [14, p. 101] In his second article he concluded that ". . . split-ups produced no lasting real gains . . . whether . . . in a normal market or in an outstanding bull market." [15, p. 551]

More recent studies of splits have shown that companies announcing stock splits have generally experienced a price improvement in the months before the announcement of the split, but that after the announcement no significant improvement remained.

The most extensive study of stock splits was conducted by Eugene Fama et al. [79], who monitored the behavior of 940 stocks for the 30 months before and after stock splits. The relative performance (that is, with market comovements removed) of a portfolio consisting of these stocks is shown in Figure 10–1. It is important to note that information on the

FIGURE 10–1: Relative pre- and post-split performance of 940 stocks

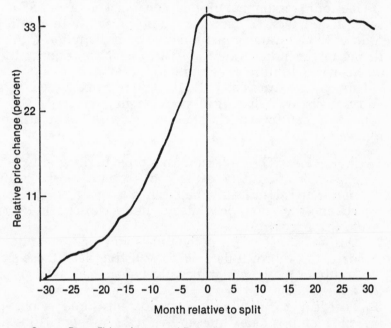

Month relative to split

Source: Fama, Fisher, Jensen, and Roll [79].

splits was not available until immediately before the splits occurred (designated by 0 on the horizontal scale of Figure 10–1)—the point at which the relative price growth *stops*. Those who believe that news of impending splits is useful should note that on the average, for two and one-half years after each split, *the relative price remained within 1 percentage point of the split price*.

This research, plus other evidence reported by Hausman, West, and Largay [121], indicates that splits are a *consequence*, and not a *cause*, of rising stock prices. Thus, it can be concluded that there is no evidence to support buying stocks on news of impending splits. Such information is apparently useless!

NEW LISTINGS

To be eligible for listing on the NYSE, a company must have a minimum of $2.5 million in annual pretax earnings, $16 million in net tangible assets, and $14.5 million in publicly held common stock representing at least 1 million shares spread among 2,000 round-lot shareholders. Needless to say, not all companies can meet these criteria.

One could reason that the decision to list on the NYSE represents the pinnacle of management optimism. In line with this train of thought, news that a company has applied for NYSE listing might indicate that its shares offer an opportunity for above-average future rates of return.

Numerous researchers [79, 177, 276] have examined the pre- and post-listing behavior of stocks traded on the NYSE. The consistent pattern which emerged may be summarized as follows:

1. *Pre-listing.*   Over a period from three to six months before the application date to the application date, these stocks performed significantly better than the market. Such price advances are doubtless a factor in the subsequent decision to list a security.
2. *During listing.*   During the time spanning the application date, the approval date, and the listing date, these stocks continue to show significantly better than average price appreciation.
3. *Post-listing.*   Whether the period measured is one day, one month, or one, three, or five years from the listing date, the rate of return for these stocks is, on average, *below that for the general market.*

Based on these studies, *stocks which have recently moved their trading to the NYSE do not, on the average, represent a likely source of above-average returns.*

PROFESSIONAL INVESTMENT RECOMMENDATIONS

Consistently superior investment analysis must meet three rather severe tests:

1. The analysis must be correct.
2. The "market" must realize that the analysis was correct in "time."
3. The analysis must not be widely used.

One of this author's acquaintances once confided that he had developed a sophisticated technique for selecting undervalued securities. His problem was that the market did not have the benefit of his careful analysis and his favored securities remained "undervalued."

At the other extreme, it is possible that regardless of the underlying "correctness" of an investment recommendation, the publicized opinion of a respected professional could precipitate dramatic price changes. Such stock market opinions could, in fact, become self-fulfilling predictions. If this is so. it might be a useful investment strategy to respond quickly to the recommendations of widely circulated advisory services.

Researchers have long been intrigued by the possibility that advisory services either make forecasts which turn out to be correct or, alternatively, issue forecasts which cause market shifts which, in turn, render the forecasts correct. As long ago as 1933, Alfred Cowles studied the forecasting ability of 16 financial services, 20 insurance companies, and 25 financial publications. Cowles concluded that the 16 financial services underperformed the market by 1.43 percent per annum, the 20 insurance companies underperformed by 1.20 percent, while the 25 financial publications underperformed by 4 percent per annum. [52]

Several modern studies have measured the market's response to published investment advice. In 1958, Robert Ferber, at the University of Illinois, studied the price movements related to recommendations of four major advisory services. After removing market and industry comovements, Ferber found that "in the very short run, stock market service recommendations tend to influence the prices of approximately two-thirds of the stocks in the direction indicated. . . ." [85, p. 94] By the end of the first week after publication, the average profit attainable from this information was 1.1 percent. However, after this very short-run adjustment, Ferber found no evidence of a longer run impact. Ferber also concluded that the short-run price adjustments were *caused* by the recommendation, and not *predicted* by them. He based this conclusion on ". . . the failure of the recommended stocks . . . to outpace the market . . . in the week or two immediately preceding the recommendation." [85, p. 94]

Other studies by Ruff [235] and Stoffels [264] confirm the general conclusion that professional recommendations accurately foretell future price changes and that there is a measurable short-term price adjustment to reflect the "news." Further evidence by Colker [47] indicates that stocks recommended by advisory services and brokerage houses tend to outperform representative market averages over the following year. It can be concluded, therefore, that *widely distributed professional opinions can to some degree presage short-term and (to a lesser extent) long-term relative price changes.*

SUMMARY

Several conclusions are possible from the examination of information on splits, new listings and professional investment recommendations. First, to the chagrin of many advocates, stock splits typically signal the *end* of price growth and *not* its continuation! Second, new listings do not offer the potential for better-than-average rates of return. Third, professional opinions can *cause* price movements. Since such publicly available information apparently is not efficiently assimilated into stock prices, *the semistrong form of the efficient market hypothesis is not valid* in this regard.

Chapter 11

Market information

This chapter examines the usefulness of information about new issues, secondary distributions, block trades, odd-lot transactions, short-interest positions, and odd-lot short sales.

NEW ISSUES

The new issue market channels investment capital into companies. The creation of a new issue requires three steps: origination, underwriting, and distribution. Origination includes the negotiations between investment banking firms and the issuing corporation to determine price and assure compliance with legalities. Underwriting refers to the purchase or guaranteed sale of the issue by participating investment banking firms. Finally, distribution involves the sale of the shares to the public and the public's financial intermediaries.

In these transactions, the underwriter has a "two-hat" role of trying to obtain the "highest" offering price for the issuing company while, at the same time, ensuring that the offering price will be "low" enough to enable the issue to be fully subscribed. If the shares offered are priced above what the market is willing to pay, the underwriter guaranteeing the sale at the offering price can sustain large losses. Thus, one could reason that to play it safe, underwriters will tend to underprice new issues.

Such underpricing was alleged in a 1963 Securities and Exchange Commission (SEC) study and later refuted by Professor George Stigler at the University of Chicago. In a pointed article criticizing the SEC, Stigler [263] showed that between 1923 and 1955 the relative long-term performance of new issues was consistently below that of the market.

In a contradictory study on the post-offering behavior of seasoned new issues between 1953 and 1963, Irwin Friend et al. reported ". . . no evidence of any penalty or premium associated with new issues. . . ." [104, p. 492] Still another contradictory study by Frank Reilly and Kenneth Hatfield, at the University of Kansas, traced the relative appreciation of 53 new issues between 1963 and 1965 for a week, a month, or a year after their respective offerings. All tests showed superior results for investors in new issues. [219, p. 80]

Results paralleling those of Reilly and Hatfield were reported by Dennis Logue in his doctoral dissertation at Cornell in 1971. Logue studied 250 new issues marketed between 1965 and 1969 and reported that "on the average, the risk-adjusted rates of return of new issues bought at the offerings were significantly greater than they sould be in an efficient market no matter if the holding period is two weeks, three months, or one year." [172]

Still different results were reported in a recent study by John McDonald and A. K. Fisher [176] at Stanford University. They examined the post-offering performance of 142 unseasoned new issues during 1969 and 1970. Their findings showed extremely large positive returns if measured one week after the offerings. However, the end of the first week to the end of the first year, 51 weeks later, they found that average returns were negative. McDonald and Fisher also showed that the size of the price change in the first week was unrelated to future performance.

Hence, studies on the performance of new issues over different time periods appear contradictory. To resolve these differences, it might be useful to examine only measures of "risk-adjusted" performance. Specifically, it would be valuable to know: (a) the comparative level of risk that is inherent in the new issue market and (b) the prevailing "price of risk" (i.e., the "character" of the market) in each of the time periods studied. These topics are discussed in subsequent chapters.

SECONDARY DISTRIBUTIONS

Any offering of stock after its new issue offering is termed a "secondary." When a secondary distribution is so large in size that it might swamp the exchange's auction process, the offering is generally organized off the floor of the exchange. The sellers are typically institutional investors or the trusts of families of the company's founders. The reasons for such sales are as varied as the reasons for any sale. But the fact that these sellers consist of knowledgeable investors, who are sometimes presumed to have superior information—in combination with the fact that *they* are disposing of their shares—is viewed by many as a "sell signal."

A detailed study of secondary distributions has been made by Myron Scholes [236] at the University of Chicago. By tracing the average relative performance (that is, with market comovements removed) for 345 stocks from 26 days before the offerings to 14 days after, Scholes found that secondary distributions were followed by an abrupt drop in market price of approximately 2 percent.

To study the long-term consequences of secondary offerings, Scholes traced the monthly performance of 1,207 stocks for 18 months preceding and following the sales. Here Scholes found that the market, on the average, interprets a secondary distribution as a signal that "something" is wrong with the stock. Further, when Scholes classified the relative pre- and post-secondary distribution performance by the kind of seller, he found some interesting differences. These are shown in Figure 11–1.

These data indicate that individuals typically sell after a substantial price rise (relative to the market). Further, the market does not react to the "news" embodied in individuals' sales. While firms and officers also frequently sell their own stock after a substantial rise, the market clearly interprets this "information" as a signal to sell and adjusts relative share

FIGURE 11–1: Comparative performance of secondaries by type of seller

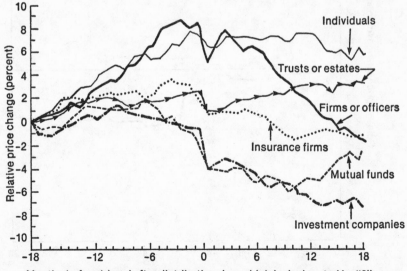

Months before (-) and after distribution day, which is designated by "0"

Source: Scholes [236].

prices downward. Whether or not from the herd (or if you prefer, "heard") effect, when mutual funds and investment companies sell, this information has lead to a further markdown in share prices.

Thus, whether superior analysis or self-fulfilling prophecies were responsible, Scholes found that stocks sold by mutual funds and investment companies were destined to exhibit relatively poor performance. The price drops that are observed after large secondary distributions may be the result either of the sellers' wisdom or of the market's assumption of their wisdom, but the result remains the same—large secondary distributions, on the average, precede price declines.

BLOCK TRADES

Alan Kraus and Hans Stoll [155] have studied the price behavior of stocks before and after block trades. (A block trade is

FIGURE 11–2: Relative price performance for 1,121 blocks on minus ticks

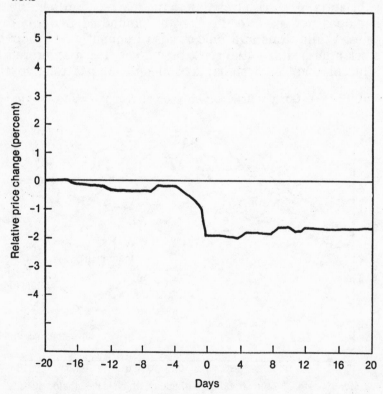

Source: Kraus and Stoll [155].

a transaction of 10,000 shares or more.) They reasoned that block trades occurring on minus ticks might portend further selling pressure. (A minus tick means that the transaction was at a lower price than the immediately preceding transaction.) Similarly, they proposed that a block trade occurring on plus ticks might presage further demand.

To test these possibilities, Kraus and Stoll studied 2,199 block trades on the NYSE from July 1968 to September 1969. The results of the study for 20 days before and after each block trade (adjusted for the movement of the market) are shown in Figures 11–2 and 11–3.

FIGURE 11–3: Relative price performance for 345 blocks on plus ticks

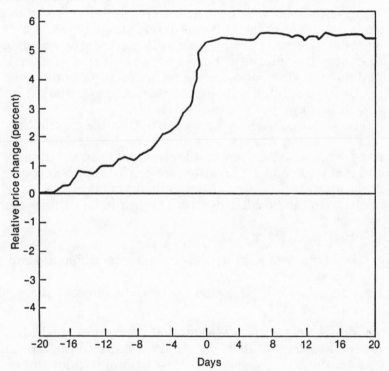

Figure 11–2 summarizes their findings for minus ticks. Notice that the prices on day zero (the day of the trade) averaged 2 percent below the prices of a day earlier. This figure vividly illustrates the validity of the semistrong form of the efficient market hypothesis. By the time the information was

publicly available (day zero), the price adjustment was complete.

Figure 11–3, showing the average performance preceding and following block trades on plus ticks, presents a similar picture of the market's efficiency. Throughout the 20-day period preceding the day that the block trade occurred, average prices made a significant upward adjustment. This adjustment process was complete, however, by the time the news of the block trade became publicly available.

ODD-LOT TRANSACTIONS

If asked to rank various classes of investors in terms of their "closeness" to important information, one would probably begin with management insiders, closely followed by market professionals. In last place would probably be the small amateur investor. Given such a ranking, there is a temptation to expect the informed, presumably skillful, professional investors to attain above-average rates of return. Conversely, the relatively unskilled and uninformed amateurs might be expected to show below-average returns.

The so-called odd-lot theory is based on the assumption that odd-lot trading (transactions involving less than 100 shares) reflects the sentiments of small, presumably amateur, investors and that these odd-lot investors are consistently below-average performers. If this is so, this simplistic notion goes, by acting contrary to the odd-lot investor one can obtain above-average returns.

This raises two questions:

1. Is the performance of odd-lot investors different from that of round-lot investors?
2. Can odd-lot information be used to forecast share price movements?

Odd-lot versus round-lot market performance. D. J. Klein [153], at Michigan State University, compared the rates of return on the 20 most sold and most bought odd-lot stocks. Regardless of the period measured, the odd-lotters' purchases yielded lower rates of return than did the stocks they sold. This conclusion was subsequently confirmed by Stanley Kaish [141]. The studies of such performance differences have not been as numerous or as definitive as one would like, and there is some countervailing evidence, but the research leans toward the conclusion that odd-lot investors are relatively unsuccessful.

Odd-lot trading rules. Unfortunately, a big step in logic is required to move from modest evidence that odd-lot investors as a group achieve below-average performance, to the use of information about their trading activities to develop a market strategy. Nonetheless, some people believe that useful trading rules can be developed from odd-lot statistics. The problem is that the strategies based on odd-lot statistics [see 146, 147] which have performed well have been "fined tuned" on historical data. But without some reason why odd-lot sale/purchase ratios should work, there is neither empirical nor theoretical justification for their use.

SHORT-INTEREST POSITIONS

One contrary opinion approach to stock selection and market timing is based on short-interest statistics. Short sales are made by people who expect the market to go down. In a regular securities transaction, shares are bought first and sold later. In a short transaction, the sale comes first, the purchase later. A short sale is effected by borrowing stock through a broker and selling it at the current market price. The proceeds of the sale are then held as collateral for the loan of the stock. To close out the short position, the borrowed stock must be replaced. This is done by buying[1] an equivalent number of shares at the then current market price. If a short sale is made at $100 and the short can later be covered by buying the stock at $90, there will be a $10 per share profit (before any intervening interest on the loan and repayment of any dividend income).

Market technicians know that each short position must eventually be closed out with a purchase. Hence, they reason, an increase in outstanding short interest represents an increase in potential demand, which serves as a downside cushion for the stock. Conversely, followers of this system believe that a reduction in short interest reflects a decline in latent demand and makes the market for the stock weak.

To assess the usefulness of short-interest information, it is necessary to answer three basic questions:

1. Do short-interest traders consistently attain above-average performance?

---

[1] Short sales "against the box" are not replaced by market purchases. The term "against the box" means the sale is made against stock held in a safe-deposit box. For a full description of this trading strategy and when it might be used, see Cohen, Zinbarg, and Zeikel [44].

2. Can short-interest statistics be used to forecast general market movements?
3. Can short-interest statistics be used to predict the movements of individual stocks?

Performance of short-interest traders. A *trader* is a short-term, in-and-out speculator. Most short sellers are traders, as evidenced by SEC statistics showing that most short positions are held for only about two weeks. In view of the fact that short sellers (a) receive no dividends, (b) pay interest on the borrowed stock, and (c) must deal with the difficulties inherent in predicting short-term price movements, one would expect short sellers to do *worse than the average* investor.

Not surprisingly, studies of short-interest transactions [189] have concluded that on the average, short sellers have absolutely no market timing ability and, as a result, incur large losses. Their poor performance does not, however, bear on the question of whether such behavior serves as a market predictor. Regardless of their success or failure, the asserted cushioning effect resulting from short-interest profit taking in a price decline is a separate issue.

Short-interest market indicators. According to several researchers [see 35, 187], the aggregate level of short interest is not correlated with market levels. But because the level of short interest fluctuates with the market's overall volume, a better relative measure of this activity is the ratio of short interest to average daily volume. Tests of this measure indicate that there is a slight correlation between the short-interest ratio and the market [see 35, 119, 238, 239]—as predicted by proponents of short-interest indicators. There is no evidence, however, that such information can be translated into a profitable trading strategy.

Short-interest stock indicators. To test the usefulness of short-interest statistics for predicting the movement of individual stocks, Randall D. Smith [260] studied the performance of portfolios of NYSE and AMEX stocks that were selected according to the short-interest statistics. Smith found that the portfolios picked on this basis favored extremely volatile stocks. This is easily explained by the proclivity of the short-interest trader for quick action. A portfolio of such stocks would also be expected to amplify the market's movement. Indeed, Smith found that the stocks selected by using short-interest statistics as a guide showed wide fluctuations in profits and losses. But the overall performance of stocks picked on the basis of the short-interest statistics was in line with that of randomly chosen stocks with similar risk.

ODD-LOT SHORT SALES

Many people who believe that both odd-lot transactions and short sales are plausible indicators reason that together—in other words, odd-lot short sales—they provide a useful, but quite different, indicator. The reasoning behind this indicator is based on the assumption that small investors are usually not short sellers. When the small investors do move to the short side, it is because they feel strongly that the market is going down. If the little guy is always wrong, this clear indication of small-investor pessimism is interpreted as a sure sign that a market bottom is near.

The conclusion that small investors do not obtain dependable advice (or if they do, shun it in favor of intuition) is further buttressed by the fact that odd-lot investors, with remarkable consistency, do sell short at market lows. Manown Kisor and

TABLE 11–1: Relation between levels of odd-lot short-sales ratio and changes in market index over subsequent month, 1960–1969

Odd-lot short-sales ratio	Number of occurrences	Percentage of occasions that market rose	Average market change (by percent)
0.0–1.0	1,222	56.1	0.2
1.0–2.0	652	71.0	1.1
2.0–3.0	181	63.0	0.4
3.0–4.0	65	67.7	1.8
4.0–5.0	43	72.1	2.3
5.0–6.0	35	88.6	3.3
Greater than 6.0	50	96.0	6.1

Source: Kisor and Niederhoffer [152].

Victor Niederhoffer [152] documented this phenomenon by contrasting the odd-lot short-sales ratio with the general level of the market between 1960 and 1969. Their results, reproduced in Table 11–1, show that the "little guy" who sold short consistently misjudged the market during that period.

SUMMARY

The research reported in this chapter leads to the general conclusion that the market is efficient. While it appears that the new issue market has not provided abnormally high, or low, risk-adjusted returns, there is evidence that secondary distributions by "knowledgeable" sellers preceed price declines. Conversely, block trades provide a classical illustration of market efficiency—by the time the information is publicly available, the price adjustment is complete. The studies of odd-lot transactions and short sales, both individually and together, tend to support the belief that both short-sellers and small (odd-lot) investors have below average performance. Nonetheless, the case for using trading schemes based on these statistics is far from persuasive.

In short, the evidence supports the semistrong form of an "almost" efficient market. That is, while careful analysis of historical data can, from time to time, reveal selected inefficiencies, there is no evidence that these inefficiencies can be translated into investment strategies that will provide above-average performance.

Inside information

Under the strong form of the efficient market hypothesis, even investors with privileged information cannot use it to produce consistently superior investment performance. This chapter examines that assertion.

INSIDERS

Insiders (i.e., exchange specialists, substantial owners, directors, and corporate officers) are required to report their security dealings to the SEC. Relatives of these insiders, various employees, and banks which might have access to the same confidential information are not subject to SEC monitoring. Obviously, it would be extremely difficult to monitor the stock transactions of every insider's friends and relatives. So, to protect against the possibility of abuse by secretly informed outsiders, the law considers any individual who trades on the basis of nonpublic information to be a de facto insider.

In one landmark case concerning the use of nonpublic information, it was alleged that Merrill Lynch had advised certain institutional clients that Douglas Aircraft would soon report disappointing earnings. The SEC hearing examiner, Warren E. Blair, used the term "tippees" to refer to persons who, through a corporate insider, came into the possession of confidential information. He held that it was the responsibility of a tippee receiving "material inside information" from insiders either to disclose the information publicly or to refrain from trading on it.

The SEC has subsequently reaffirmed that acting on a tip is a violation of the law if there is reason to believe that the information was not made public. In fact, the SEC has ruled that people who use information which innocently comes into their possession are in violation of the law if they have reason to know that the information was intended to be confidential. The law is thus explicit: *all parties to securities transactions must have access to the same material facts.*

The significance of the preceding point cannot be overemphasized. This rule obligates all publicly owned companies to ensure that disclosed changes in material facts are widely disseminated. If information is disclosed to one analyst, it must be made available to all analysts. This constructively limits all investment research to the gathering and analysis of publicly available facts.

The law notwithstanding, the prospective buyer of a share of stock faces two groups of people who have access to confidential information. First, the management of the company knows, or certainly should know, more about that company than the average investor. Second, when a purchase order reaches the floor of a stock exchange, the specialist in that stock is privy to nonpublic information on pending buy and sell orders at specific prices.

Thus, four important questions are:

1. Do management insiders profit from their privileged information?
2. Do specialists profit from their privileged information?
3. Do the actions of management insiders provide investors with useful information?
4. Do the actions of specialists provide investors with useful information?

MANAGEMENT INSIDERS

Of all groups, management insiders are in the best position to foresee the future of their companies. This does not mean that insiders use such information for personal profit. There are two deterrents to such insider transactions. First, there is the moral obligation of corporate officers to honor their fiduciary responsibilities. Second, certain SEC restrictions (preventing short-term gains, for example) constrain those who might otherwise neglect their moral and fiduciary obligations.

Nonetheless, insiders can and do make fully disclosed purchases and sales of their companies' stock. After a clerical and printing delay of about one month, a complete record of these transactions is available in the *Official Summary of Security Transactions and Holdings.*

Several researchers have attempted to find out whether management insiders display better than average foresight in their company-related investment decisions. Donald Rogoff [221] studied the relationship between insider trades and subsequent stock performance in his doctoral dissertation at Michigan State University. Based on a sample of 98 companies between 1957 and 1960, Rogoff found that in 162 cases of predominant insider buying, the stock outperformed the market during the next six months in 102 cases and underperformed the market in only 54 cases. Of 210 instances of predominant insider selling, 112 sales preceded relative declines, while 98 were followed by relative gains.

In a study of insider activity during 1963–64, James Lorie and Victor Niederhoffer [175], at the University of Chicago, found that predominant insider buying preceded 36 advances, compared with 19 declines. Of the 124 instances of predominant selling, 81 sales were followed by declines and 43 preceded advances.

Shannon Pratt and C. W. DeVere [215] took the issue of insider trading a step further and studied the profitability of 52,000 insider transactions between 1960 and 1966. They defined an "insider consensus" as three or more buys or sells, respectively, with none of the opposite transaction. The average relative stock performance following such insider activity is shown in Figure 12–1.

Notice that one year after a consensus of insider sales, those stocks showed an average positive return of 9.6 percent. This is a respectable rate of return and reflects the general market uptrend during the period covered by the study. The results following insider buying, however, are almost too good to be true. Stocks bought by three or more insiders during one month had appreciated 27.1 percent a year later. Further, there was an obvious long-run difference between the performance of the two groups. Clearly, the information depicted in Figure 12–1 does not support the strong form of the efficient market hypothesis.

It should also be asked whether the publicly available knowledge of insider activities is useful to outsiders seeking above-average returns. Studies on the usefulness of the published reports of insider activities are encouraging. Pratt and DeVere found that imitating insiders' actions even one or two months after the record of their actions was published provided above-average performance.

It is not really surprising that management insiders are bet-

FIGURE 12-1: Performance of stocks experiencing unusual insider activity—no lag

Source: Pratt and DeVere [215].

ter than average investors in their own stocks—a refutation of the strong form of the efficient market hypothesis. What is surprising is that this advantage is available to anyone who reads the *Official Summary of Security Transactions and Holdings*—or listens to someone who does.

EXCHANGE SPECIALISTS

Another group of insiders—the specialists who maintain markets in securities on the floor of a stock exchange—also has confidential information. They know the size and prices of standing buy and sell orders. Under exchange rules, this information is confined to the specialist. So, again, the questions which need to be answered are:

1. Do specialists profit from their privileged information?
2. Do any of their actions provide useful information?

As discussed earlier (Chapter 4), successive intraday price changes on the NYSE do not occur in accordance with the random-walk model. The question remains, however, whether the specialists use of the private information on their books is responsible for the nonrandom intraday pattern. This question can be answered by taking a closer look at the behavior of intraday price changes.

There is a pronounced tendency for stock prices to cluster around whole numbers, halves, quarters, and odd one eighths—in that order. M. F. M. Osborne [211] probed this phenomenon by studying what he called "partially reflecting barriers." He hypothesized that if a stock's price is "reflected" back down as it rises to a whole number level, we should find an inordinately large number of daily highs ending in 7/8 fractions. Similarly, if prices are reflected back up as they sink to whole numbers, we should find an abnormally large number of daily lows with 1/8 fractions.

Osborne found such a distribution of prices; that is, whole number and half number price levels acted as partially impenetrable barriers. Thus, many stocks showed daily highs of 7/8 or 3/8 because they were unable to attain the "barrier" price level. Conversely, an inordinate number of lows were observed at price levels just above integers and halves—at 1/8 and 5/8. Thus, as stock prices move either up or down toward whole or half numbers, there is a tendency for prices to reverse. This tendency for prices to reflect off of whole-number "resistance" or "support" points is illustrated in Figure 12–2. Victor Niederhoffer [203, 204] later confirmed Osborne's results for a much larger sample of stocks.

Research conducted by this author (see Hagin [116]) provides further evidence of this phenomenon. Intraday lows and highs for 784 major stocks, classified by price range, are summarized in Table 12–1. The data in the first column of this table were compiled by comparing the number of times over a four-year period each stock's daily high ended with a 1/8 fraction with the number of times its daily low ended with a 1/8 fraction. If the number of lows ending with a 1/8 fraction exceeded the number of highs with a 1/8 fraction, that stock was tallied in the column labeled "more lows at 1/8." The other columns were calculated in a similar fashion.

If prices do not meet resistance at whole numbers, there would be only slight differences between the entries in each column. If, however, prices do tend to be reflected off whole

FIGURE 12–2: Reflection tendency

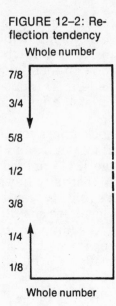

Whole number

7/8

3/4

5/8

1/2

3/8

1/4

1/8

Whole number

numbers, there would be a predominance of "more lows at ⅛" and "more highs at ⅞" as shown in Figure 12–2.

To best examine the data in Table 12–1, place a sheet of paper across the page so that only the information for the first price range ($0–$9) is visible. For stocks priced in the $0–$9 range, there is no evidence of reflection. In the next price range

TABLE 12–1: Comparison of intraday lows and highs at ⅛ and ⅞ fractional prices for stocks classified by average price range

Average Price Range ($)	More lows at ⅛	More highs at ⅛	More lows at ⅞	More highs at ⅞
0–9	60	59	60	57
10–19	90	43	28	108
20–29	102	17	8	112
30–39	132	6	3	135
40–49	108	6	2	113
50–59	70	2	0	73
60–69	40	0	0	40
70–79	23	0	0	23
80–99	12	1	0	13
100–999	9	1	0	9
Total	646	135	101	683

Source: Hagin [116].

($10–$19), however, the excess of more lows at ⅛ and more highs at ⅞ provides overwhelming evidence of reflections. Further, the tendency toward such reflection increases with the price of the stock. Clearly, one would not expect this kind of reflection in a perfectly efficient market.

The specialist system is a curious anomaly. Evolving legal theory holds that *all* parties to a stock transaction must have equal access to information. Yet, the exchanges allow specialists, who trade with the public for their own accounts, to have access to private information. This author has discussed elsewhere (see Hagin [117]) how specialists can use their information on pending buy and sell orders for personal profit. This activity causes the reflection phenomena illustrated in Table 12–1. While it has not been documented, it is reasonable to assume that investors who know that there is an inordinately high probability that a daily high will be at the ⅞ fraction, and an inordinately high probability that a daily low will be at the ⅛ fraction, can use this knowledge to improve their decisions on purchase and sale points.

Chapter 13

Conclusion: Efficient market hypothesis

WEAK FORM

The weak form of the efficient market hypothesis holds that information on the past movements of stock prices and volumes cannot be used to predict future stock prices. In examining the validity of this hypothesis, it is useful to divide the empirical tests into certain categories. First, since any discussion of the weak form of the hypothesis requires an explicit definition of "past," it is useful to discuss three categories of "past"—intraday, between 1 and 40 days, and more than 40 days. Second, since certain results can be statistically significant and still not provide the basis for a profitable investment strategy, it is useful to differentiate between two categories of "significant" research—statistical and practical.

When the evidence in support of the weak form of the efficient market hypothesis is viewed in this context, the conclusions are both clear and consistent. Beginning with the shortest possible time periods (intraday price changes), there is statistical evidence that such changes are not random. While this would imply that someone who could trade without commissions (such as a specialist) might be able to implement inordinately profitable trading strategies, this level of nonrandomness has no practical significance for someone who must pay transaction charges. This research is emphatic in the conclusion that practices such as tape reading are useless!

In the next time interval, the period between 1 and 40 days, there is absolutely no reliable evidence that historical price and volume information is statistically, much less practically, significant. In the third time interval, in excess of 40 days, there is statistical evidence of the phenomenon of relative strength continuation, where the best performing stocks tend to show above-average performance in subsequent periods. Attempts to translate these statistical phenomena into reliable, practical trading strategies, however, have met with failure.

Thus, two conclusions can be drawn with regard to the weak form of the efficient market hypothesis:

1. The weak form of the efficient market hypothesis is a valid description of the market for anyone who is interested in developing profitable investment strategies from historical price or volume information.
2. There is neither a theoretical foundation nor empirical support for technical analysis based on historical price and volume data.

SEMISTRONG FORM

The most widely used form of fundamental security analysis rests on developing projections of price-earnings multiples and earnings per share. Unfortunately, price-earnings multiplies are subject to wide swings for which there is neither a theoretical nor empirical basis for prediction. Nonetheless, even though the vagaries of price-earnings multiples compromise the basis for this kind of analysis, it can be shown that accurate earnings estimates would provide above-average investment performance.

The semistrong form of the efficient market hypothesis, however, raises serious questions about an analysts' ability to develop useful earnings forecasts. Specifically, this form of the hypothesis holds that the analysis of any publicly available information is pointless because all such information is already reflected in stock prices.

The evidence here is again clear. First, it has been shown that period-to-period earnings changes behave in accordance with a random-walk model. This means that the common practice of basing future earnings projections on historical patterns of earnings changes is of no value.

Second, studies which have examined the behavior of stock prices prior to unexpected earnings changes dramatize that the market is remarkably efficient at accurately anticipating such fluctuations. This evidence indicates that the marketplace is filled with competent analysts who, as a whole, accurately forecast earnings. In this extremely competitive arena it is doubtful that a few superior earnings forecasters *consistently* "beat the market to the punch."

Dividend information raises a significant challenge to the efficient market hypothesis. There is evidence to support the contention that dividend changes mirror management's largely correct assessment of a firm's future.

A systematic examination of other levels of the information hierarchy reveals only isolated exceptions to a purely efficient market setting. There is evidence, for example, that professional opinions on stocks can cause price movements and that secondary distributions by sellers, whom the market views as "knowledgeable," precede price declines.

STRONG FORM

In its strong form, the efficient market hypothesis holds that even investors with privileged information cannot use that information to develop profitable investing strategies. Not surprisingly, there is little support for this hypothesis. Management insiders do have extra insight into their company's future. Also, there is evidence that stock exchange specialists cause abnormal patterns of fractional price movements.

Significance of the findings

Given the evidence, the stock market can accurately be described as a "nearly efficient" marketplace. Unquestionably, if an opportunity for inordinate profit presents itself in the market, it will not go unnoticed. In such a marketplace one would not expect prices to deviate by much, or for long, from what is perceived to be a "fair" price by the myriad market participants.

The conclusion that the market is "reasonably efficient" is important for two reasons. First, if the market was inefficient (i.e., there were feasible strategies for attaining consistently above-average performances) it would not be necessary to study MPT. But, given the fact that the market is reasonably efficient, it is naïve to assume that the diligent pursuit of traditional forms of analysis will provide above-average returns. Second, a "reasonably efficient" market is a prerequisite for the use of MPT. Without such a high level of efficiency, the theoretical foundation upon which MPT rests would not exist.

PART TWO

MPT: BUILDING BLOCKS

Chapter 14

Forms of risk

Risk is the possibility that the actual return from an investment will differ from the expected return. Embedded in this definition is a subtle, but important, distinction between "risk" and "uncertainty." In situations involving "risk," the probabilities of various outcomes are known. But under "uncertainty," there is no knowledge of the probability distribution of the possible outcomes. In roulette, for example, while there is no way of predicting what the next outcome will be, explicit knowledge is available on the underlying probabilities of all possible outcomes. Hence, in roulette, the exact risk associated with any situation can be calculated. At the other extreme, a prospective investor in a new and unseasoned company has no reliable means of estimating the likelihood of sales, earnings, or stock price distributions. Technically, the latter situation is characterized by uncertainty, not risk.

Recent research has succeeded in eliminating much of the uncertainty previously associated with investment decisions. Much as someone interested in playing roulette might tally the frequency of the various occurrences on a particular wheel in order to derive the probability of certain outcomes, Fisher and Lorie [91, 92, 93] and Ibbotson and Sinquefield [127, 128] have meticulously tallied the results of investing in various markets over varying lengths of time. Through such research, much of the uncertainty and guesswork which would otherwise be associated with investment decision making has now been upgraded to the status of "calculated risk."

While it is useful to bear the distinction between risk and uncertainty in mind, most practitioners do not make this distinction. Thus, from the traditional investment perspective, there are several different kinds of risk: interest-rate, liquidity, purchasing power, market, and business. Modern portfolio theorists have recast and extended these notions under the rubric of investment risk.

INTEREST-RATE RISK

Most investments provide current income, such as bond interest, common or preferred stock dividends, or rental income from real estate holdings. The relative worth of these returns varies over time as interest rates (the rental charges for money) fluctuate in line with the changing supply of, and demand for, this "commodity."

When interest rates rise, a bond paying a fixed return will become a less desirable investment. Thus, an interest rates rise, bond prices fall. Suppose that the prevailing long-term interest rate is 8 percent. This means that an investor can enter into a long-term contract under which $1,000 can be rented to the issuer of the bond in return for 8 percent, or $80 a year. Once consummated, there is a long-term contractual obligation to accept $80 a year until the end of the "rental period"—when the $1,000 will be returned.

If, however, the investor decides to sell the contract before the end of the rental period, the price that someone else would be willing to pay for it will depend on prevailing interest rates. For example, when prevailing rates are at 10 percent, a contract yielding 8 percent on its face value will be worth less than the 10 percent contracts which are currently available in the market. Similarly, fixed-income contracts increase in value as interest rates decline. Since dividends derived from common stock ownership are similar to the interest derived from bonds, stock prices are influenced by fluctuations in the prevailing interest rates on alternative investments.

LIQUIDITY RISK

Liquidity refers to the ease with which an investment can be converted into cash. Liquidity risk, therefore, represents the possibility of sustaining a loss from current value just by the process of "liquidation," or converting an asset into cash. Generally speaking, shares of an NYSE listed company are highly liquid. Even here, as institutions try to build extremely large positions in a particular stock, the adverse impact on liquidity must be considered.

PURCHASING POWER RISK

We hear a lot about inflation these days, and its threat is indeed a serious one. Since 1967 the average increase in the Consumer Price Index (CPI) has been more than 6 percent per year. To understand and appreciate (or if you prefer, respect) the significance of such an index it is necessary to examine its impact on some "benchmark" item.

There are several ways to measure the historical impact of inflation. One is to contrast current spending requirements with historical requirements. Another is to examine the current worth of "old" money. Both are illustrated in Table 14–1.

TABLE 14–1: Impact of inflation (CPI): 1967–1979

	Year	
	1967	1979
Equivalent purchasing power	$1,000	$2,012
Purchasing power of $1,000	$1,000	$ 476

* Under the assumption of an average annual increase in the Consumer Price Index (CPI) of 6 percent.

These data show that spending $2,012 in 1979 would be the equivalent of spending $1,000, 12 years before. Similarly, it would take a $1,000 bill in 1979 to purchase the same quantity of consumer goods which $476 could have bought in 1967.

Probably the most useful perspective from which to view inflation is to think of it as a *tax on income*. Using $10,000 held in a bank savings account which earns 5 percent annually as an example, consider the scenarios shown in Table 14–2.

Scenario 1 combines annual income consisting of the 5 percent interest payment with 5 percent inflation and zero income tax. Scenario 2 combines an annual interest income of 5 percent with zero inflation and a 100 percent income tax rate. Notice that the year-end purchasing power under each scenario is identical. This means that for an investor who earns 5 percent from a savings account, the effect of 5 percent inflation is equivalent of a 100 percent income tax rate!

Since the inflation rate has averaged more than 6 percent annually since 1967, scenarios 3 and 4 more accurately describe the pretax impact of rising price levels on a 5 percent savings account. Here, for an investor who earns 5 percent, the effect of a 6 percent inflation rate is the same as a 120 percent

TABLE 14–2: Inflation as a tax on income

In each scenario it is assumed that:
Start $10,000
Plus: Annual income (5%)   500

SCENARIO 1:	Inflation 5% Income tax 0%	SCENARIO 2:	Inflation 0% Income tax 100%
Start	$10,000	Start	$10,000
Plus: Annual income (5%)	500	Plus: Annual income (5%)	500
Less: Inflation (5%)	−500	Less: Inflation (0%)	0
Less: Income tax (0%)	0	Less: Income tax (100%)	−500
Year-end purchasing power	$10,000	Year-end purchasing power	$10,000

SCENARIO 3:	Inflation 6% Income tax 0%	SCENARIO 4:	Inflation 0% Income tax 120%
Start	$10,000	Start	$10,000
Plus: Annual income (5%)	500	Plus: Annual income (5%)	500
Less: Inflation (6%)	−600	Less: Inflation (0%)	0
Less: Income tax (0%)	0	Less: Income tax (120%)	−600
Year-end purchasing power	$ 9,900	Year-end purchasing power	$ 9,900

tax rate. In reality, however, we have both—inflation and taxation. But, of the two, inflation is far more damaging than any tax enacted by legislators.

Unfortunately, tax-exempt investors are also "taxed" by inflation. As a final illustration of the "tax" of inflation, consider a tax-exempt investor who earns 8 percent from a bond portfolio during a year in which the inflation rate is 7 percent. In this case the "tax rate"—the seven-eighths of the return drained away by inflation—is 87.5 percent!

Clearly, the penny postcard, nickel ice cream cone, $800 Ivy League tuition, and $1,000 Chevrolet are long past. Investing in a world with inflation is in some ways an *Alice in Wonderland* situation: "If you want to keep in the same place, you must run. If you want to go someplace else, you must run twice as fast."

MARKET RISK

The market value of sound, well-managed companies can be adversely affected by overall stock market declines. This is not surprising because the fortunes of individual companies, as well as the fortunes of the overall market, are subject to many of the same overall economic forces. (More on this subject later.)

BUSINESS RISK

The degree to which an investment fulfills an investor's expectations depends to some measure on the future prosperity of the business. Unfortunately, not all firms which issue bonds remain solvent long enough to repay their obligations. Similarly, not all firms which issue stock reward their investors with profitable performance.

An investor assumes little business risk in U.S. government bonds or the bonds of broad-based, well-financed, blue-chip corporations such as AT&T. It is very doubtful that these institutions will, in the foreseeable future, become unable to meet their obligations. Yet, all profit-seeking enterprises face some degree of business risk.

Many factors bear on the profitability or ultimate solvency of an enterprise. Some are under the control of the company's management, while others are beyond their control, such as the actions of competitors, changes in demand, and government policies. Some amount, however, of a firm's future is dependent on management's ability to guide the organization successfully in a changing environment. By investing in a company, an investor assumes this risk.

INVESTMENT RISK

When J. P. Morgan was asked what he thought the market would do, he replied that it would "fluctuate." Clearly, as individuals continually reappraise investments, stock prices will move up or down in response to the dynamics of demand and supply. If investors frequently change their minds about a company's outlook, these changes of heart will be reflected in the fluctuations of the stock's price. If investors are consistent in their appraisal of a company, this uniformity of opinion will similarly translate into a stable stock price.

Modern portfolio theorists have sought to quantify these fluctuations under the rubric of investment risk. In keeping with the earlier definition, investment risk is the possibility that the actual return from an investment will differ from the expected return. Since, the magnitude of investment risk can be gauged by the volatility of stock price changes, explicit specifications of investment risk require estimates of the *probability* that variations (from the expected, or mean, return) of a given *magnitude*, will, or will not, occur. Fortunately, information on both the probability and the magnitude of such

volatility is contained in one statistic—the "standard deviation" of expected return.

The standard deviations for a normal distribution are shown
in Figure 14–1. The magnitude of variations from the mean is
represented by the standard deviations along the bottom of the

FIGURE 14–1: A normal distribution

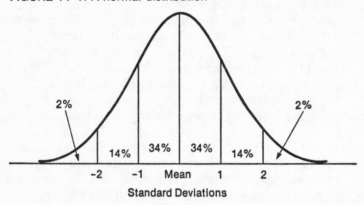

Standard Deviations

curve. The probability of such variations is represented by the
area under the curve. Thus, for normally distributed data, 68
percent of the outcomes (roughly two out of three) will be
within the range of plus, or minus, one standard deviation
from the mean. Or, again looking at Figure 14–1, 16 percent of
the observations (roughly one out of six) will be above plus one
standard deviation.

The notion of a standard deviation becomes more meaningful in the following example. Over the 51-year period from the
beginning of 1926 through the end of 1976, the mean annual
return (dividends plus capital appreciation) for the S&P Composite Index was 9.2 percent. During the same period the standard deviation of annual returns was 22.4 percent. [127] Thus,
while the average annual return was 9.2 percent, the return
corresponding to plus one standard deviation was 31.6 percent
(9.2% + 22.4%), and so on. This situation is shown in Figure
14–2.

An examination of Figure 14–2 reveals that over the 51-year
period prior to 1977, while the average annual return was 9.2
percent, the odds were roughly two out of three that the returns in any single year would be between −13.2 percent (one
standard deviation below the mean) and +31.6 percent (one
standard deviation above the mean). Similarly, since 96 percent of all normally distributed observations fall within plus or

FIGURE 14–2: Historical risk of stock market returns (1926–1976)

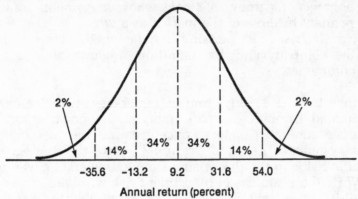

Annual return (percent)

Mean annual return 9.2%
Annual standard deviation....................... 22.4%

Source: Abbotson and Sinquefield [127].

minus two standard deviations, there was better than a 96 percent chance that the returns in any one year were within the range of −35.6 percent (two standard deviations below the mean) and +54.0 percent (two standard deviations above the mean).

Standard deviations can also be used to specify the likelihood that the return in any particular period will be outside of some range. That is, since 16 percent of all normally distributed observations fall below minus one standard deviation, there was a 16 percent chance—roughly one out of every six years—that the return in any single year would be less than −13.2 percent (one standard deviation below the mean).

When dealing with market aggregates, such as the S&P Composite Index, the ex post (historical) measure of risk (the historical standard deviation of return) can reasonably be used as an ex ante (forward-looking) estimate of investment risk. Unfortunately, when dealing with individual stocks, the ex post standard deviation of return is not a reliable guide for predicting future risk.

When working with individual stocks, it is necessary to delve into the three sources of investment risk:

1. *Systematic risk.* Risk that is related to market covariance—the tendency for an individual security's return to fluctuate with the return on the market portfolio.

2. *Extramarket risk.* Risk arising from comovements of homogenous groups of stocks whose movements are independent of those of the market as a whole.
3. *Specific risk.* Risk arising from factors that are specific to the company and, by definition, are unrelated to other companies.

Since the risk arising from extramarket covariance can be eliminated through diversification, many modern portfolio theorists and practitioners concentrate on the prediction of only systematic risk and "residual" risk—the aggregate of specific risk and the risk arising from extramarket covariance.

While these sources of investment risk will be discussed in detail in subsequent chapters, a few words about diversifiable and nondiversifiable risks are in order here. Systematic risk—the risk derived from the tendency for an individual security's return to fluctuate with the return of the market portfolio—is a nondiversifiable risk. Clearly, if an investor held a portfolio with equal proportions of all stocks this risk would still be present. For this reason, systematic risk is said to be a nondiversifiable risk.

Extramarket risk—the risk derived from comovements of homogeneous groups of stocks whose movements are independent of those of the market as a whole—is a diversifiable risk. This means that a portfolio that has an equal representation of all groups can diversify away the risks that are associated with holding only one or more of the homogeneous groups that en toto comprise the market. Specific risk—the risk derived from factors that are specific to a company—is also a diversifiable risk.

This is best understood by thinking of a portfolio composed of all available stocks. Assume that the annual performance of this portfolio was +10 percent. This means that for every security that appreciated more than 10 percent, there had to be another security, or, securities, that had offsetting below-average performance. In such a portfolio the unique characteristics of any company are lost. As a result, the market portfolio did not derive any incremental return (i.e., any return above the 10 percent for holding the market portfolio) from company sources. The performance of the average company, or industry, by definition, is the same as the average performance of the market.

Given that neither individual stocks nor selected homogenous groups of stocks add incremental return to the average return of the market portfolio, it follows that neither stocks, nor homogenous groups of stocks, add risk to the market portfolio. This means that a portfolio that has an equal representation of all stocks has neither group-related (extramarket) nor security-related (specific) risk—only the market-related (systematic) risk. Thus, two of the three sources of investment risk can be eliminated through proper diversification. Conversely, portfolios that do not match the market possess these risks—as well as these potential sources of excess return.

SUMMARY

The process of investing involves selecting from the available alternatives those investments with the risks and expected returns that best meet the investment objectives. It is a fact of life that in this process one must incur risks in order to attain excess returns. To attain returns in excess of those available from riskfree investments, an investor must incur systematic (market-related) risk. To attain returns in excess of the market's return, an investor must incur risks in excess of the market's purely systematic risk.

Of the wealth of stock market research which has emerged in the last decade, it will become clear in subsequent chapters that the most far-reaching contribution has been the explicit integration of risk into both investment analysis and the measurement of investment performance.

Chapter 15

Professional performance

The first in-depth analysis of the performance of professional investment managers examined mutual funds. At the time only mutual funds, among all institutions, had to disclose their performance figures. Now, bank trust departments, pension funds, and insurance companies have all come under closer scrutiny.

The first comprehensive study of the mutual fund industry, released in 1963, was prepared under the supervision of Professor Irwin Friend and has come to be referred to as the "Wharton School Study of Mutual Funds." The startling conclusion of the analysis was that, on the average, mutual fund performance "did not differ appreciably from what would have been achieved by an unmanaged portfolio consisting of the same proportion of common stocks, preferred stocks, corporate bonds, government securities, and other assets as the composite portfolios of the funds." [100]

In 1965, Friend and Douglas Vickers, also at Wharton, published another study of portfolio performance. They compared the common stock portfolios of 50 mutual funds with 50 randomly selected common stock portfolios over a six-year period. Friend and Vickers reported that "for the six-year period as a whole, from the end of 1957 through 1963, the random portfolios experienced a slightly higher average return than the mutual funds." [102, p. 398] They concluded that "there is still no evidence—either in our new or old tests, or in the tests so far carried out by others—that mutual fund performance is any better than that realizable by random or mechanical selection of stock issues." [102, p. 412] These data prompted Friend and Vickers to remark that their results "raise interesting questions about the apparent inability of professional investment management on the average to outperform the market." [102, p. 413]

Another segment of Friend and Vickers' research raised a crucial issue. During a certain period, the mutual funds performed significantly better than the randomly selected portfolios. Did this mean that mutual fund managers indeed obtained above-average results during that period?

It so happened that the variability of the returns for mutual funds was consistently higher than it was for the randomly generated portfolio returns. The mutual funds were, on the average, riskier than the random portfolios. In such a case, the mutual funds would be expected to do better than average in a year of sharp upward movement for the overall stock market. Could risk differences, asked Friend and Vickers, explain this aspect of their findings? Clearly, there was a need to factor risk into measurements of performance.

TREYNOR AND THE MEASUREMENT OF RISK

Jack Treynor, the editor of the *Financial Analysts Journal*, was the first to incorporate the vital ingredient of risk into a study of investment performance. [271] He devised a way to compare the distinctive risk characteristics of different mutual funds. Prior to Treynor's research, investigators had noted that rates of return for mutual funds typically show wide variations from year to year. The problem was, as it is to a lesser degree even today, to devise a stable risk-related parameter to include in the measurement of "performance." Treynor approached the problem by showing the remarkable stability of a fund's "characteristic line," which can be used to measure risk.

The rate of return history of two hypothetical portfolios over ten years is plotted in Figure 15–1. The horizontal axis records the rate of return for the general market, while the vertical axis measures the return for each fund. Notice that the lines, known as characteristic lines, which are fitted to the points describing the two funds in Figure 15–1 provide two quite different pictures.

Drawn in this way, Treynor's "characteristic lines" illustrate the historical relationships between the rate of return of the portfolio and market over the period studied. The slope of Treynor's characteristic line provides a graphic measure of a fund's volatility in relation to that of the general market. Notice that a steeply sloping characteristic line (such as that of Fund A) means that the historical rate of return for the fund has magnified the general market's return. By contrast, Fund

FIGURE 15-1: Characteristic lines representing different historical
risk postures

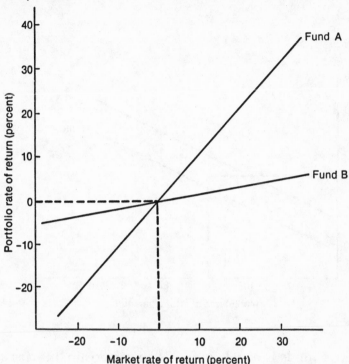

B's characteristic line is less steep than that of Fund A. A
characteristic line such as Fund B's indicates less sensitivity to
general market fluctuations. Fund B carries a lower component
of general market risk.

Treynor observed, "the slope-angle of the characteristic line
obviously provides a more refined measure of a fund's volatility than the usual categories of 'balanced fund," 'stock fund,'
or 'growth fund.' " [271, p. 66] Treynor reported further that
"the range of volatility observed in actual practice is enormous." He found, for example, that a 1 percent change in the
rate of return of the Dow Jones Industrial Average was often
accompanied by changes in rates of return of certain funds
that were more than twice as large.

Besides comparing the historical risk of any two funds, the
characteristic line discloses other performance information.
Notice that the slopes of the characteristic lines for Fund X and
Fund Y in Figure 15-2 are identical. The volatility, or risk, of

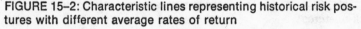

FIGURE 15–2: Characteristic lines representing historical risk postures with different average rates of return

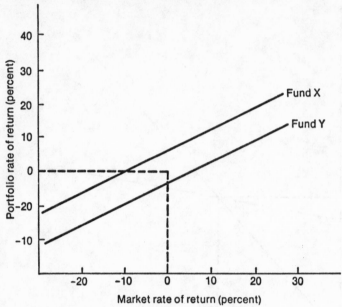

the two funds is equal. Fund X's characteristic line lies above the characteristic line for Fund Y, however. This means that Fund X has historically demonstrated consistently higher returns than Fund Y—in good years and bad. Thus, Treynor's "characteristic line" reflects two distinctive ingredients of a fund's performance history—return and systematic (market-related) risk.

In his now-classic paper, Treynor used this graphic technique to compare the performance of 54 mutual funds. He noted that over a ten-year period (1954–63), roughly 80 percent of the funds studied maintained a constant posture toward systematic risk.

SHARPE'S REWARD TO VARIABILITY MEASURE

William Sharpe also studied the performance of mutual fund portfolios. Sharpe utilized a ratio, similar to that devised by Treynor, which measured the "reward per unit of variability." Like Treynor's measure of performance, Sharpe's statistic gauged the reward provided to the investor for assuming risk. Sharpe was able to confirm large differences in the way the 34 mutual funds he studied rewarded their investors for assuming risk.

Sharpe also examined the relationship between the efficient market hypothesis and performance. If as the hypothesis holds, elaborate and expensive security analysis is useless, the mutual funds which spend the least on research should show the best net performance records. In Sharpe's words, "the only basis for persistently inferior performance would be the continued expenditure of large amounts of a fund's assets on the relatively fruitless search for incorrectly valued securities." [244, p. 121] Conversely, if security analysis is worthwhile, funds spending the most on such research should have shown better net performance. After much careful investigation, Sharpe reported that "the results tend to support the cynics: good performance is associated with low expense ratios." [244, p. 132]

Sharpe also compared the 34 mutual funds with the Dow Jones Industrial Average, using his reward to variability performance measure. Based on this measure of performance, Sharpe reported that in terms of a reward to risk ratio, the odds were "greater than 100 to 1 against the possibility that the average mutual fund did as well as the Dow Jones portfolio from 1954–1963." [244, p. 137]

Sharpe traced the cause of these remarkably bad mutual fund results to differences between their gross and net performance. He had hypothesized that if the security analysis practiced by Wall Street professionals was indeed useless, the funds' gross performance before fees and expenses would equal that attained from random selection of securities with similar risks. If the hypothesis is correct, it means that, counter to intuition, the investment companies which have spent most heavily on security selection in fact have compiled the worst net performance!

After much careful study, Sharpe reported ". . . all other things being equal, the smaller a fund's expense ratio, the better the results obtained by stockholders." [244, p. 137] On the basis of this evidence, Sharpe was able to conclude, ". . . the burden of proof may reasonably be placed on those who argue the traditional view—that the search for securities whose prices diverge from their intrinsic values is worth the expense required." [244, p. 138]

THE CASE AGAINST "PROFESSIONAL" MANAGEMENT GROWS STRONGER

By 1968, there was a growing body of evidence challenging professional management's ability—as typified by mutual fund results—yet several unanswered questions remained. The 1963 Wharton study, and subsequent research by Friend and Vickers, did not adequately relate performance differences to risk. Treynor and Sharpe examined risk, but their work was not sufficiently comprehensive. A study was needed which analyzed the performance of a large number of mutual funds. Fortunately, investors did not have to wait long.

In 1968, Michael Jensen, building upon the theoretical models derived by Treynor and Sharpe, devised a measure for comparing fund performance across "different risk levels and across differing time periods irrespective of general economic and market conditions." Jensen used this measure to evaluate the "ability of the portfolio manager or security analyst to increase returns on the portfolio through successful prediction of future security prices. . . ." [132, p. 389] In seeking evidence of portfolio managers' predictive ability, Jensen studied the performance of 115 open-end mutual funds in the 1945–64 period. Jensen's measure of performance tested the managers' ability to forecast market behavior as well as price movements of individual issues. His findings are summarized as follows:

> . . . the mutual fund industry (as represented by these 115 funds) shows very little evidence of an ability to forecast security prices. Furthermore, there is surprisingly little evidence that indicates any individual funds in the sample might be able to forecast prices. . . .
>
> The evidence on mutual fund performance . . . indicates not only that these 115 mutual funds were on average not able to predict security prices well enough to outperform a buy-the-market-and-hold policy, but also that there is very little evidence that any individual fund was able to do significantly better than which we expected from mere random chance. It is also important to note that these conclusions hold even when we measure the fund returns gross of management expenses (that is, assume their bookkeeping, research, and other expenses except brokerage commissions were obtained free). Thus on average the funds apparently were not quite successful enough in their trading activities to recoup even their brokerage expenses.
>
> The evidence . . . indicate[s] . . . a pressing need on the part of the funds themselves to evaluate much more closely both the costs and the benefits of their research and trading

activities in order to provide investors with maximum possible returns for the level of risk undertaken [132, pp. 414–15].

In a subsequent study, Jensen reported

> . . . mutual fund managers on the average are unable to forecast future security prices [133, p. 170]
>
> . . . it appears that on the average the resources spent by the funds in attempting to forecast security prices do not yield higher portfolio returns than those that could have been earned by equivalent risk portfolios selected (a) by random selection policies or (b) by combined investments in a "market portfolio" and government bonds. [133, p. 170]
>
> [Even though] analysts . . . operate in the securities markets every day and have wide-ranging contacts and associations in both the business and the financial communities . . . the fact [is] that they are apparently unable to forecast returns accurately enough to recover their research and transaction costs. . . . [133, p. 170]

In another study, John O'Brien evaluated the performance of 119 funds during the ten years spanning 1959–68. He concluded that "there are no more managers than predicted by chance occurrence either exceeding or failing to exceed the rate of return predicted for them based upon the level of uncertainty they assume." [208, p. 102]

One of the most extensive research studies of mutual fund performance and that of other institutional investors was published in August 1970 by three faculty members of the Wharton School. In this study Irwin Friend, Marshall Blume, and Jean Crockett reported on the performance of 299 leading funds for the years 1960 through 1968. These researchers reported that:

> The overall annual rates of return on investment in 136 mutual funds [essentially all the larger, publicly owned funds for which data were available] averaged 10.7 percent for the period January 1960, through June 1968 (9.0 percent for the period January 1960, through March 1964, and 12.8 percent for the period April 1964, through June 1968). Unweighted investment in all stocks listed on the Big Board in the same periods would have yielded 12.4 percent (7.0 percent in the first part and 17.8 percent in the second).

> * * * * *

> When funds were classified by fund size, charges, management expenses, portfolio turnover, and investment objectives, no consistent relationship was found between these factors and investment performance properly adjusted for risk. To the ex-

tent that a relationship exists between performance and sales charges, the funds with the lowest charges, including the "no-load" funds, appear to perform slightly better than the others.

*   *   *   *   *

The apparent absence of any consistent relationships between the nonrisk characteristics of mutual funds and their investment performance suggests that, for the industry as a whole, there may be no consistency in the performance of the same fund in successive periods. [103, pp. 19–21]

*   *   *   *   *

The performance analysis gave no indication that higher sales charges, management costs, or trading expenses are consistently linked with performance either above or below that of random portfolios. Because no clear payoff results from higher management and trading expenses, a new type of mutual fund and minimal management and trading may be desirable. Such a fund would resemble the fixed or semifixed trusts of former years. These trusts deliberately duplicated the performance of all NYSE stocks or of some other broad range of investments.

This new kind of fund would provide, at a minimal cost, the risk diversification which seems to be the most important continuing service rendered by today's mutual funds. The larger this fund might be, the smaller would be the relative management expenses, and the easier it would be to duplicate the performance of the entire market. Such large funds would become sufficiently well known to the investing public for their shares to be sold at commission rates appreciably lower than the sales loads now charged by mutual funds. [103, p. 23]

CONCLUSION

A long series of research studies dating from 1963 has sought to measure the performance of mutual funds. While the methodology has differed somewhat, the conclusions unanimously cast serious doubt on the "management" ability of mutual funds. Their performance has been no better than could be attained through random stock selection. Despite some debate on research technique, no substantial evidence indicates that mutual funds can outperform the workings of chance.

Chapter 16

Historical performance

In spite of the evidence supporting the existence of an "almost" efficient market, some investment managers do perform better than others. Clearly, when many people "play the game," some must win. Unfortunately, the winner's investment selection process is not necessarily responsible for his or her success. Suppose, for example, that all investment managers were to select their stocks in a completely random fashion—barring a tie, one manager would still outperform the others.

Investors hear much about so-and-so's "expert performance." But how much of the performance is luck, and how much is attributable to astute investment selection? To answer this question, we need to know something about (a) what is considered "average," and (b) expected variations from "average."

If thousands of investment managers each "randomly" selected one NYSE-traded stock, what results could be expected one year later? One might anticipate the performance of these managers' "selections" to parallel that of the market. It would also be expected, however, that many of these stocks would show widely divergent results, with some better, and others worse, than the average. The distribution of the performance of a large number of one-stock portfolios can be represented by the bell-shaped, or normal, curve shown in Figure 16–1.

An understanding of what can be expected from purely random stock selection provides an important benchmark against which to compare the results obtained by "skilled professionals." As Figure 16–1 shows, purely random selection of stocks produces a cluster of results around some average value. Also, purely by chance, some perform better, and some perform worse, than others.

FIGURE 16-1: Expected distribution of performance for many separate one-stock portfolios

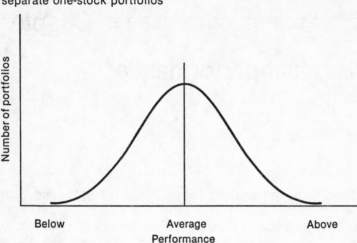

STANDARD DEVIATION

Because the concept of "standard deviation" plays an important role throughout MPT, the salient characteristics of this popular statistical measure should be thoroughly understood. A standard deviation is a measure of variability around a mean (i.e., a mathematical "average"). If it is assumed that the observations of a given characteristic, or value, cluster around the mean in a "normal" fashion, the computed standard deviation has a very convenient property: 68 percent of the values will fall within one standard deviation (plus or minus) from the mean; 95.5 percent of the values will be within two standard deviations from the mean; and 99.7 percent of the values will fall within three standard deviations from the mean.

Because 68 percent is very close to two thirds (66.7 percent), a convenient "rule of thumb" is that the chances are two out of three that an expected value will fall within one standard deviation (plus or minus) of the mean. The key point to remember is that the smaller the standard deviation, the greater is the probability of achieving the expected or "average," result. In turn, a higher likelihood of some average expectation being realized goes hand in hand with a reduction in the standard deviation.

DIVERSIFICATION—AN INTRODUCTION

Suppose that thousands of investment managers were each to buy two-stock portfolios, again using random selection. It would be expected that the average performance of the two-stock investors would again equal that of the overall market, but also that their results should cluster more tightly around that average. Fewer two-stock portfolios would demonstrate the extreme returns exhibited by some one-stock portfolios.

What causes the differing distributions in Figure 16–2? The results for the two-stock investors—the same average perfor-

FIGURE 16–2: Performance outcomes from random selection of one-stock and two-stock portfolios

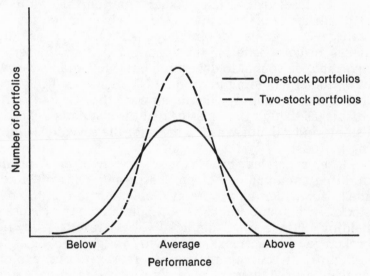

mance, but with less variation—do not reflect more accurate forecasts of the market. The investors in this case still could not, on the average, beat the market. They were, however, able to avoid large negative variations through diversification (discussed more fully in Chapter 18). If this example were carried further, it would be shown that holding an increasing number of stocks tends to yield results which increasingly approach the market average. In turn, this market average provides a benchmark against which to measure the *value* of professional investment management.

FISHER AND LORIE

The first comprehensive study of the stock market's long-term rate of return was conducted by Lawrence Fisher and James Lorie [91] at the University of Chicago during the mid-1960s. Using an extensive computer-readable file, Fisher and Lorie determined the historical rate of return of all NYSE common stocks between 1926 and 1960. Fisher and Lorie calculated what would have happened if one had held all stocks traded on the NYSE during 22 different, but overlapping, periods between January 1926 and December 1960. Most of the rates of return they reported were greater than 10 percent compounded annually, although the year-to-year returns ranged from a negative 48 percent to a positive 17 percent.

In a subsequent article, Fisher reported the results of an elaborate study of random investments in common stocks. The earlier work, published jointly by Fisher and Lorie, studied all stocks in composite for the specified periods. Fisher's later investigation sought to determine how well an investor would have done by holding individual NYSE stocks. The stocks selected were randomly chosen, as were the buy and sell dates (that is, as though the investor had thrown darts at both stock listings and calendars as the basis for the selections and holding periods).

Fisher generated, by computer, the investment results for multiple combinations of purchases and sales of individual stocks for which data were available. For the 1,715 common stocks in his study, 56,557,538 combinations of stocks and holding periods were tabulated. These results (allowing for brokerage commissions) are shown in Figure 16–3.

Figure 16–3 reveals that annual rates of return exhibited a marked central tendency, or "normal" grouping about the average. Taking brokerage commissions-into account, Fisher reported that "78 percent of the time common stocks yielded a positive net return. Over two thirds of the time, the rate of return exceeded 5 percent . . . [and] the median rate of return was 9.8 percent. . . . Nearly one-fifth of the time, the rate of return exceeded 20 percent per annum, compounded annually." [89, pp. 153–54]

Other conclusions by Fisher are worth noting. The variability of rates of return was much greater for short-term investments than for long-term positions. On the average, the probability of a gain on a long-term investment was greater than 78 percent. Furthermore, "long-term" holdings of more than one

FIGURE 16–3: Frequency distribution of rates of return on investment in each common stock listed on the New York Stock Exchange, 1926–1960, using all possible combinations of month-end purchase and sale dates (based on 56,557,538 cases)

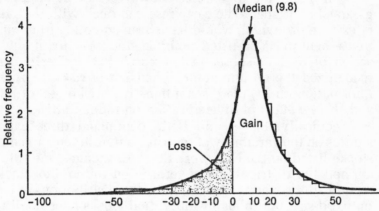

Percent per annum compounded annually

Source: Fisher [89, p. 54].

stock at a time would have yielded, on the average, positive returns far more than 78 percent of the time and, in fact, would have generated returns in excess of 9.8 percent per annum substantially more than half the time. [89, p. 159]

Fisher's work is highly significant. By investing in the most random, haphazard fashion imaginable, an investor would have profited 78 percent of the time during the periods studied. Portfolios of many stocks would be expected to be profitable an even larger percentage of the time. Further, Fisher has shown that risk, or the variation in rates of return, is much greater for short-term investments. Investments held for several years were much less likely to produce absolute losses. Fisher also calculated that the average rate of return, compounded annually, for NYSE common stocks was almost 9.8 percent per annum. In short, using stock price charts, fundamental analysis, or Ouija boards, an investor could have expected to do this well!

Fisher and Lorie's early and now classic studies on average rates of return thus provided important benchmarks for evaluating investment performance. Their finding that the average compounded annual rate of return from NYSE common stocks was 9.8 percent over the period studied may well be one of the best remembered and most frequently quoted of all investment statistics.

Their more recent studies, however, are of significantly greater importance. The early research dealt with the *average* rates of return which would have been compiled from random investment in NYSE-listed common stocks—*without any indication of risk*. In subsequent research [93] Fisher and Lorie recognized the all-important dimension of risk by providing information on (a) the distributions (i.e., riskiness) of returns and (b) the effect of diversification on reducing risk.

Specifically, Fisher and Lorie conducted three extensive studies on the variability of returns on investments in common stocks listed on the New York Stock Exchange. One study examined the distributions of returns on *individual* stocks. A second study examined the aggregated distributions of returns on *fixed-size portfolios* of individual stocks over holding periods ranging from 1 to 20 years. A third study examined returns from *different size portfolios* (containing from as few as 6 stocks to as many as 128 stocks).

They found that in general, returns[1] increased with the length of the holding period. These results, while not surprising, verify the precept of MPT that risk increases with the uncertainty of time. They confirm that investors are indeed risk averse and demand (and hence, through their market action, attain) higher rates of return for longer holding periods. (The significance of these findings is discussed in Chapters 19–26.)

Of major importance to other researchers were Fisher and Lorie's observations of positive skewness (relating to the fact that one can occasionally earn more than 100 percent on an investment). Fisher and Lorie also verified this author's (see Hagin [116]) observations of an abnormally high number of very large returns. In their second study, Fisher and Lorie aggregated the distributions. This aggregation, much like tallying the results of a roulette wheel, has provided important information on the historical risk of various investment strategies. With this data, we can ask questions such as, "How frequently would one have realized a gain of more than 20% on an investment in a single randomly selected stock that was held for a randomly selected calendar year between 1946 and 1965?"

---

[1] Fisher and Lorie defined "return" by means of "wealth ratios" (the ratio of the value of an investment at the end of a period to the amount invested).

Another important part of their research has dealt with how increasing the number of stocks in a portfolio can reduce the variability of returns—an important topic which will also be discussed in Chapters 19–26.

Fisher and Lorie's largest tabulation of historical investment results, *A Half Century of Returns on Stocks and Bonds,* was published in 1977. In all, 51 tables provide comparative rates of return on portfolios of NYSE stocks and U.S. Treasury securities, as well as their performance in relation to changes in the Consumer Price Index.

Tables 16–1 and 16–2 have been abstracted from this mass of data in order to contrast the inflation-adjusted returns for

TABLE 16–1: Returns from all NYSE common stocks with equal initial weighting and dividends reinvested (tax-exempt)

	If held until the end of 1976 and purchased at end of				
	1950	1955	1960	1965	1970
Current dollars	11.0%	9.4%	9.6%	6.7%	7.1%
Deflated by CPI	7.5	5.5	5.1	1.0	0.5

Source: Fisher and Lorie [94, pp. 24–27].

TABLE 16–2: Returns from holding short-term U.S. Treasury bonds and notes with interest reinvested (tax exempt)

	If held until the end of 1976 and purchased at end of				
	1950	1955	1960	1965	1970
Current dollars	3.9%	4.4%	4.7%	5.6%	6.9%
Deflated by CPI	0.6	0.6	0.5	0.0	0.3

Source: Fisher and Lorie [94, pp. 136–37].

common stocks with those on short-term government securities. The period covers the 26-year span from the last trading day of 1950 until the close of 1976. The first line of Table 16–1 shows annualized rates of return that would have been realized by a tax-exempt investor who reinvested all dividends on the assumption that an equal amount had been invested in each of the NYSE common stocks at the beginning of each designated period. The next line shows annual rates of return *after inflation* (but still before taxes)!

Thus, Table 16–1 shows that over the 26 years from the end of 1950 to the close of 1976, the real (after inflation) annual total return (dividends plus capital appreciation) would have averaged 7.5 percent per year. However, in the more recent 11-year period spanning the end of 1965 to the end of 1976, the real (after inflation) annual rate of return for common stocks averaged only 1.0 percent.

Table 16–2 presents an even more startling picture. *Over the 26-year period from the end of 1950 to the end of 1976, the real (after inflation) return from short-term U.S. Treasury securities has never averaged more than 0.6 percent ($^6/_{10}$ of 1 percent) per year.*

Clearly, over the "long run," common stocks have provided a superior real rate of return. This is totally consistent with the forthcoming discussion of how one would *expect* assets to be priced. Clearly, common stocks are riskier than short-term government securities. Thus, the only incentive to buy common stocks is that in the "long run," investors should be compensated for the additional risk through higher returns.

Obviously, "the long run" is not a very precise time period. As the famous economist John Maynard Keynes said, "the long run is when we are all dead." Nonetheless, the relationship between risk and long-term average returns is crucial. The only inducement for buying common stocks is that the market's pricing mechanism, over time, will reward investors through higher long-run average returns. Conversely, investors in common stocks should be aware of their riskiness—their likely short-term deviations from the long-run expectation.

Viewed from this perspective, the statistics shown in Tables 16–1 and 16–2 are not at all surprising. They reflect the fact that returns from common stock investments have been both higher and more volatile than those on short-term government securities.

Chapter 17

Expected returns and variance

A market performance study co-written by Roger Ibbotson at the University of Chicago and Rex Sinquefield at the American National Bank and Trust Company of Chicago has attracted considerable attention since its publication in 1977. Basically, Ibbottson and Sinquefield

1. Calculated historical returns and variances during the period 1926–77 for common stocks, long-term U.S. government bonds, long-term corporate bonds, U.S. Treasury bills, and the inflation rate (based on the Consumer Price Index), and
2. Simulated probabilities, future returns, and variances for each of these asset classes for the period 1977–2000.

HISTORICAL RETURNS

Ibbotson and Sinquefield's data on the returns of common stock were derived from a historical analysis of the Standard and Poor's (S&P) Composite Index. This is a market-value weighted index, which means that the weight given each stock corresponds to the market value of that company's outstanding shares. (Although the S&P Composite includes the 500 U.S. stocks with the largest market value, prior to March 1957, the index consisted of 90 of the largest stocks. Nonetheless, the value-weighted data used by Ibbotson and Sinquefield constitute a reasonable proxy for the overall market.)

Figure 17–1 shows comparative growth rates (including capital gains plus dividends or interest income) for three asset classes and inflation (measured by the Consumer Price Index) over a 52-year period. In each case it is assumed that $1 was invested at the end of 1925. Since the vertical scale is

121

FIGURE 17–1: Comparative growth for inflation and three asset classes, 1926–1977 (assumed initial investment of $1.00 at year-end 1925, includes reinvestment of income without taxes or transaction costs)

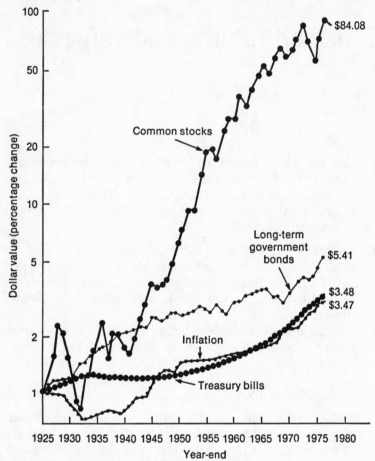

Source: Ibbotson and Sinquefield [127, p. 3].

logarithmic, equal vertical distances represent equal percentage changes.

Figure 17–1 dramatizes the relatively superior long-term performance of common stocks. Specifically, if $1.00 had been invested at year-end 1925 and all subsequent dividends were reinvested (without being taxed and without transaction costs), the $1.00 investment would have been worth $84.08 at year-end 1977. By comparison, at the close of 1977, a dollar put into long-term (20-year) government bonds would be worth only \$5.41—having grown only about one-fifteenth as rapidly as common stocks during the identical period.

Possibly the most discouraging trend portrayed by Figure 17–1 is the difference between the *real* and *nominal* rates of return for U.S. Treasury bills. (A *real* rate of return is an inflation-adjusted return; while a *nominal* return refers only to the pure, unadjusted numerical value). On a nominal (unadjusted) basis, a \$1.00 investment in U.S. Treasury bills would have grown to \$3.48 over the 52-year period. Inflation took its toll, however. Based on the Consumer Price Index, \$3.47 would be necessary at the end of 1977 to equal the purchasing power of \$1.00 in 1925. This means that after 52 years, the real (inflation-adjusted) return on an investment in U.S. Treasury bills would have been a paltry \$0.01 (still before taxes and costs to reinvest the interest).

Looking only at returns provides just half of the picture. The other key dimension is risk. Before examining the data on the comparative risk of each of the asset classes studied by Ibbotson and Sinquefield, the conceptual difference between an *arithmetic* and a *geometric* mean should be clearly understood.

Consider the following two-year performance record:

Year	Performance (percentage change)	Year-end value of \$1
0	—	\$1.00
1	+50%	1.50
2	−50	0.75

What is the average performance? Arithmetically, the average of +50 percent and −50 percent is 0 percent. Yet, a computed average change of zero seems inconsistent with the fact that the initial \$1.00 is now worth \$0.75. This is the reason for including the geometric mean when reporting average performance. This mean indicates the average annual rate of return which, when compounded annually, would produce the final result. In the above case, the geometric mean is −13.4 percent.[1] Thus, the two-year performance record using the geometric mean would be as follows:

---

[1] Readers interested in the formula for the calculation of the geometric mean are referred to Ibbotson and Sinquefield [127, p. 8].

Year	Performance (geometric mean)	Year-end value of $1
0	—	$1.00
1	−13.4%	0.87
2	−13.4	0.75

In practice, both measures are useful. When results for a single period are considered, the arithmetic mean is generally used. When the average performance over more than one period is computed, the geometric mean is used.

Returning to the Ibbotson and Sinquefield study, Table 17–1 summarizes the geometric means, the arithmetic means, and

TABLE 17–1: Total annual returns, 1926–1976

Series	Geometric means (percent)	Arithmetic mean (percent)	Standard deviation (percent)
Common stocks	9.2%	11.6%	22.4%
Long-term corporate bonds	4.1	4.2	5.6
Long-term government bonds	3.4	3.5	5.8
U.S. Treasury bonds	2.4	2.4	2.1
Inflation	2.3	2.4	4.8

Source: Ibbotson and Sinquefield [127, p. 10].

the standard deviation (corresponding to the arithmetic mean) for the total returns (with dividends and interest reinvested) for each of five series for the period 1926–76.[2]

The data in Table 17–1 indicate that over the 51-year period spanning 1926 and 1976, stocks returned an average of 9.2 percent per year (compounded annually). During the same period, U.S. Treasury bills returned an average of 2.4 percent, while the Consumer Price Index grew at a nearly offsetting compounded annual rate of 2.3 percent!

These data reveal that while common stocks outperformed other classes of assets, their returns were far more volatile. The standard deviation of common stock annual returns was 22.4 percent. This means that in approximately two out of every

---

[2] The data illustrated in Figure 17–1 show data through 1977—reflecting the *partial* update (available from the Financial Analysts Research Foundation) of the more complete study that is tabulated in Table 17–1 for the period 1926–76.

three years the return was between −13.2 percent and +31.6 percent (as shown earlier in Figure 14–2).

EQUITY RISK PREMIUM

A concept which will be developed more fully in Chapters 19–26 is that capital markets are dominated by risk-averse investors. Investors could invest solely in risk-free assets such as U.S. Treasury bills. For investors to be persuaded to buy common stocks, they must anticipate higher returns. More specifically, this "excess" return (i.e., the return in excess of the risk-free rate) must be high enough to compensate investors for the assumption of the risk entailed in common stock investments.

The difference between the rate of return available from risk-free assets (such as U.S. Treasury bills) and that on common stocks is called the *equity risk premium*. It is the net return from investing in common stocks rather than U.S. Treasury bills.

This relationship is illustrated by the capital market line shown in Figure 17–2. If an investor assumes no market risk,

FIGURE 17–2: Capital market line

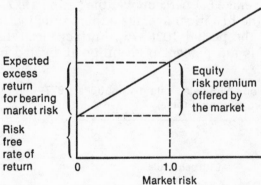

represented by the zero point on the horizontal axis, that investor can obtain the prevailing risk-free rate of return. If an investor invests in the market (i.e., with an investment in all stocks in proportion to their capitalization), represented by 1.0 on the horizontal axis, that investor must *expect* a return that is in excess of the return available without market risk. Otherwise, there would be no reason to invest in the market!

Historical data for the equity risk premium are shown in Table 17–2. (Because of year-to-year compounding effects, the values for the annual equity risk premiums are not precisely equal to the simple differences between the two basic annual returns).

TABLE 17–2: Total annual returns, 1926–1976

Series	Geometric mean (percent)	Arithmetic mean (percent)	Standard deviation (percent)
Equity risk premium	6.7%	9.2%	22.6%

Source: Ibbotson and Sinquefield [127, p. 19].

SIMULATING THE FUTURE

To simulate probabilistic distributions of *future* returns for the period 1977 to 2000, Ibbotson and Sinquefield combined their historical data on the distributions of various rates of return with information on the term structure of interest rates (discussed in Chapter 30). Their simulated inflation figures are shown in Figure 17–3. This study projects the compounded inflation rate to average 5.4 percent over the period 1977–2000 (compared with the historical average annual inflation rate of 2.3 percent over the period 1926–76). Further, according to this study, there is a 5 percent probability (indicated by the

FIGURE 17–3: Inflation—Simulated rate distributions, 1977–2000 (geometric average annual rates)

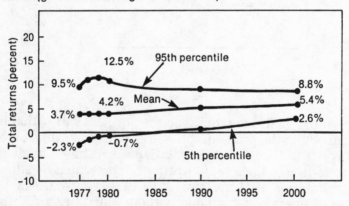

Source: Ibbotson and Sinquefield [127, p. 53].

95th percentile) that, over the length of the forecast period, the inflation rate will average more than 8.8 percent and a 5 percent chance that it will average less than 2.6 percent. On a shorter time horizon, such as the 1977–80 period, the range of probable outcomes is much wider.

Figure 17-4 shows the simulated total return distributions. Specifically, the expected nominal (before inflation) return on

FIGURE 17–4: Common stocks—Simulated total return distributions, 1977–2000 (geometric average annual rates)

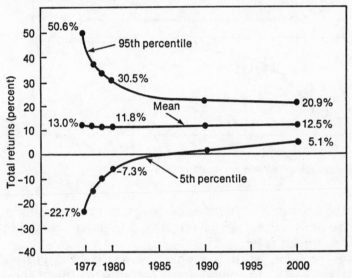

Source: Ibbotson and Sinquefield [127, p. 49].

common stocks for the period is 12.5 percent per year compounded. There is a 5 percent probability that, over the length of the forecast period, the nominal returns will average in excess of 20.9 percent per year. There is also a 5 percent probability that, over the period, the nominal return will average less than 5.1 percent per year. Again, on a shorter time horizon, such as the 1977 to 1980 period, the range of probable outcomes is much wider.

Figure 17–5 portrays the results of an inflation-adjusted simulation of common stock returns by Ibbotson and Sinquefield. Here the expected real (inflation-adjusted) compounded returns on common stocks for the period 1977–2000 work out to 6.8 percent per year. As before, the 95th and 5th

FIGURE 17–5: Common stocks, inflation adjusted—Simulated total return distributions, 1977–2000 (geometric average annual rates)

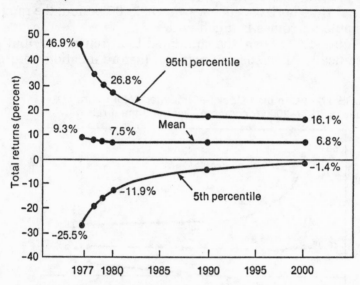

Source: Ibbotson and Sinquefield [127, p. 55].

percentile "funnels" define the range, over increasingly long time periods, within which 90 percent of the inflation-adjusted returns are expected to fall.

One problem with the data presented in Figures 17–3 through 17–5 is that the ever-decreasing width of the probabilistic bands wrongly implies a reduction in uncertainty over time. The graphic representations of the so-called stock and bond wealth indexes in Figures 17–6 and 17–7 illuminate this shortcoming. (A wealth index compares all investments on the assumption that they were worth $1.00 at year-end 1976).

Figure 17–6 shows the simulated distribution of the nominal wealth index for the period 1977–2000. According to this forecast, an investment of $1.00 in common stocks at year-end 1976 will be worth $27.04 at year-end 2000. The dispersion of the simulated results around the mean, or expected value of $27.04, shows that there is a 5 percent probability that in the year 2000 the $1.00 could be worth more than $95.91 and a 5 percent probability that it could be worth $3.27 or less.

Figure 17–7 shows the simulated distribution of the real (inflation-adjusted) wealth index for long-term corporate

FIGURE 17–6: Common stocks—Simulated distributions of nominal wealth index, 1977–2000 (year-end 1976 equals $1.00)

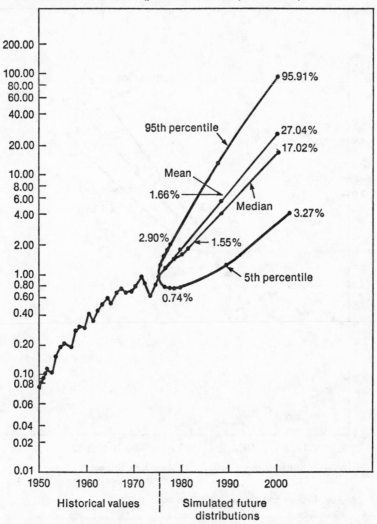

Source: Ibbotson and Sinquefield [127, p. 48].

bonds over the period 1977–2000. Under the forecast, an investment of $1.00 at year-end 1976 has an inflation-adjusted expected value of $6.10 at year-end 2000. Similarly, the simulated results indicate a 5 percent probability that in the year 2000, the $1.00 could be worth more than 9.44 times the initial inflation-adjusted investment. Also, there is a 5 percent proba-

FIGURE 17–7: Long-term corporate bonds—Simulated distributions of
wealth index, 1977–2000 (year-end 1976 equals $1.00)

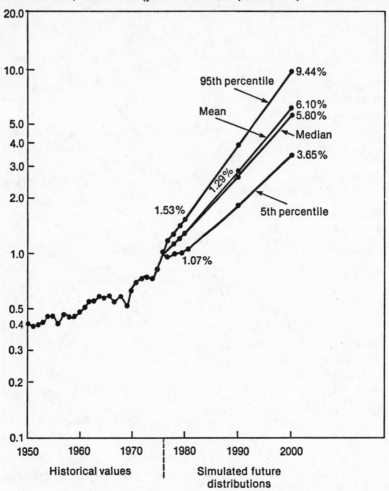

bility that the inflation-adjusted value of the investment will
be worth less than 3.65 times the initial inflation-adjusted
amount.

These notions of expected returns will be used in subsequent chapters to provide an important perspective on
forward-looking portfolio risk. Before that, however, it is
important to understand the relationship between risk and
diversification.

Chapter 18

Diversification

Broadly speaking, there are two categories of investors—those who prefer to concentrate their holdings, and those who would rather diversify. Investors who concentrate their assets in a relatively small number of issues typically reason that they can better focus their attention on a limited group of stocks. Conversely, other investors believe that it is difficult to do a consistently better than average job of investment selection. Members of this group typically diversify their holdings among a wide variety of stocks so as to achieve approximately the market's average rate of return.

A BYGONE ERA—PORTFOLIO CONCENTRATION

Most of the "go-go" performers of the 1960s relied on the concentration approach. In this "star" era, those managers with "genius for picking stocks" generated such demand for certain stocks that their recommendations became selfful-filling prophecies and enhanced their reputations even further.

Today's perspective reveals that the go-go investments of the 1960s were concentrated in high-risk glamour stocks. Individually, these stocks would be expected to do well in rising markets and poorly in downturns. Also, portfolios which mainly consisted of a few basically similar companies could be expected to undergo severe declines during a general market downturn—because of the absence of meaningful diversification. This indeed proved to be the case. The supermen of the go-go era ultimately encountered a special kind of kryptonite—a falling market for their glamour stocks.

131

THE OTHER WAY TO PLAY THE GAME—DIVERSIFY

Many successful investors have adopted the opposite philosophy of diversification. One of the wealthiest and shrewdest
investors to espouse a philosophy of diversification was the
famous Texan Clint Murchison, Sr. After a roaring start in
wildcat oil drilling in the 1920s, Murchison started to diversify
his holdings. At one point he was said to control 115 companies stretching from Canada to South America. Murchison
undoubtedly had an awareness of industrial and national market "comovements" and protected himself against them
through diversification. His philosophy on diversification was
a simple one: "Money is like manure—when it stacks up, it
stinks; when you spread it around, it makes things grow."

The rationale for stock market diversification is that the
overall risk from owning many stocks is lower than the risk of
holding a few stocks. The fewer stocks held, the greater the
injury if one issue does poorly. The effect of diversification in
reducing the overall risk of a portfolio was studied extensively
by Jack Gaumnitz [106] in his doctoral dissertation at Stanford
University in 1967. Gaumnitz found that until the number of
independently chosen securities in a portfolio reached 18, significant reductions in overall risk could be derived by holding
more securities.

In 1968, John Evans also studied the effects of diversification
in his doctoral dissertation at the University of Washington.
Evans randomly constructed 2,400 portfolios which were
composed of from 1 to 60 stocks. His findings which are summarized in Figure 18–1, are important.

Evans' calculations show that a portfolio with maximum
diversification (that is, equal dollar amounts in all stocks studied) would be expected to have a rate of return fluctuation
(hence, risk) of 11.9 percent during a six-month period. Yet, if
the investor held only one stock, a six-month variation in the
rate of return of approximately 20.5 percent could be expected.

The startling part of Evans' research is what can be expected
when an investor places equal dollar amounts in portfolios
consisting of two, three, four, five, and ten securities, respectively. Notice in Figure 18–1 that the additional reduction in
risk is relatively minor as one moves from a portfolio containing 10 securities to one containing 20 or even 40 securities. In
fact, a randomly selected portfolio with equal dollar amounts
in just five stocks has only slightly more risk than a portfolio
with equal dollar amounts invested in all of Evans's stocks.

FIGURE 18–1: Impact of number of securities held on risk level of portfolio

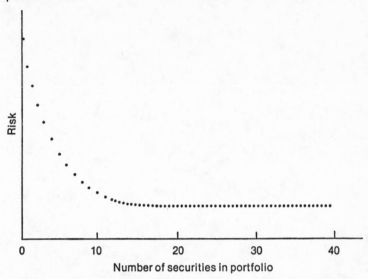

Source: Evans [67, p. 765].

Thus, the importance of portfolio management lies not in the number of holdings, but rather in both the nature and degree of the combined risk of the underlying stocks. Brealey [34] has shown quite dramatically what can happen when one considers both the nature and degree of risk in portfolio composition. He reported that a portfolio containing only 11 securities, which were carefully selected for their risk-diversifying characteristics, would be less risky than a portfolio of 2,000 securities which were selected without regard to risk.

CONCLUSION

A prudent investor must have serious reservations about both the inherent usefulness of traditional forms of security analysis and the ability of investment managers who use these techniques to attain consistent above-average performance. This does not mean, however, that prudent investors should disassociate themselves from the stock market. There is strong evidence that there is merit in using diversification to control risk while predicting the collective behavior of groups of securities.

PART THREE

MPT: CONCEPTUAL FOUNDATION

Chapter 19

Capital asset pricing model

In this chapter, two key concepts—efficient capital markets and risk premiums—are brought together in the *capital asset pricing model (CAPM)*.

The concept of an efficient capital market leads to the conclusion that prices cannot be expected to diverge "by much" or "for long" from the consensus view of an equitable rate of return for a given level of risk. The rationale of a risk premium is basically that investors must be paid to take any risk above that of a "riskless" investment.

The classical example of a riskless investment is a short-term obligation of the U.S. government. Since the government can always print money, there is no dollar risk with such an instrument. This is not, of course, a truly riskless investment. Any investment which returns a fixed number of dollars is subject to the risks inherent in the fluctuations of the future purchasing power of the dollar. For the time being, however, the notion of purchasing-power risk will be set aside. Unless noted, "risk" will be used in the narrow sense of the dollar risk inherent in market- and company-related investments.

According to the CAPM, investors who select a risk-free investment (such as short-term government securities) can expect to be compensated for the use of their money, but not for market- or company-related risk. This riskless compensation can be thought of as the amount which the government is willing to pay to "rent" money. As such, it is the "pure" (risk-free) interest rate.

Other investors, however, opt for risky investments, including common stocks. Such investors logically expect a higher rate of return as compensation for the risk that they assume. As discussed earlier, the difference between the risk-free rate of return and the total return from a risky investment is called a

137

risk premium. The capital asset pricing model provides the framework for determining the relationship between risk and return and the amount of the risk premium.

LINEAR RELATIONSHIPS: A KEY PART OF MPT

Since many of the relationships that are examined within the context of MPT are linear in nature, it may be worthwhile to review a little high school math, specifically, the *formula for a straight line*. The basic (zero intercept) equation for a line is

$$Y = \text{Slope } X$$

where the *slope* describes the relationship between the two variables. Graphically

$$\text{Slope} = \frac{\text{Units of vertical ``rise''}}{\text{Units of horizontal ``run''}}$$

Using the formula, it is possible to develop explicit definitions of the relationships shown by the lines in Figure 19–1. Inspection of the slope of line d shows, for example, that for each

FIGURE 19–1: Linear relationships with a zero intercept

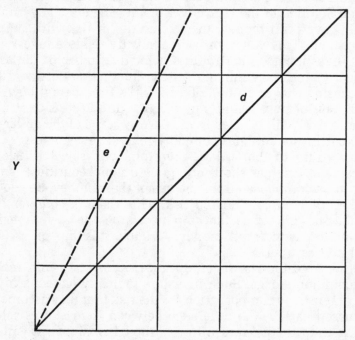

unit of vertical "rise" there is one unit of horizontal "run." Thus, the formula for line d is

$$Y = 1X$$

This means that according to the relationship described by this line, for each unit increase in X there will be a corresponding unit increase in Y. The slope of line e characterizes a relationship between the two variables in which two units of vertical "rise" correspond to one unit of horizontal "run." Thus, the slope of line e (the rise of 2 divided by a run of 1) equals 2. Therefore, the formula for line e is

$$Y = 2X$$

That is, $2X$ is the number of units that Y will increase by for each unit increase in X.

Using the more general form, the equation for a line (with a zero intercept) is

$$Y = bX$$

where b denotes the slope of the line. Note that the greater the value of b, the more rapid the rise of the line.

Figure 19–2 illustrates lines where zero units of X do not

FIGURE 19–2: Linear relationships with a nonzero intercept

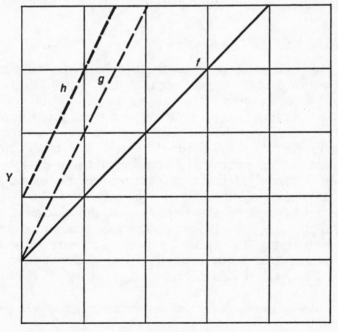

correspond to zero units of Y; i.e., relationships in which the vertical intercept is not zero. To describe these lines, we can use the most general form of the equation for a straight line

$$Y = a + bX$$

where a is the intercept on the vertical axis and b is the slope. Thus, the formula for line f is

$$Y = 1 + 1X$$

The formula for line g is

$$Y = 1 + 2X$$

The formula for line h is

$$Y = 2 + 2X$$

Moving from the general equation to describe a linear relationship between two variables, X and Y

$$Y = a + bX$$

to the equation which represents the linear relationship between a security's expected return and the market's return (discussed in forthcoming sections),

Security's expected return = alpha + beta (market return)

we find basically the same equation!

CAPITAL MARKET LINE

The capital asset pricing model can be portrayed graphically by means of the *capital market line.* Theoretically, the "market" encompasses all securities in proportion to their market value; however, in practice, value-weighted indexes, such as the NYSE or the S&P Composite indexes, are used as proxies for the "market." Given the assumption of an efficient capital market, the pricing of the market portfolio, at any point in time, accurately reflects an equilibrium relationship between the market's consensus of risk and expected return.

Figure 19–3 graphically depicts the capital market line, which represents the relationship between risk and expected return underlying the capital asset pricing model.[1] The horizontal axis measures risk (defined as the standard deviation of return). The vertical axis measures expected return. Note that

---

[1] For consistency, the notation used here, and in other diagrams, is the same as that of Sharpe [252].

FIGURE 19–3: Capital market line

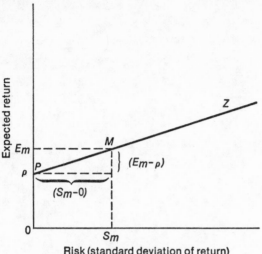

Where

S_m—Standard deviation of market return.
ρ—Riskless rate of interest.
E_m—Expected return of market portfolio.
M—Market portfolio.

and

PMZ—Capital market line.
Slope—Reward per unit of risk borne.

when risk is zero, the expected return is ρ—the riskless rate of interest (return). Note also that the risk of holding the market portfolio (S_m) corresponds to the expected return of the market portfolio (E_m). The difference between the expected return of the market portfolio (E_m) and the expected riskless rate of return (ρ) is the risk premium for the market portfolio.

By assuming that both lending and borrowing are used (explained in detail in Chapter 22), it is possible to select combinations of riskless and risky investments which will plot along line PMZ—the capital market line. The slope of the capital market line (the difference between the expected return on the market portfolio and the expected riskless rate of return, divided by the difference in their risks) can be thought of as the expected reward per unit of risk.

Chapter 20

Balancing risk and return

The prudent application of MPT requires significant departures from the "old school" investment selection processes. The most fundamental of these changes is the shift in emphasis from examining the characteristics of individual investments toward the analysis of investments within the context of a complete, appropriately designed portfolio.

MPT has demonstrated that the investment selection process requires far more than just assembling a portfolio of what we believe to be the "best" available securities. Similarly, MPT has shown us that portfolio evaluation should go far beyond simply determining, and then summing, the characteristics of the individual component securities. MPT has demonstrated that investors undertaking either the construction or analysis of portfolios must address the *relationships* between the individual securities which comprise the aggregate portfolio.

RELATIONSHIPS BETWEEN SECURITIES

The relationships between securities which make up a portfolio are easy to understand but difficult to measure. It is obvious to most people, for example, that holding two substantially different securities is less risky than holding a single security. If two quite different securities are held and one suddenly turns "sour," there is a chance that the second security, possibly in a different industry, will turn in an offsetting "good" performance.

But what *is* the chance? The answer to this question depends on the degree to which the two securities can be expected to move together. One would not expect, for example, the same degree of offsetting performance from a two-stock portfolio drawn from the airline industry, as from a two-stock portfolio representing two widely different sectors of the economy.

Most portfolio managers are intuitively aware of the various kinds of market *comovements*—the tendency for certain stocks, or groups of stocks, to move in the same, or opposite, directions. It is a giant step, however, to move from this intuitive awareness of interrelationships between securities to the development of techniques to measure and forecast these interrelationships. Given the complexity of the problem, it is not surprising that the evolution from modern portfolio *theory*, to practical *applications*, to widespread *acceptance*, and to effective *use* by investment practitioners has spanned more than 25 years.

HARRY MARKOWITZ—THE FATHER OF MPT

The duration of the MPT evolution is best illustrated by the fact that Harry Markowitz (accurately referred to as the father of MPT) published the theoretical foundation for MPT in 1952. [185] In this now classic article, as well as a later book [186], Markowitz set forth the analytical process by which to measure the impact of diversification on risk. While it has taken many years to move from the theory espoused in the 1952 article to widespread acceptance and use by the investment community, Markowitz's work has permanently changed the course of investment-related thought.

Before Markowitz's article, it was more or less taken for granted that the proper way to construct an investment portfolio was just to select the "best securities." It was erroneously assumed that this technique would maximize the expected return for the resultant portfolio. Markowitz correctly pointed out, however, that *the goal of modern portfolio management is not solely to maximize the expected rate of return.* (If this were the only aim, rather than diversifying, investors should concentrate all of their assets in those securities with the highest expected returns—regardless of risk.) Markowitz demonstrated instead that *the objective of modern portfolio management is to maximize what he called "expected utility."*

THE CONCEPT OF UTILITY

The concept of utility is based on the fact that different consumers have different desires, and individuals derive personal satisfaction in varying ways. Consumers purchase goods which satisfy their needs or desires. To avoid the complex task of attempting to measure the relative importance of these needs and desires, economists have devised the concept of utility. Thus, from the perspective of an economist, purchases are said to provide the consumer with some measure of "utility."

In the context of MPT, the concept of "utility" is used in much the same way. Basically, *utility* embraces "all that an investor wants to get and all that an investor wants to avoid . . . ." [287, p. 291] If we set the complexities aside, "utility" can be viewed as being synonymous with "satisfaction"—as the consumer sees it. If satisfaction is translated into investment terms, each investor's preferred combination of investments depends on his or her preference for positive returns relative to his or her distaste for risk. In turn, then, the goal of all rational investing can be thought of as that of maximizing "satisfaction" (or, in economic jargon, "utility").

The trouble with this definition is that it ends up exactly where it starts. We say that investors seek to maximize utility. But what is utility? It is what investors seek to maximize! Of what use, then, is the economist's assumption that investors seek to maximize utility? The answer is that if all investors are attempting to maximize this thing called utility, all investors must behave in the same way. Consistent behavior by investors means that very specific statements can be made about their aggregate behavior. This, in turn, permits accurate descriptions of their future actions.

A means of somehow measuring utility and determining precisely how much utility someone would attain from a given amount of consumption would be very desirable. Unfortunately, no one has ever been able to devise a satisfactory method for measuring utility. This makes it impossible directly to gauge *marginal utility*—the additional unit of satisfaction the consumer gets for each additional dollar of expenditure.

The inability to measure marginal utility is not a problem, however. Although utility cannot be gauged on an absolute scale, it is possible to evaluate it on a relative scale—much as temperature might be gauged without a thermometer. That is, various states of hot and cold can be distinguished even if the absolute differences cannot be determined. Similarly, a consumer, without an explicit scale of measurement, can still express judgments about relative levels of satisfaction and dissatisfaction. For any individual, these relative judgments can be put in the form of indifference curves.

CLASSIC INDIFFERENCE CURVES

The indifference curve technique is not new. Francis Y. Edgeworth, a British economist, first introduced the concept in the early 1880s. Later, in the 1930s, the approach was popularized by two other British economists, John R. Hicks and R. G. D. Allen. Since then, indifference curve analysis has become a standard and necessary tool of economics.

The significance of the concept lies in the fact that indifference curve analysis eliminates the need to measure utility directly. *Indifference curves* are a graphic representation of consumer tastes and preferences. In Figure 20–1, for example, the consumer is limited to choosing between two commodities—meat and poultry.

Assume that the consumer's household is currently consuming 25 pounds of meat and 20 pounds of poultry per month. This combination is shown as point E in Figure 20–1. Notice that any point in quadrant B gives the consumer more meat and more poultry—presumably a situation that the con-

FIGURE 20–1: Classic indifference curve

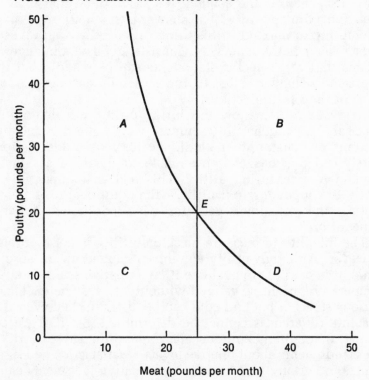

sumer would find preferable. Also notice that any point in quadrant C gives the consumer less meat and less poultry—presumably a less desired situation. In quadrants A and D, it is not as clear what the preferred, or less desirable, situations will be. In quadrant A the consumer will receive more poultry and less meat; in quadrant D, more meat and less poultry.

The line in Figure 20–1 is the hypothetical consumer's indifference curve. This means that the consumer views all combinations of meat and poultry along this line as *equally satisfactory alternatives*. Specifically, this hypothetical consumer would be indifferent to accepting five pounds less meat in exchange for ten pounds more poultry. Similarly, this con-

FIGURE 20–2: Indifference curves

A. Perfectly substitutable goods

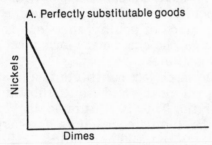

B. Perfectly complementary goods

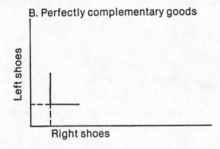

C. Approximately substitutable goods

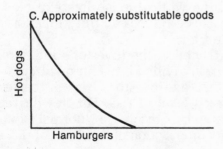

sumer would be willing to substitute ten pounds more meat for ten pounds less poultry. Thus, the consumer is indifferent to any combination of items represented by points *along* the curve.

Technically, the indifference curve represents a single contour line of the investor's utility function. In Figure 20–1 any points above and to the right of the indifference curve give the consumer *more* satisfaction. Similarly, any points to the left and below the curve give the consumer less satisfaction.

The slope of an indifference curve at any point indicates the *marginal rate of substitution*—the rate at which a consumer is willing to substitute one product for another. Between 30 and 40 pounds of poultry, the slope ("rise" divided by the "run") is 2.0. This means that in this range the consumer is willing to substitute two pounds of poultry for one pound of meat. However, between 10 and 20 pounds of poultry, the slope is 1.0. This means that in this range, the consumer views meat and poultry as perfect 1-to-1 substitutes.

The indifference curve for a *perfect substitute* is a straight line; however, as in the case of nickels and dimes, substitution need not be in a 1-to-1 ratio. This is illustrated in Figure 20–2A. By comparison, the indifference curve for *perfect complements*—products which go together as units—is shown in Figure 20–2B. Finally, the shape of an indifference curve for approximately substitutable goods is shown in Figure 20–2C.

INVESTOR'S INDIFFERENCE CURVE

A typical investor's *indifference curve* (or *utility function*) is shown in Figure 20–3. Notice that while economists usually draw indifference curves that are "downward sloping to the right," as they were depicted in Figures 20–1 and 20–2, the curves are "turned" for MPT applications so that the axes can be labeled to match those of the capital market line. Specifically, the horizontal axis shows risk (measured as the standard deviation of return), and the vertical axis plots expected return. This labeling of the axes produces a utility function that is "upward sloping to the right."

To provide a point of reference, the investor's indifference curve in Figure 20–3 has been divided into four quadrants—*A*, *B*, *C*, and *D*. Imagine that an investor's risk is currently *M*—designating the market's level of risk. For this degree of risk, the investor is assumed to receive a "normal" rate of return, *N*. Moving from the intersection of this level of risk and

FIGURE 20-3: Investor's indifference curve

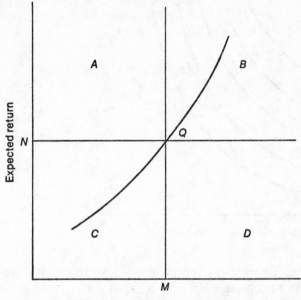

Risk (standard deviation of return)

expected return, Q, the investor would prefer any point in quadrant A—with a higher expected return and less risk. Conversely, the investor would be less satisfied with any point in quadrant D—with a lower expected return and more risk.

As with other indifference curves, the choice of the points in the other quadrants depends on the individual's personal preferences; in this case, the preference for return and the distaste for risk. Thus, moving along the curve in quadrant B, this "typical" investor will be willing to accept more risk since the proportionate increases in expected return would progressively exceed the increases in risk. Conversely, moving along the curve in quadrant C, the "typical" investor will be willing to accept a lower expected return so long as the proportionate decline in risk progressively exceeds the reduction in expected return.

Importantly, however, by moving to different points along the line, the investor neither increases nor decreases the total level of satisfaction derived from the various combinations of risk and expected return. Hence, the investor is indifferent to being at any point along his or her indifference curve.

Figure 20-4 shows a typical investor's indifference map—a

FIGURE 20–4: Investor's indifference map

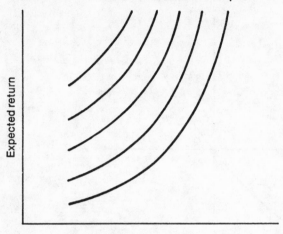

Risk (standard deviation of return)

set of indifference curves which profile an investor's willingness to trade off changes in risk against changes in expected
return. The important characteristic of an investor's indifference map is that each successive curve moving upward to the
left represents a higher level of utility (or, if you prefer,
satisfaction).

It should not be presumed that all of the curves on the indifference map are possible. Instead, what the indifference map
shows is that depending on the available alternatives, a rational investor would always prefer a higher curve—one with
less risk and a greater expected return. Again, given the highest available curve, the investor's personal preferences are
such that he or she will be indifferent to any combination of
risk or expected return along that particular curve.

Importantly, different investors have varying indifference
curves. Figure 20–5 shows two extreme cases in which the
indifference curves (in these cases they are actually "lines")
labeled 1 through 3 provide different types of investors—
"fearless" and "fearful"—with increasing levels of satisfaction. The fearless investor in Figure 20–5A is oblivious to risk
since increased satisfaction (moving from indifference curve 1
to 3) is derived solely from increases in expected return—
regardless of risk. This investor will select the combination of
investments offering the highest expected return. The fearful
investor in Figure 20–5B is oblivious to return since increased
satisfaction is derived solely from reductions in risk—

FIGURE 20–5: Extreme cases of indifference

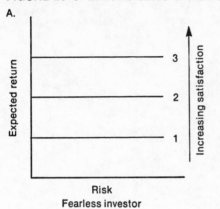

A.

Fearless investor

B.

Fearful investor

regardless of return. This investor will select the combination of investments offering the lowest risk.

Figure 20–6 illustrates two more typical cases of investor indifference. Both investors are risk averse, but the "adventuresome" investor portrayed in Figure 20–6A is willing to trade relatively smaller increases in incremental expected return for a given increment of risk than the "conservative" investor portrayed in Figure 20–6B.

FIGURE 20–6: Typical cases of indifference

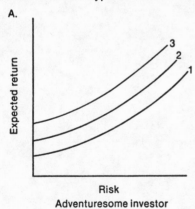

A.

Adventuresome investor

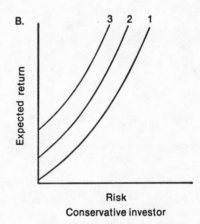

B.

Conservative investor

Chapter 21

Markowitz model

To operationalize the concept of "expected utility," Markowitz began with the valid premise that all investors want a combination of high returns *and* low risk. Stated another way, rational investors maximize their "utility" by seeking either (1) the highest available rate of return for a given level of risk. or (2) the lowest level of available risk for a given rate of return.

INEFFICIENT SETS

The relationship between risk and expected return is best illustrated by Figure 21–1. Here "expected return" is plotted on the vertical axis, and "risk" is plotted on the horizontal axis. For now, do not be concerned about how either risk or return is measured. Simply bear in mind that the expected return will increase as one moves up the vertical scale and that risk increases as one moves to the right on the horizontal scale.

Which investment in Figure 21–1 best meets the objective of maximum return with minimum risk? Investment alternatives A and B each have the same expected return, but B carries more risk. Thus, since investment A would be preferred by any rational, risk-averse investor, B can be eliminated from consideration.

Of alternatives A and C, both have the same risk, but A has a higher expected return. Accordingly, alternative C can be eliminated from consideration. A comparison of the two remaining alternatives, A and D, reveals that A has both a higher expected return and a lower risk than D. Thus, investment A—with the highest expected return and the lowest risk—is the preferred alternative.

EFFICIENT SETS

What would happen, however, if these four hypothetical investment alternatives existed in a freely competitive real-

FIGURE 21–1: An "inefficient set" of
investment alternatives

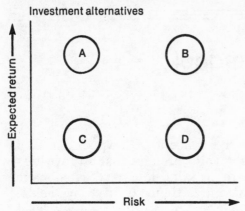

Investment alternatives

world marketplace (while maintaining the assumption that
everyone has the same estimates of expected return and risk)?
In a competitive marketplace, since all investors would prefer
investment A to the other alternatives, their demand for investment A would drive up its price. But in a real-world marketplace, as the price of investment A increased, the expected
return per unit of investment would decrease.

Suppose, for example, that the price of investment A was
originally (as shown in Figure 21–1) $1,000 and that its ex-
pected return was $80 per year. The return ($80) divided by
the cost ($1,000) times 100 gives investment A an expected
return of 8 percent. Similarly, suppose that the original price
of investment C (as shown in Figure 21–1) was also $1,000, but
that its expected return was only $75 per year. The return ($75)
divided by the cost ($1,000) times 100 gives investment C an
expected return of 7.5 percent. Since A and C have exactly the
same level of risk, investment A will be preferred to investment C as long as investment A continues to have a higher
expected return. But remember that as the demand for investment A increases, so will its price.

Carrying the example further, suppose that the increased
demand for investment A increased its price from $1,000 to
$1,066.67. If this occurred, the expected return ($80) divided
by the new cost ($1,066.67) times 100 would be 7.5 percent.
Since investment C's expected return is also 7.5 percent, the
two investments would now be equally attractive on a price
basis. (This is an oversimplification because the lack of de-

mand for investment C would drive its price down, in turn increasing its expected return.)

Through what the classical 18th-century economist, Adam Smith [259] referred to as the "invisible hand," prices in competitive markets (such as those for investment securities) quickly adjust to the forces of supply and demand. In keeping with the efficient market hypothesis, these adjustments in price eliminate any market *inefficiencies* whereby one commodity, or investment, is so attractively priced that it is preferred to all others.

Thus, while investors have different risk/return preferences, rational investors will always attempt to find portfolios which provide (a) the maximum rate of return for every level of risk, or conversely, (b) the minimum level of risk for every possible rate of return. Markets which reflect this goal are said to be *efficient*. Markets containing investments that are "out of line" with this goal, such as alternative D in Figure 21–1, are said to be *inefficient*.

Since inefficiencies are eliminated by competition, the hypothetical investment alternatives depicted in Figure 21–1 would not exist in a competitive marketplace. Instead, as long as everyone used the same estimates for expected return and risk, the "inefficient" marketplace depicted in Figure 21–1 would, through price changes, become "efficient," and the *new* investment alternatives would array themselves as shown in Figure 21–2. The line *XYZ* in Figure 21–2 thus represents the so-called *efficient boundary*, or *efficient set*, of investment alternatives. That is, the investments on this line offer the

FIGURE 21–2: An "efficient set"
of investment alternatives

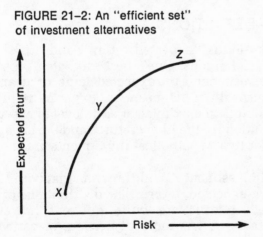

highest level of return for this degree of risk or, alternatively, provide the lowest level of risk for this rate of return.

Readers who are not familiar with the concept of an "efficient set" of investment alternatives are encouraged to note for themselves that in Figure 21–2 (1) any investments to the left of or above line XYZ would be superior investments, and (2) any investments to the right of, or below, line XYZ would be inferior investments. Further, readers are reminded that the competitive forces of the marketplace will eliminate—through price changes—any agreed-upon superior or inferior alternatives.

Working from the three investment alternatives depicted in Figure 21–2, suppose it was necessary to select an investment for someone whose investment preferences closely reflect those of a classical "widow" or "orphan." Presumably, this individual would want to attain the highest available return that is consistent with a minimum level of risk. Of the three alternatives shown in Figure 21–2, the investment with the lowest risk—the overriding consideration for this person—is investment X.

At the other extreme, suppose that an investment must be selected for a classic "speculator." Here, the objective would be to select the alternative with the lowest available risk that is consistent with the highest expected return. Of the three hypothetical investments shown in Figure 21–2, the one with the highest expected return—the overriding preference for this person—is investment Z. The middle ground between the two extremes—essentially a balance between risk and expected return—is represented by investment Y.

RISK AND RETURN—DEFINITIONS

At this point, the terms "expected return" and "risk" require more explicit definitions. One's best estimate of the future return of any investment is the expected value, or mean, of all of the likely returns. It is this mean, or "expected return," that an investor attempts to maximize at each level of acceptable risk. The distributions of the likely returns and the mean, or expected, returns for two hypothetical investments are shown in Figure 21–3.

A comparison of investment A and B reveals that both have the same average, or expected, return. The distributions of the likely, or expected, returns are quite different however. Specifically, investment A has more dispersion, or variance,

FIGURE 21–3: Comparative distributions of likely returns

Investment A

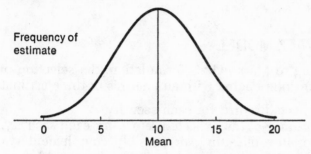

Estimates of expected annual return (percentages)

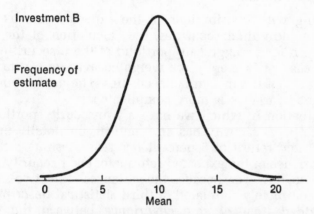

Estimates of expected annual return (percentages)

around the mean than the distribution of likely returns for investment B. Thus, based either on a comparison of the graphic representations in Figure 21–3, or on the explicit numerical measures for the variance of the distributions of the expected returns for the two investments, investment B emerges as superior because it offers the same expected return but with less variance of estimated returns.

Figure 21–3 dramatizes the importance of variance. The higher an investment's variance, the more its actual return is likely to deviate from the expected return. From an investor's point of view, the more assurance that the actual results will parallel the expected results, the better the investment. Thus, as we operationalize the maxim that rational, risk-averse investors will always seek investments with a minimum level of risk for a given level of expected return, it becomes clear that the statistical variance (or its square root, the *standard deviation*) of the distribution of possible expected returns can be used as a measure of risk.

THE MARKOWITZ MODEL

According to Markowitz's formulation, the selection of an efficient portfolio begins with an analysis of three estimates:

1. The *expected return* for each security.
2. The *variance of the expected* return for each security.
3. The possibly offsetting, or possibly complementary, interaction, or *covariance*, of return with every other security consideration.

Beginning with distributions of the expected returns for each of the individual securities, the calculation of the expected return for an aggregate portfolio of these securities is relatively easy. It is merely the weighted average of the expected returns of the individual securities. The calculation of the combined variance is more complicated.

For a situation in which we have a two-security portfolio, assume that each security has an identical, but totally unrelated, expected return of 8 percent per year. Assume further that the variance of the expected returns for *each* security is 2 percent. Also, however, because the variances of the two securities are completely unrelated, a third statistical description can be added—that of zero *covariance* between the two securities.

Thus, investing in either of the two securities separately will produce an expected return of 8 percent with a 2 percent variance of return. It can be shown, however, that if the returns on the two securities are completely unrelated, then the variance in the rate of return if the two securities are combined into a two-security portfolio is only half the variance for each security considered alone. In fact, as long as the expected rates of return of the two stocks are not perfectly correlated, the variance (i.e., risk) of a two-security portfolio will always be lower than the variance of either of the securities considered alone.

To determine the most efficient set from a large number of investments requires what is known as "quadratic programming." (Rather than explain how this is actually done, we will ask the reader to take it on faith that the portfolios resulting from this analysis—which is admittedly taxing for even large-scale computers—do indeed define the efficient set.)

SUMMARY: THE MARKOWITZ MODEL

Markowitz demonstrated that the two relevant characteristics of a portfolio are

1. Its expected return.
2. Some measure of its risk—operationally defined as the dispersion of possible returns around the expected return.

Markowitz also demonstrated that rational investors will choose to hold efficient portfolios; that is, portfolios which maximize each investor's utility by

1. Maximizing expected return for a given degree of risk.
2. Minimizing risk for a given level of expected return.

Markowitz further demonstrated that the identification of efficient portfolios would require information on *each* security's

1. Expected return.
2. Variance of return.
3. Covariance of return with *every other security under consideration.*

Finally, Markowitz demonstrated that once prepared, the foregoing security descriptions could be manipulated by *portfolio optimization* programs (i.e., quadratic programming techniques) to produce an explicit definition of the efficient portfolio in terms of

1. The securities to be held.
2. The proportion of available funds to be allocated to each.

PORTFOLIO OPTIMIZATION PROGRAMS—THE "VALUE ADDED"

It is important to know whether or not portfolio optimization programs generate portfolios which are basically the same as those produced by people who rely on "professional judgment" and "traditional" approaches. In short, are the portfolio optimizers that are derived from MPT really "much ado about nothing"?

While there is a shortage of definitive research data, many organizations which use portfolio optimization techniques to "shadow" professionally constructed portfolios have found a significant number of "inefficient" portfolios (i.e., portfolios that do *not* strike the optimum balance between risk and return). More importantly, given the portfolio selection techniques described here, it is *impossible* to envision a more effective and accurate way to translate a unique set of forecast assumptions and portfolio objectives into an optimal portfolio.

The increasing availability of portfolio optimization programs is causing the traditional role of the portfolio manager to be redefined. *It is an undisputed fact that the translation from security-related forecast assumptions and a set of portfolio objectives and constraints (such as no more than 5 percent in any single security, at least four percent yield, and so on) to optimal portfolios can be done more effectively, and more accurately, by portfolio optimization programs.*

This does not mean, however, that the job of the portfolio manager will be eliminated by the widespread use of portfolio optimization programs. Quite to the contrary, a portfolio optimization program is merely a tool by which a portfolio manager translates "assumptions" on the risk and return characteristics of a universe of potential investments into a portfolio with certain predefined "characteristics." Both the "assumptions" about the universe of available investments and the "characteristics" of the portfolio must be supplied by the portfolio manager.

Chapter 22

Asset allocation line

William Sharpe extended Markowitz's work in two important dimensions. First, Sharpe broadened the analysis to include riskless assets (such as short-term government securities) and the possibility of borrowing. Second, he developed a simplified model that alleviates the burdensome data collection and computing problems inherent in the Markowitz model. These refinements are discussed, in turn, in the next two chapters.

COMBINING RISKLESS AND RISKY SECURITIES—THE ASSET ALLOCATION LINE

In the earlier discussion of the capital market line, it was stated that various combinations of lending and borrowing will generate a linear continuum of alternative investment possibilities. These return and risk combinations ranged from the risk-free rates of return on a riskless investment through the expected rate of return commensurate with the risk of a fully diversified market portfolio.

As such, the capital market line is a special case of the more general notion of an *asset allocation line*. Although the capital market line employed lending and borrowing to develop a continuum of investment possibilities ranging from risk-free assets to the market portfolio, the same line can be developed to range from risk-free assets to *any* portfolio. The basis for this important notion comes from the work of William Sharpe. Sharpe demonstrated that "when a risky security or portfolio is combined with a riskless one, the risk of the combination is proportional to the amount invested in the risky component." [245, p. 85] Suppose, for example, that an investor divides his or her funds between a common stock portfolio and an insured

161

(presumably riskless) savings account. Here the only amount "at risk" is the portion in common stock.

This is best illustrated by the hypothetical portfolios shown in Table 22–1. Portfolio A is fully invested in an insured savings account, and the investor is acting as a "lender." For

TABLE 22–1: Investment alternatives: Combinations of risky and riskless holdings

Portfolio designation	Composition of the portfolio	Expected rate of return (percent)	Standard deviation of return (percent)	Whereby an investor is:
A...................	100 percent in insured savings account	5.0	0.0	Lender
B	100 percent in common stock portfolio	10.0	20.0	Owner
C	60 percent in portfolio A and 40 percent in portfolio B	7.0	8.0	Lender and owner
D	40 percent in portfolio A and 60 percent in portfolio B	8.0	12.0	Lender and owner
E...................	20 percent in portfolio A and 100 percent in portfolio B	11.0	24.0	Borrower and owner

purposes of illustration, the expected return of portfolio A is assumed to be 5 percent, and the standard deviation of return (the square root of the variance) is assumed to be 0 percent. The "riskless" portfolio appears as point A in Figure 22–1.

By comparison, portfolio B in Table 22–1 consists of a portfolio of common stocks, so that an investor purchasing this portfolio of common stocks, is acting as an "owner." In keeping with the valid presumption that a common stock portfolio would carry both a higher expected return and greater risk than an insured savings account, portfolio B is assumed to have an aggregate expected rate of return of 10 percent and a standard deviation of return of 20 percent. (Note these figures are very much in keeping with Ibbotson and Sinquefield's historical data that was discussed in Chapter 17.) Portfolio B is designated as point B in Figure 22–1. (The reader is encouraged to "plot" point B at the intersection of an expected return

FIGURE 22–1: A hypothetical asset allocation line—Available combinations of risky and riskless investments

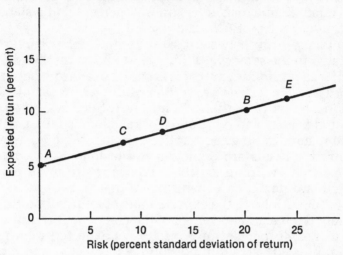

of 10 percent and a standard deviation of return of 20 percent.)

In a situation with two such investment alternatives, an investor could

1. Invest everything in portfolio A.
2. Invest everything in portfolio B.
3. Divide the investment, in any proportion, between the two alternatives A and B.

The latter case, in which funds are divided between the two alternatives, is represented by portfolios C and D in Table 22–1 and Figure 22–1.

Portfolio C, where an investor is acting as both a lender and an owner, was made up by allocating 60 percent of the available funds to portfolio A (an insured savings account) and the remaining 40 percent to portfolio B (a common stock portfolio). Since the expected rate of return for a combined portfolio is merely the weighted average of the component returns, the expected rate of return of portfolio C is 7 percent (i.e., 60 percent of portfolio A's expected return of 5 percent, plus 40 percent of portfolio B's expected return of 10 percent).

Further, since it can be shown that the risk of a portfolio resulting from the combination of a risky security with a riskless one is proportional to the amount invested in the risky security, the standard deviation of return for portfolio C is 8 percent (i.e., 40 percent of the standard deviation of return of portfolio B). The relationship between risk and expected return for portfolio C is shown as point C in Figure 22–1 (i.e., at the intersection of an expected return of 7 percent and a standard deviation of return of 8 percent).

The relationship between risk and return for portfolio D is calculated in the same way. Table 22–1 shows that portfolio D is similar to portfolio C in that it is constructed from both risky and riskless assets. The proportion of the two types of assets differs from that of portfolio C, however. Specifically, 40 percent of the assets in portfolio D are deployed in portfolio A—the insured savings account. The remaining 60 percent of portfolio D's assets are deployed in portfolio B—a common stock portfolio with an expected rate of return of 10 percent and standard deviation of return of 20 percent.

As with portfolio C, the expected rate of return of portfolio D is merely the weighted average of the component returns, or 8 percent (i.e., 40 percent of portfolio A's expected return of 5 percent, plus 60 percent of portfolio B's expected return of 10 percent). Also, since the risk of portfolio D is proportionate to the amount invested in the risky security, the standard deviation of return for portfolio D is 12 percent (i.e., 60 percent of the standard deviation of return of portfolio B). As with portfolio C, the relationship between risk and expected return for portfolio D is shown as point D in Figure 22–1. (Again, the reader is encouraged to "plot" this point).

As now developed, Figure 22–1 illustrates a continuum of investment alternatives—ranging from 100 percent in riskless assets (point A) to 100 percent risky assets (point B). That is, an investor could choose to place all his or her assets in a riskless portfolio—point A. Alternatively, all of an investor's assets could be placed in the common stock portfolio—point B. An investor could, however, select any combination of the first two investment alternatives. All possible combinations of riskless assets (portfolio A) and risky assets (portfolio B) fall on the *asset allocation line ACDB* in Figure 22–1.

Extending this analysis one step further, it is possible to think of the expected return on a *loan* as a riskless investment with a guaranteed loss. Take, for example, the case of a person with $10,000 to invest who, because of a willingness to increase his or her risk through borrowing, takes out a loan of an additional $2,000 with a promise to repay the principal plus interest of 5 percent. This investor could now invest a total of $12,000 in common stock portfolio B. This situation is depicted as portfolio E (where the investor is acting both as a borrower and an owner) in Table 22–1.

The expected rate of return of such a combined portfolio is still the weighted average of the respective component returns. Thus, we have a situation in which the investor is investing 120 percent of his or her available assets in a portfolio that has an expected rate of return of 10 percent, but 20 percent of these available assets are *also* in a portfolio with an expected return of −5 percent. Combining the 12 percent expected return from common stock portfolio B (120 percent of the 10 percent expected return) with the 1 percent expected loss from borrowing (20 percent of the 5 percent negative expected return) indicates an expected return of 11 percent for portfolio E.

Similarly, this investor, through borrowing, will increase the risk (standard deviation of return) to 120 percent of that of the underlying portfolio, or 24 percent. Graphically, portfolio E is shown in Figure 22–1 as point E (i.e., the intersection of the 11 percent expected return and the 24 percent standard deviation of return).

Beyond the details of the foregoing example, it is important to note that the *asset allocation line* in Figure 22–1 illustrates the risk and expected return for all possible allocations of assets between a riskless and risky investment. Specifically,

1. Riskless investing through leading—represented by point A.
2. Risky investing without lending—represented by point B.
3. Any combination of riskless investing *and* risky investing—represented by a continuum of possible points along the line AB.
4. Any feasible combination of borrowing and risky investing—represented by the continuum of possible points along the line BF.

Figure 22–1 illustrates the important concept that with only three investment alternatives—generally termed risk-free lending, owning, and borrowing—an investor can "mix and match" these alternatives to attain a continuum of possible asset allocations.[1]

---

[1] An important subject that is beyond the scope of this book deals with the amount of debt that should be used to finance a firm's operations. If investors, through their selection of combinations of investment instruments, can indeed acquire any combinations of debt and equity that they desire, we could presume that this market efficiency would adjust the firm's cost of capital so as to minimize the importance of the firm's internal decisions regarding capital structure. Readers who are interested in this topic are referred to the classic article on the M–M hypothesis by Franco Modigliani and Merton Miller [193].

Chapter 23

Single- and multi-index models

Aside from the omission of the lending and borrowing alternatives, the original Markowitz formulation of the theoretical solution to portfolio selection poses several problems in implementation. Certain simplifications which facilitate implementation are discussed in this chapter.

The "efficient portfolios" resulting from the Markowitz (or any other) model are based on the analysis of estimates of future risk and expected returns which are available at a particular point in time. These estimates, and hence the resultant "efficient portfolios," can be expected to change over time—as price fluctuations raise or lower expected returns and as analysts revise their forecasts of risks and returns.

Thus, the "portfolio selection problem" is not simply that of determining the most efficient portfolios. Instead, investment managers are continually challenged to keep the analysis up to date and to weigh the potential advantages to be derived from changes in a portfolio against transaction costs.

This, in turn, demands both that human resources continually update the required estimates and that the computational resources translate the estimates into efficient portfolios. Logically, the longer one waits to repeat such analysis, the further the once-efficient portfolios can be expected to deviate from the new efficient set. As a result, frequent updates are needed.

Unfortunately, the Markowitz approach requires enormous amounts of both human and computational resources. For example, to evaluate 100 securities, an analyst must prepare 100 timely estimates of both risk and expected return. In addition, *the Markowitz solution requires an explicit estimate of the covariance of returns between each possible pair of securities.* Thus, the evaluation of the covariance between 100 pairs of securities necessitates the estimation and processing of 4, 550 estimates of covariance.[1]

Aside from the sheer volume of the data, imagine the practical problems facing an expert in the analysis of automobile stocks who is asked to estimate the degree of expected comovement between Ford, American Motors, General Motors, and each of 500 other stocks drawn from 60 other industries! Going one step further, even if the automobile analyst prepared such estimates, it would be difficult to place any confidence in their accuracy.

The problem with gathering both this kind and quantity of information was probably best expressed by Markowitz himself when he wrote, "it is reasonable to ask security analysts to summarize their researches in 100 carefully considered expected returns, and 100 carefully considered variances of return. It is not reasonable, however, to ask for [almost] 5,000 carefully and individually considered covariances." [186, pp. 96–97]

To bridge the gap between his theoretical solution and the practical problems of estimating the covariance for each pair of securities under consideration, Markowitz suggested using the relationship between each security's rate of return and the rate of return on a market index as a substitute for explicit data on the covariance of each pair of securities under study. William Sharpe [242] pursued this approach with the so-called single-index model.

There is considerable evidence that securities tend to move with the market. Whether based on such time-honored Wall Street aphorisms as "when they raid the brothel, they take all the girls," or Brealey's less colorful statement, "when the wind of recession blows, there are few companies that do not lean with it" [34, p. 104], it is true that in major market moves, most securities move in the same direction. However, even though securities have many common characteristics and, as a result, tend to move together, their numerous individual and distinguishing properties cause stocks to comove with the market at *different rates*. Accordingly, how *sensitive* a security's price is to changes in the overall market is of crucial importance.

Thus, while the ideal way to select a portfolio would be to develop precise estimates of how every pair of securities under consideration would, or would not, move together, the ap-

---

[1] The number of pairs which can be drawn from a sample of N securities is $N(N-1)/2$. Thus, the Markowitz analysis of 100 securities requires the estimation and processing of $100(99)/2$ covariances—one for each pair of securities.

proach is difficult to implement. To develop an easier to implement alternative, Sharpe focused on the sensitivity of individual stock prices to fluctuations in a single market index— hence, the term "single-index model."

THE INPUTS TO A SINGLE-INDEX MODEL

Aside from reducing the amount of information Sharpe's model requires a significantly different *kind* of information. The Markowitz approach calls for an *unconditional* forecast of the rate of return for each stock. Sharpe's model, on the other hand, employs *conditional forecasts*; that is, forecasts which are conditional on market levels.

It is an important feature of Sharpe's analysis that it does not depend on an absolute forecast of how well a stock will, or will not, perform. Basically, when using the Sharpe approach, security analysts are asked to forecast expected rates of return under several alternative sets of market conditions. Because these analysts are *not* required directly to speculate about future market conditions, the functions of market-level forecasting and company-level forecasting are clearly delineated.

This separation has two major advantages. First, for the investment decision maker, an analyst's forecasts do not represent a composite opinion on both the overall trend of the market and how the security is expected to move within that market context. Imagine the difficulties facing a portfolio manager who receives performance or price estimates from more than 50 security analysts. Each of these estimates may have been derived from the analyst's assumptions about the market, plus his or her outlook for the company. Happily, the Sharpe model separates market- and security-level forecasts.

The second advantage of this separation is that it allows the responsibility for each decision level to be vested with the people who are best qualified to provide each type of forecast. Further, conditional forecasts keep the element of risk in its proper perspective—both as it relates to the security and to the overall market.

Unfortunately, not every organization uses such procedures. In the words of Sharpe, "people continually ask for, and get, single estimates, ignoring the influence of overall market moves and the presence of uncertainty. Such procedures are, however, too simplistic: *most returns are uncertain, and they do depend on market moves.* These two factors are too important to be ignored [italics added in the last sentence]." [252, p. 108]

SUMMARY—SHARPE'S SINGLE-INDEX MODEL

Sharpe's portfolio selection approach does not require estimates of the comovement among individual securities. Instead, the Sharpe approach uses estimates of each security's comovement with one general market (single-index) indicator. As a result, the data required to "drive" the Sharpe single-index model is significantly simpler and less burdensome than that required for the Markowitz model. Specifically, the three estimates that are required for each security to be analyzed by the Sharpe approach are:

1. The amount of specific, or nonmarket, return (alpha).
2. A measure of responsiveness to market movements (beta).
3. The variance of the nonmarket return.

MULTI-INDEX MODELS

The Markowitz portfolio selection model can be viewed as the ultimate multi-index model. Since the model is based on the estimation of the covariance between each pair of securities, every security is, in fact, an "index," or reference point, for analysis. At the other extreme, Sharpe proposed a single market-related index as the reference point for analysis. Logically, then, there is an entire continuum of possible multi-index models in the "middle ground" between the Sharpe and Markowitz approaches.

Unfortunately, Sharpe's single-index model reflects one disquieting assumption. The model assumes that *the only movements which are common to all securities are related to movements of the overall market.* Other comovements, however, such as those of industries, have been shown to exist [see King, 149, 150]. It is reasonable to expect, therefore, that the use of "middle ground indices," such as those built around significantly different industries, could produce better results than those of a single-index model—without introducing the burdensome data collection and computational problems associated with the Markowitz full covariance approach.

Thus, the limited multi-index approach, while still minimizing data collection requirements offers the advantages of:

1. "Fine tuning" the comovement of homogeneous companies to some subclassification of the general market index.

2. Explicitly estimating the comovements between each pair of subclassifications, in much the same manner as between pairs of individual securities in the Markowitz full covariance approach.

Although it holds out the promise of improved results, the concept of a multi-index model poses a new problem. The market must be segmented into distinctly homogeneous and unrelated groups; that is, securities that are homogeneous in the sense that they move together as a group but are unrelated in that group movements are unrelated. Discouragingly traditional industry classifications—assumed by most people to be the "natural" basis for multi-index classification schemes—have provided disappointing results.

SINGLE- VERSUS MULTI-INDEX MODELS

Kalman Cohen and Jerry Pogue [45] working at the Carnegie Institute of Technology, developed the first multi-index model in the late 1960s. Working with historical data from a fairly large universe of common stocks, they found, surprisingly, that a single-index model usually performed better than their ten-industry, multi-index model.

James L. Farrell, Jr., who now heads the Citibank Investment Management Group, has shown, however, that the reason the Cohen and Pogue multi-index model failed to outperform the single-index model can be traced to deficiencies in their industry indexes. In Farrell's words, "[Cohen and Pogue's] . . . results do not necessarily lead to the conclusion that the single-index model is preferable to the multi-index model. The main implication is that [the] industry indexes [used by Cohen and Pogue] are basically deficient as inputs to the multi-index model." [83, p. 12]

Following Benjamin King's conclusion that stock price movements can be traced to four factors—the market, the basic industry, the industry subgroup, and the company—Farrell reasoned that a broader than industry classification of "growth, cyclical, or stable" characteristics might provide the basis for an improved multi-index model.

Using data on 100 stocks and a technique known as "cluster analysis," Farrell separated stocks into groups or clusters within which price movements were highly correlated, but between which price movements showed little correlation. Four homogeneous groups emerged from this analysis—

growth, cyclical, stable, and, surprisingly, oil stocks. That is, these four groupings of stocks were found to be homogeneous in the sense that intragroup price movements were highly correlated at the same time that there was an insignificant amount of correlation between intergroup price movements. This kind of group homogeneity is the prerequisite for a multi-index portfolio selection model and encouraged Farrell to proceed with the development and testing of a model based on these groups.

A comparison of efficient portfolios generated by a single-index model and Farrell's multi-index model showed that the multi-index model selected "portfolios with lower risk over a broad range of the efficient frontier." Further, the multi-index model diversified more efficiently than the single-index model owing to its facility for distributing the portfolio more evenly across the four homogeneous groups. [83, p. 47]

Having established that his groups remained stable over time, Farrell used historical data from 1961–69 to develop inputs to the two models and then tested their comparative performance against large all-stock mutual funds and the S&P 500 over the period spanning 1970–74. Farrell found that both models outperformed the mutual funds and that his multi-index model outperformed the single-index model.

Chapter 24

Market model

The *market model* provides the conceptual foundation for the single-index model (which is also known as the diagonal model, or the one-factor model). The market model *describes the relationship between returns on individual securities (or portfolios) and the returns on the market portfolio.* Specifically, the market model holds that the returns on an individual security (or portfolio) are linearly related to an index of market returns.

EX POST VERSUS EX ANTE INFORMATION

All investment information is a "before the fact" prediction or an "after the fact" result. Much of the confusion over MPT can be traced to the failure to keep the distinction between "before the fact" estimates and "after the fact" results in mind.

The literature on MPT generally makes the distinction between "before the fact" and "after the fact" by referring to *ex ante* and *ex post* variables. While other terminology might be employed, the academic convention is used here both to familiarize the reader with the quantitative jargon and to parallel the more rigorous discussions of the material.

Much as poker players "ante" before the deal, ex ante is the Latin term used by MPT theorists to indicate "before the fact." Similarly, ex post is taken to mean "after the fact." The need to make this distinction stems from the fact that information such as a stock's beta—its price sensitivity to that of the market— can be an ex ante (i.e., predicted) or an ex post (i.e., historical) value. Moreover, ex post outcomes are occasionally used as estimates for ex ante expectations. This is the case, for example, when historic, or ex post, betas are used as estimates of

173

future, or ex ante, betas. Thus, when necessary, the distinction between ex ante and ex post information will be made.

CAPM VERSUS MARKET MODEL

The capital asset pricing model (CAPM) discussed in Chapter 19 is a very distinct model. Neither the market model nor the CAPM depends in any way on the other. The CAPM *provides an explicit expression of the expected returns for all assets.* Basically, the CAPM holds that if investors are risk averse, high-risk stocks must have higher expected returns than low-risk stocks. In equilibrium, a security with zero risk will have an expected return equal to that of a riskless asset. Increases in risk beyond that of a riskless asset will be accompanied by proportional increases in expected return.

Thus, the CAPM is indeed a pricing model—it indicates *the price of immediate consumption and the price of risk.* That is, when consumers choose to direct their funds into immediate consumption, they do so in favor of the alternative of investing these funds in riskless securities. The "price" of immediate consumption is consequently the "reward" which could have been earned from waiting. Similarly, when investors choose risky investments, they do so in favor of the alternative of holding riskless investments.

However, in order to attract capital to the risky alternatives, the marketplace must reward investors in proportion to the amount of risk they undertake. Since "price" to the buyer is the "reward" to a seller, these returns can also be thought of as rewards—the reward for waiting and the reward for taking market risk. From the opposite point of view these returns can be thought of as the "price of immediate consumption" and the "price of risk."

While the CAPM is an abstraction and simplification of capital market theory, the market model is not explicitly linked to a particular theory. The market model is merely a description of the relationship which exists between security and market returns. As such, the market model tells us nothing about what determines returns. The model merely describes the relationship which has been shown to exist between market and security returns. The construct that is used to describe the market model relationship is the security characteristic line.

SECURITY CHARACTERISTIC LINES

The market model describes the relationship between the return on a security and the overall market (represented by a single market index). The best way to summarize this relationship is through a *"security characteristic line."* This concept divides a security's "excess return" into two components: (1) market-related (or, systematic), and (2) nonmarket-related (or, residual) return.

"Excess return" as used here is the return that is expected to be derived from the security (during a specified holding period) *less* the estimated return from holding a riskless security (such as a short-term government obligation) during the same period.

Figure 24–1 illustrates the important features of a security characteristic line. The horizontal axis plots excess return on

FIGURE 24–1: Security characteristic line

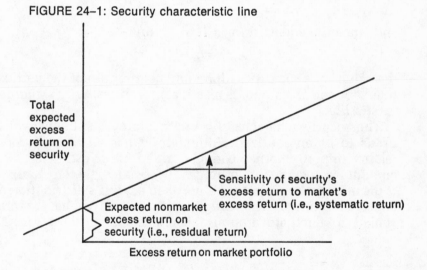

the market portfolio. This is defined as the return on the market portfolio minus the riskless rate of return. The vertical axis measures the excess return on any security. Specifically, the total expected excess return on a security equals the before the fact estimate of the security's return less the riskless rate of return.

The estimation of a security's expected excess return may be best understood from the following verbal representation of the underlying equation:

Since a security's

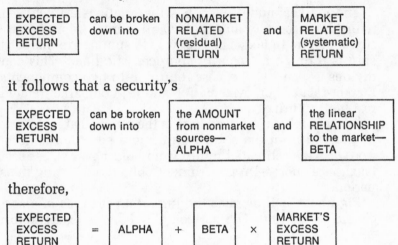

and since the equation for a straight line is:

$$Y = a + bX$$

the values of a security's *alpha* and *beta* represent the vertical intercept and the slope, respectively, of the *security's characteristic line.*[1]

The security characteristic line contains a subtlety which needs to be emphasized. Although *beta* is an estimate of a *relationship* to another variable, *alpha* is an estimate of an *amount*—a specific rate of return. In practice, therefore, alpha is the average, or expected value, of an analyst's *distribution* of expected returns. Accordingly, estimates of alpha are presumed to fluctuate around the expected, or "best guess," value.

---

[1] In specific technical terms:

$$\tilde{R}_i - \rho = [\alpha_i + \tilde{r}_i] + [\beta_{im} (\tilde{R}_m - \rho)]$$

where

$\sim$ = Variable not known in advance.

R_i = Holding period return on security i.

ρ = Riskless rate of return.

α_i = Expected nonmarket excess return on security i.

r_i = Actual deviation from the expected value.

β_{im} = Sensitivity of security i's excess return to the market's excess return.

R_m = Holding period return on the market.

$\tilde{R}_i - \rho$ = Total expected excess return on security i.

$\tilde{R}_m - \rho$ = Excess return on the market portfolio.

Before the fact alpha represents the expected nonmarket excess return. After the fact, however, one should expect the actual results to deviate from this expectation. This is best explained by reference to Figure 24–2. Suppose that the security characteristic line *AB* was drawn at the beginning of a

FIGURE 24–2: Illustration—Nonmarket (residual) variance

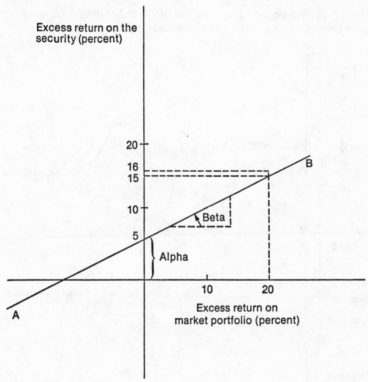

given time period. At the end of that period, it is determined that the estimated beta (the slope of the characteristic line) of 0.5 was correct. Further, it is determined that at the end of the time period, the excess return on the market portfolio was 20 percent and the excess return on the security was 16 percent. The forecast, derived from forward-looking estimates of alpha (5 percent) and beta (0.5), called for an excess return on the security of 15 percent. The discrepancy between the expected and actual results is explained by the difference between the estimated and the actual values for alpha—the nonmarket component of the security's excess return.

The fact that an estimate of alpha is really the mean of a distribution of estimates of nonmarket return is illustrated in Figure 24–3. While both security characteristic lines have the same intercept (alpha) and slope (beta), they present two quite different pictures. The estimate of alpha's dispersion from the expected value is significantly greater in Figure 24–3A than in Figure 24–3B. For this reason, an explicit statement of a secu-

FIGURE 24–3: Security characteristic lines illustrating differences in the variance of estimated nonmarket (residual) returns

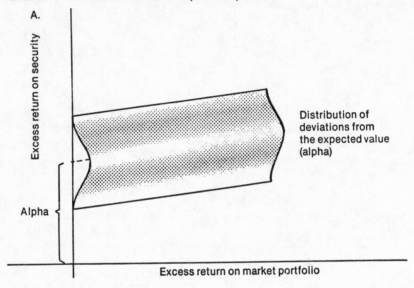

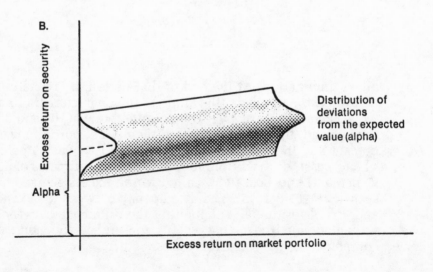

rity's characteristics requires three estimated values: (a) alpha, (b), beta, and (c) an estimate of alpha's dispersion—the variance of the residual component of return (i.e., the amount by which alpha is likely to diverge from its expected value). Looked at another way, since alpha is an estimate of the nonmarket contribution to return, a measure of the dispersion of the residual component of return (typically its standard deviation) is a measure of the security's nonmarket risk.

CLASSIFICATION OF RISK

It follows that if a security's excess return can be broken down into two components—alpha (nonmarket related) and beta (market related)—a security's risk can also be divided into the same categories. As discussed earlier, risk, as the term is used within the context of MPT, is the possibility that the actual return from an investment will differ from the expected return. The estimates of risk used by MPT practitioners are attempts to categorize and quantify this lack of assurance that the future will materialize as expected.

Thus, the risk associated with an investment outcome can be broken down into two parts: (1) the *systematic* part related to relationship of the security to the market and (2) the *residual* part related to the deviation between the expected and actual results for the *nonmarket* component of return. Therefore,

TOTAL SECURITY RISK	=	RISK OF THE RESIDUAL (NONMARKET) COMPONENT	+	RISK OF THE SYSTEMATIC (MARKET) COMPONENT

The equation for an expected security characteristic line[2] can be expressed as follows:

EXPECTED VALUE OF A SECURITY'S EXCESS RETURN	=	EXPECTED VALUE OF THE RESIDUAL (NONMARKET) COMPONENT OF EXCESS RETURN	+	EXPECTED VALUE OF THE SYSTEMATIC (MARKET) COMPONENT OF EXCESS RETURN

---

[2] The formal equation is

$$\text{Exp}(\tilde{R}_i - \rho) = \alpha_i + \beta_{im} \text{Exp}(\tilde{R}_m - \rho)$$

(cont.)

Since the standard deviation of the distribution of a security's expected excess returns quantifies the likelihood that deviations of certain magnitudes will occur, it is an appropriate measure of risk.

Conceptually, therefore,

TOTAL SECURITY RISK	=	STANDARD DEVIATION OF THE RESIDUAL (NONMARKET) COMPONENT OF EXCESS RETURN	+	STANDARD DEVIATION OF THE SYSTEMATIC (MARKET) COMPONENT OF EXCESS RETURN

The problem with this conceptually accurate representation is that, mathematically, standard deviations are not additive. However, given the relationship

$$\text{STANDARD DEVIATION}^2 = \text{VARIANCE}$$

and the fact that variances of two independent sources of risk —nonmarket and market—can be combined, it is possible to square the two standard deviations and then combine the two resulting variances. Thus, the equation[3] for a security's risk is

TOTAL SECURITY RISK (VARIANCE)	=	VARIANCE OF THE RESIDUAL (NONMARKET) COMPONENT OF EXCESS RETURN	+	VARIANCE OF THE SYSTEMATIC (MARKET) COMPONENT OF EXCESS RETURN

---

where:

Exp = Expected value.
$\sim$ = Variable not known in advance.
R_i = Holding period return on security i.
ρ = Riskless rate of return.
R_m = Holding period return on the market.
α_i = Expected nonmarket excess return on security i.
β_{im} = Sensitivity of security i's excess return to the market's excess return.

[3] The formal equation is

$$\text{Var } (\tilde{R}_i - \rho) = \text{Var } (\tilde{r}_i) + \text{Var } [\beta_{im} (\tilde{R}_m - \rho)]$$

---

or

$$\text{Var}\,(\tilde{R}_i - \rho) = \text{Var}\,(\tilde{r}_i) + \beta_{im}^2\,\text{Var}\,(\tilde{R}_m - \rho)$$

where:

Var = Variance.

$\sim$ = Variable not known in advance.

R_i = Holding period return on security i.

ρ = Riskless rate of return.

R_m = Holding period return on the market.

β_{im} = Sensitivity of security i's excess return to the market's excess return.

r_i = Probability distribution of residual returns for the ith security.

Notice that in the formal equation for the expected value of a security's excess return, alpha is not designated as an "expected value." The reason is that alpha, by definition, is already an expected value. Specifically, alpha is the expected value of a probability distribution of excess security-related returns (designated $\tilde{r}_i$). Thus, the residual (non-market) component of risk in the equation is the variance of $\tilde{r}_i$ (and alpha does not appear in the equation).

Chapter 25

Risk: Classification and measurement

To better understand the classification of risk, it may be useful to imagine a "market portfolio"—one consisting of all outstanding stocks. The total return for accepting the level of risk associated with the market portfolio is the aggregate rate of return society pays to suppliers of risk capital. This return and its associated risk are tied to the overall capital market system. Accordingly, such *returns* are called *systematic* or *market-related* returns. Similarly, the *risk* that is linked to the overall capital market system is referred to as *systematic* or *market-related* risk.

Any risk beyond market-related or systematic risk is known by a variety of names, including residual risk, nonmarket risk, unsystematic risk, and selection risk. Residual merely defines what is "left over." The nonmarket and unsystematic nomenclature parallels the "market" and "systematic" terminology. So-called selection risk pinpoints the source of the risk as coming from selecting investments which are different from the total market. In turn, residual risk can be broken down into *specific risk* (arising from factors that are specific to the company) and *extra-market risk* (arising from components of homogeneous groups whose movements are independent of the market as a whole).

From the perspective of the overall market, each investor's selection risk is always offset by some aggregation of other investors' selection risk. For the market as a whole, there is no selection risk. Looked at another way, the capital market system cannot, and does not, reward investment selection. The capital market system only rewards capital market risk. Any gains derived solely from astute investment selection are at the

183

expense of the investors who have the offsetting selection losses.

PORTFOLIO CHARACTERISTIC LINES

An approach similar to that used to construct a security-related characteristic line can be used to generate a *portfolio characteristic line*[1] where

EXCESS RETURN ON A PORTFOLIO	=	RESIDUAL (NONMARKET) COMPONENT OF A PORTFOLIO'S EXCESS RETURN	+	SYSTEMATIC (MARKET-RELATED) COMPONENT OF A PORTFOLIO'S EXCESS RETURN

A portfolio's characteristic line is derived from the estimates for the individual securities that comprise the portfolio. In the case of alpha and beta, the relationship is straightforward. A portfolio's alpha is merely the weighted average (using relative market values as weights) of the alpha values of its component securities. Similarly, a portfolio's beta is the weighted average of the beta values of its component securities.

The residual or nonmarket risk of a portfolio (the probability and the amount by which the actual results will deviate from the expectation) is more difficult to estimate. This difficulty arises from the fact that the amount by which the actual non-market component of the portfolio's excess return deviates from its expected value, alpha, depends on the degree to which the security-level equivalents of these components are correlated.

---

[1] In technical terms

$$(\tilde{R}_p - \rho) = (\alpha_p + \tilde{r}_p) + (\beta_{pm} (\tilde{R}_m - \rho))$$

where:

- $\sim$ = Variable not known in advance.
- R_p = Return on portfolio P.
- α_p = Expected value of the nonmarket component of portfolio P's excess return.
- r_p = Deviation of the actual nonmarket component of portfolio P's excess return from its expected value.
- β_{pm} = The sensitivity of portfolio P's excess return to the market portfolio.
- R_m = Return on market portfolio.
- ρ = Riskless rate of return.

If, for example, a portfolio consists of a few oil stocks, the correlation between the individual securities' nonmarket component of excess return would likely be very high. As a result, nonmarket risk would be very high. If, at the other extreme, the portfolio consists of a well-diversified selection of holdings, it is possible to assume that the deviations of the actual nonmarket component of excess return will be uncorrelated. In this case, the portfolio's nonmarket risk is the weighted average of the variance for the nonmarket component of excess return for its component securities.

R-SQUARED

It has been shown that alpha is the expected value of the nonmarket component of a security's excess return. Alpha is, by definition, uncorrelated with beta—the market-related component of a security's excess return. It has also been shown that a security's total risk consists of two independent components—alpha (nonmarket related) and beta (market related).

The so-called R-squared is a measure of the proportion of the total risk that is market related. Therefore,

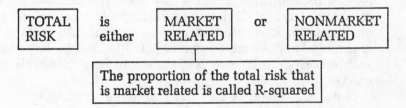

Thus, much as general terms such as alpha and beta have taken on very narrow and explicit meanings within the context of MPT, *R-squared* defines the proportion of either a security's or a portfolio's total risk that is attributable to market risk.

In a portfolio context, R-squared measures the completeness of diversification relative to that of the overall market. The market portfolio, for example, is completely diversified. Thus, in the market portfolio, systematic, or market, risk is the only source of uncertainty. Since R-squared is a measure of the proportion of the total risk that is market risk, the R-squared of the market portfolio is 1.00. Put another way, a portfolio with an R-squared of 1.0 will have zero selection risk. Technically, R-squared is the *coefficient of determination* (R^2).

The formula for computing R-squared, the proportion of total risk (measured by variance) that is attributable to the overall market, is[2]

$$R^2 = \frac{\text{VARIANCE OF THE MARKET COMPONENT OF RETURN}}{\text{VARIANCE OF BOTH COMPONENTS OF RETURN}}$$

The value of R-squared for a typical stock is about 0.30. This means that around 30 percent of a typical stock's behavior (and, hence, risk) is explained by the behavior of the market. On the other hand, the R-squared for a well-diversified portfolio will typically exceed 0.90. *This means that more than 90 percent of a well-diversified portfolio's total price movements can typically be explained by the market's behavior.*

EFFECT OF DIVERSIFICATION

Research examined in Chapter 18 demonstrated that only relatively minor reductions in total risk can be achieved as the size of a portfolio is increased beyond 20 or so unrelated securities. Figure 25–1 goes one step further by showing the relationship between portfolio size and (a) total portfolio risk, as well as (b) the nonmarket component of total portfolio risk. The assumptions underlying the figure approximate the findings of the empirical studies of market performance. Specifically, the standard deviation of the annual excess return on the market portfolio is assumed to be 20 percent, and each security is assumed to have an R-squared of 0.30. (That is, 30 percent of each security's total risk is assumed to be attributable to the market).

Figure 25–1 shows that the nonmarket component of total portfolio risk "washes out" as the number of securities in a portfolio increases. The significance of this phenomenon is that in well-diversified portfolios, the relevant measure of risk for a security is beta—its relationship to the market, or systematic risk. As illustrated in Figure 25–1 while most nonmarket risk can be diversified away, a significant amount of systematic risk remains. Thus, in a diversified portfolio, the only relevant measure of risk for a security is its volatility. In Sharpe's words, "the unsystematic risk is irrelevant, it will 'wash out' when the security is combined with others." [245, p. 97]

---

[2] Technically, a security's R-squared value—the proportion of total risk measured by variance attributable to market risk—is

$$R^2 = \frac{\beta_{im}^2 \, \text{Var}(\tilde{R}_m - \rho)}{\text{Var}(\tilde{R}_i - \rho)}$$

FIGURE 25–1: Effect of diversification on risk

Number of securities in portfolio

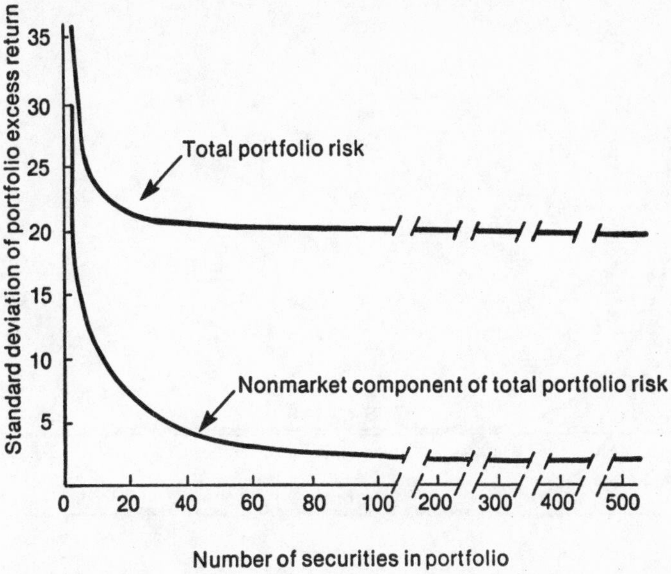

Source: After Sharpe [252, pp. 115–16].

INTERNATIONAL DIVERSIFICATION

It should be clear from the preceding section that diversification reduces risk. While the nonmarket component of risk can be diversified away (by holding the market portfolio), market risk is unavoidable. The only way this systematic market risk can be lowered is to expand the definition of "market" to include other dissimilar markets.

Bruno Solnik [261, 262] has pursued this avenue of research by studying the effect of international diversification on risk. Figure 25–2 contrasts the total risk of portfolios drawn exclusively from securities traded on the New York Stock Exchange with the risk of an international portfolio drawn from exchanges in the United States, the United Kingdom, France, Germany, Italy, Belgium, the Netherlands, and Switzerland. As expected, Solnik's results show that internationally diversified portfolios are much less risky than those limited to NYSE issues.

THE MEANING OF RISK

It is possible to focus too closely on curves that show a progressive reduction of risk. The hazard is that the remaining

FIGURE 25–2: International diversification

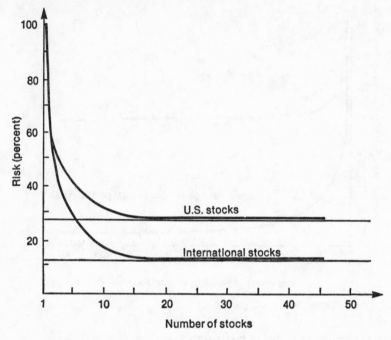

Source: Solnik [261, p. 51].

levels of systematic risk lose their proper perspective. Figure 25–3 shows that the standard deviation of the market (NYSE) portfolio is approximately 20 percent. This means that, on average, in every two out of three years, the market's return will fall within plus or minus 20 percent of the expected return.

Using data from the Ibbotson and Sinquefield study, Figure 25–3 shows a capital market line—the average historical rate of return provided by the marketplace for various levels of risk. On the average, the market portfolio (with a beta of 1.0) has provided an annual return of 9.2 percent. However, given the historical standard deviation of return of 22.4 percent, the market portfolio had a 68 percent probability of providing an annual return of between 31.6 percent (the average of 9.2 percent plus one standard deviation of 22.4 percent) and a negative 13.2 percent (the average of 9.2 percent minus one standard deviation of 22.4 percent). The funnel-shaped pattern in Figure 25–3 illustrates an important concept—the expansion

FIGURE 25–3: Capital market line's "risk funnels"

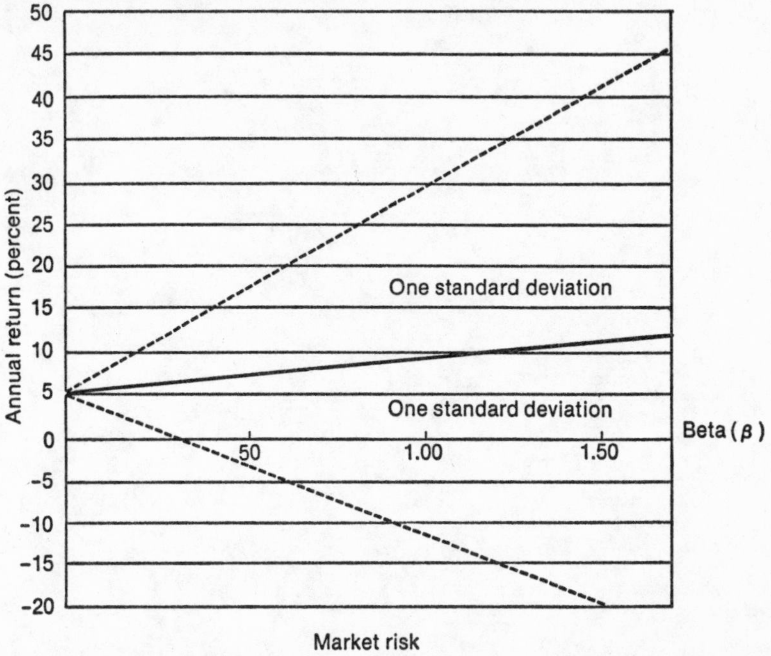

Market risk

Source: Based on historical data from 1926–1976 taken from Ibbotson and Sinquefield [127].

in total risk (in this case the one standard deviation range) as the level of market risk (beta) increases.

The key point to remember is that the higher the beta, the greater is the standard deviation. While high-beta portfolios can be expected to outperform good markets they can be expected to underperform bad markets. This is, of course, no news to most investors. What is news, however, is that MPT allows these expectations to be quantified in advance!

Chapter 26

Structure of MPT

At this juncture, it may be useful to review the importance of the possibly bewildering array of "hypotheses," "theories," "models," and "lines" that comprise MPT.

THE EFFICIENT MARKET HYPOTHESIS

Early chapters examined the pivotal notion of the efficient market hypothesis in its three forms. The importance of the hypothesis is that if the market is largely inefficient, the study of MPT need not, and in fact, could not proceed. First of all, if the market were inefficient, it would not be necessary to bother with approaches such as MPT. Enormous profits could be realized by detecting and capitalizing on the opportunities posed by the inefficient marketplace. Second, a "relatively" efficient market is a prerequisite for MPT and the existence of "widespread" inefficiencies would invalidate MPT's theoretical foundation.

The research chronicled in earlier chapters established that the market is "reasonably" efficient. Given this research, and the number of astute and knowledgeable competitors, it is logical to assume that the market price for a security will not diverge *by much*, or *for long*, from the market's consensus of an equitable return for a given level of risk.

PORTFOLIO THEORY

Portfolio theory is a *normative* theory. Normative means "normal" or "standard." In economics, a normative theory refers to the "normal" way consumers behave. Accordingly, portfolio theory (or Markowitz theory) delineates the decisions that will be made by a population of normal investors—each exercising his or her personal preferences.

Specifically, portfolio theory holds that all investors are risk averse. This means that, other things being equal, all rational investors will avoid risk. Thus, faced with the four investment alternatives in Figure 26–1A, all rational investors would choose alternative A—offering the best combination of low-risk and high expected return.

However, as a result of the unanimous preference for alternative A, the inefficiencies depicted in Figure 26–1A will diminish until the available alternatives comprise the efficient set depicted in Figure 26–1B. It should be stressed, however, that portfolio theory says nothing about the way prices of individual assets adjust. The theory describes only the way in which normal investors behave.

Consequently, the importance of portfolio theory is that it provides a normative description of an investor's trade-off between two important dimensions—risk and expected return. This trade-off between what is not wanted (risk) and what is wanted (expected return) can be uniquely represented for any investor by an indifference curve. Figure 26–1C illustrates three indifference curves from a hypothetical investor's indifference map. Moving downward to the right, from curve 1 to 3, each of these curves represents a decreasing level of investor's utility, or satisfaction.

The matching of the available investment alternatives (from the efficient set of alternatives shown in Figure 26–1B) with the investor's most desired alternative (as represented by the highest feasible indifference curve in Figure 26–1C) is the final step in the investment selection process. This selection of the optimal combination of risk and return from the efficient set of many such alternatives is shown in Figure 26–1D.

Importantly, the fact that all investors agree about the optimal combination of risky securities in Figure 26–1B does not mean that all investors will choose the same portfolio. Different sets of indifference curves, representing either more defensive or more aggressive investors, would lead to the selection of different investments from the wide-ranging set of efficient alternatives.

Adding the assumption that every investor can borrow and lend changes the optimal combinations of risk and expected return that are available in the marketplace—the efficient set of investment alternatives on curve XYZ in Figure 26–1B. Figure 26–1E shows the asset allocation line—the set of investment

FIGURE 26–1: Portfolio theory—Summary

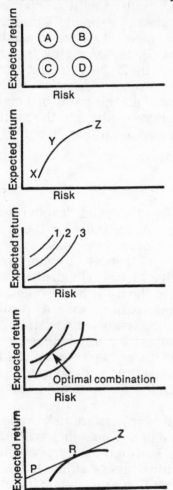

A. Inefficient set of investment alternatives.

B. Efficient set of investment alternatives (without borrowing and lending).

C. Investor's indifference map.

D. Investor's optimal combination of risk and expected return (without borrowing and lending).

E. Asset allocation line (with borrowing and lending) connecting the riskless rate of return and the optimal portfolio.

F. Investor's optimal combination of risk and expected return with borrowing and lending.

alternatives which become available with lending and borrowing. These range from the riskless rate of return, obtained by lending to the Treasury at the riskless rate (point P), through to choosing to be fully invested in the most desirable combination of risky investments (point R), to leveraging that risky portfolio through borrowing to point Z. Next the investment that best matches the investor's personal preferences with the available alternatives is selected (i.e., the point of tangency between the highest level of investor utility and the available alternatives shown on the asset allocation line PRZ in Figure 26–1F.

CAPITAL MARKET THEORY

This theory could appropriately be called "capital market theory based on portfolio theory." As explained in the preceding section, portfolio theory is a normative construct which explains how investors "normally" behave. By comparison, capital market theory is a *positive* theory. The distinction between a normative and a positive theory is best explained by an analogy to a machine. In a mechanical sense, a "positive" mechanism is "definite, unyielding, constant or certain," the outcomes of which are "determined by unyielding parts, or controlled movements." In this sense, capital market theory can be thought of as the unyielding and constant price-setting mechanism that is driven by the "normal" behavior of investors.

Portfolio theory holds that all investors are risk averse and that in satisfying their individual preferences they will act in a consistent, predetermined way. Portfolio theory says nothing about the way prices of individual assets adjust to investor behavior. It follows, however, that if investors are rational, risk averse, and act as portfolio theory suggests (all of which are logical assumptions), the price-setting mechanism relating risk and expected return will be consistent and can be predicted. This is the function of capital market theory—to describe (and, hence, allow us to predict) the relationship between expected risk and expected return.

CAPITAL ASSET PRICING MODEL (CAPM)

William Sharpe has aptly described models as "toy worlds." The advantage of these toy worlds is that key relationships can be defined and analyzed without extraneous information.

Once the key relationships have been dissected and understood, the toy world can then be moved toward the real world by progressively adding more relationships.

One of the most important "toy worlds," or models, of the capital market theory is the capital asset pricing model (a contribution attributable to Sharpe [242], Lintner [168, 167], Treynor [270], and Mossin [197]). Broadly speaking, the simplifying assumptions on which the CAPM is based are:

1. Investors are risk averse and act as portfolio theory suggests.
2. Investors can borrow or lend at the risk-free interest rate.
3. There are no taxes.

Given these assumptions (which are, in fact, not as limiting as they appear), the CAPM provides an explicit statement of the equilibrium expected return on all assets. When the market is in equilibrium, there is no pressure for change. In disequilibrium, investors are dissatisfied with either the securities they hold or the prices of these securities and, as a result, there is pressure for change. At any moment, however, the market is in equilibrium, reflecting the combined influence of all investors' wealth, preferences, and predictions. Whenever disequilibrium occurs because of changes in wealth, preferences, or predictions, these changes are translated to the market and equilibrium is restored.

Thus, the CAPM is the facet of capital market theory that provides an explicit statement of the equilibrium expected return for all securities. Specifically, the CAPM states that the prices of assets in a capital market will be in equilibrium where the expected return on a security is equal to a riskless rate of interest plus a premium that is proportional to the amount of market-related risk—beta. Stated another way, the expected excess return for a security, or portfolio, will come entirely from the market component of return. This is because in equilibrium a security with zero systematic risk (beta) will have the expected return that is available for a riskless asset. Further, in equilibrium, the expected excess return from the nonmarket component is always zero.

According to the CAPM, for efficient portfolios

1. An appropriate measure of risk is the standard deviation of return.
2. In equilibrium, there is a linear relationship between risk and expected return.

FIGURE 26–2: Summary of linear constructs used in MPT

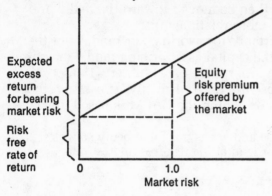

A. *Capital market line*

Concept. The price of imme-diate consumption and the price of risk (alternatively, the reward for waiting and the reward per unit of risk borne).

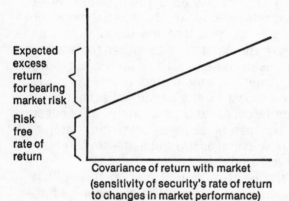

B. *Security market line*

Concept. In equilibrium, *every* security and portfolio will plot along the line.

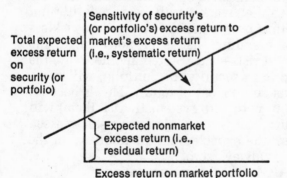

C. *Characteristic line*

Concept. Summarizes the rela-tionship between the excess re-turn on a security (or portfolio) and the excess return on the market.

A construct that is used to portray this relationship between the risk and return of a market portfolio and the riskless rate of return—thereby defining the widely held notions of the price of risk and the price of immediate consumption—is the *capital market line*. Since "price" to the buyer is the same as the "reward" to the seller, these notions can also be thought of as rewards; specifically, the reward per unit of risk borne and the reward for waiting. The format of the capital market line is shown in Figure 26–2A.

The CAPM holds that for individual securities (which may be regarded as highly inefficient portfolios) and portfolios, which are either efficient or inefficient,

1. An appropriate measure of risk is
   a. The covariance between a security's rate of return and that of the market.
   b. The volatility of a security's rate of return relative to changes in market performance.
2. In equilibrium, every portfolio and every security will show a linear relationship between risk and expected return.

The *security market line* is used to portray this relationship between risk and expected return for securities, as well as portfolios. The format of this construct is shown in Figure 26–2B.

In equilibrium, every portfolio and security will plot along the security market line. The market portfolio is no exception. Thus, the capital market line is a special case of the security market line, where the measure of risk used in the security market line (the covariance with the market) turns out to be the market's covariance with itself.

Another construct, the *characteristic line* summarizes the linear relationship between two variables: the market's excess return and a portfolio's or a security's excess return. The values of *alpha and beta* represent the vertical intercept and the slope, respectively, of the line. This relationship is shown in Figure 26–2C.

PART FOUR

MPT: TESTS, EXTENSIONS, AND APPLICATIONS

Chapter 27

Empirical tests

The market model and the capital asset pricing model (CAPM) have been subjected to a considerable amount of testing. The results of these investigations are discussed in this chapter.

TESTS OF THE MARKET MODEL

The market model, sometimes called the diagonal model, hypothesizes that a linear relationship exists between the returns on an individual security or a portfolio, and an index of market returns. To test this hypothesis, Marshall Blume [30] examined the stability of beta coefficients over time. Using successive seven-year periods between July 1926 and June 1968, Blume calculated the correlation between period-to-period betas for portfolios of varying size. He calculated, for example, the correlation between the average beta coefficient which prevailed for the period 1926–33 and that for 1933–40; the correlation between the 1933–40 and 1940–47 betas, and so on. He repeated each calculation for portfolios composed of 1, 2, 4, 7, 10, 20, 35, and 50 securities, respectively. As shown in Table 27–1, the correlations between period-to-period betas are quite high—especially for portfolios containing ten or more securities.

The square of each correlation coefficient in Table 27–1 indicates the percentage variation in the second period's beta that can be explained by the beta of the preceding period. Thus, for individual securities with an average correlation coefficient of approximately 0.60, approximately 36 percent (0.60^2) of the variation in betas can be explained by the historical betas. However, for portfolios with 50 securities, 96 percent of the variation (0.98^2) can be explained by historical betas.

TABLE 27-1: Correlation coefficients of betas for varying size portfolios between successive seven-year time periods

	Correlation of period-to-period betas				
Number of securities per portfolio	Between 1926–1933 and 1933–1940	Between 1933–1940 and 1940–1947	Between 1940–1947 and 1947–1954	Between 1947–1954 and 1954–1961	Between 1954–1961 and 1961–1968
1	0.63	0.62	0.59	0.65	0.60
2	0.71	0.76	0.72	0.76	0.73
4	0.80	0.85	0.81	0.84	0.84
7	0.86	0.91	0.88	0.87	0.88
10	0.89	0.94	0.90	0.92	0.92
20	0.93	0.97	0.95	0.95	0.97
35	0.96	0.98	0.95	0.97	0.97
50	0.98	0.99	0.98	0.98	0.98

Source: Blume [30].

Thus, for estimating the future betas of large portfolios, simple extrapolations appear to provide extremely accurate forecasts. Furthermore, Gerald Levitz [158] has shown that the forecasting accuracy associated with 30 and 40 security portfolios can be improved by adjusting for the tendency of deviant betas to return to normal.

Basically, the empirical tests support the market model hypothesis. That is, the relationship between security, or portfolio, returns and market returns (the slope of the characteristic line, or beta) remains relatively stable over time. However, *for individual securities or small portfolios, extrapolations of future betas from historical betas do not produce sufficiently accurate forecasts.*

Empirical tests of alpha also support the market model hypothesis. The ex post (after the fact) alpha coefficient is an indication of how a stock has performed with the market-related portions of the total return eliminated. Studies show that *alphas in successive periods are not related.* As a result, historic alphas have no predictive value. This is not surprising. If high alphas tended to be followed by high alphas, investors would choose to hold only stocks with high alphas. This action, however, would bid up the price of high-alpha stocks which, in turn, would lower the return.

TESTS OF THE CAPITAL ASSET PRICING MODEL

The capital asset pricing model states that in equilibrium, the expected excess return for a security or portfolio will come entirely from the market component of return. The verbal representation of this equation is

EXPECTED EXCESS RETURN ON A SECURITY	=	DEGREE TO WHICH THE SECURITY WILL AMPLIFY OR DAMPEN THE MOVEMENT OF THE MARKET (BETA)	×	EXPECTED EXCESS RETURN ON THE MARKET

Thus, the CAPM states that when the market is in equilibrium, there is a linear relationship between the *expected* returns on individual securities and *expected* returns on the market portfolio. The difficulty one encounters in attempting to test this model is that such ex ante (before the fact) expectations are not directly measurable. However, because investors' expectations are what drive the market, an exact test of the CAPM can be based on the study of ex post realizations. Basically, if both the CAPM and the market model are valid, then plots of the ex post returns on assets for any given period should cluster around the *security market line.*[1] The verbal representation of the equation for the security market line is:[2]

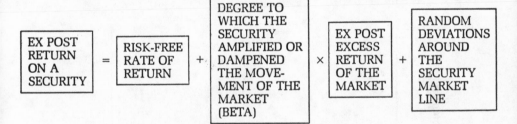

To test the validity of this model, Black, Jensen, and Scholes [26] compared the theoretical and the actual relationships between systematic risk (beta) and average monthly returns for

---

[1] For a technical description of the derivation of the security market line from the market model and the CAPM, the interested reader is referred to Jensen [135, pp. 27–33].

[2] In specific technical terms:

$$R_i = \rho + \beta_{im}(R_m - \rho) + r_i$$

where:

R_i = Holding period return on security *i*.
ρ = Riskless rate of return.
β_{im} = Sensitivity of security *i*'s return to the market's return.
R_m = Holding period return on the market.
r_i = Random deviations.

all 1,952 common stocks listed on the NYSE for the 35-year period spanning 1931–65. In order to handle the massive amount of data, for each year the investigators grouped the securities into ten portfolios of approximately equal size on the basis of that year's beta coefficient. That is, the 195 securities with the highest betas were assigned to one portfolio, the 195 securities with the next highest betas were assigned to another portfolio, and so on.

Figure 27–1 compares the average monthly returns with the systematic risk (beta) for each of the ten different portfolios (denoted by Xs) over the entire 35-year period. The market portfolio is denoted by the symbol O, and the solid line (the regression line, or line of "best fit," derived from the empirical portfolios) represents the actual relationships. The dashed

FIGURE 27–1: Systematic risk (beta) versus average monthly returns for ten different risk portfolios, and the market portfolio, for the 35-year period 1931–1965

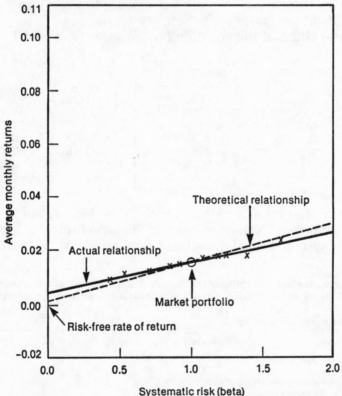

Source: Black, Jensen, and Scholes [26].

line, connecting the average risk-free rate of return and the rate of return on the market portfolio, depicts the theoretical relationship.

If the security market line correctly described reality, the theoretical (dashed) line would match the empirically derived (solid) line. The actual relationship is in fact highly linear (the correlation between return and beta was 0.996), but the actual intercept was higher, and the slope lower, than the theoretical expectation. In practical terms, this means that over the 35-year period, low-risk (low-beta) stocks earned higher returns than implied by the CAPM. Similarly, high-risk (high-beta) stocks showed lower returns than the theory predicts.

Figure 27–2 provides a closer look at the 35-year period studied by Black, Jensen, and Scholes. For four 105-month periods from January 1931 through December 1965, the systematic risk (beta) is plotted against the average monthly returns for the same ten market portfolios and the market portfolio. Here again, the actual relationships do not match the theoretical model. In the post-crash period from January 1931 through September 1939, the low-beta stocks earned less than the model implies and the high-beta stocks earned more. Thus, there is clearly a difference in slope between the theoretical and actual security market lines.

The second difference that can be noted lies in the *direction of the slope* for the actual relationships from April 1957 through December 1965. The security market line is based on the valid assumption that all investors are averse to risk. Nonetheless, the downward sloping security market line during the last 105-month period reveals that, on average, high-risk stocks earned less than low-risk stocks. Clearly, the market did not appropriately compensate investors for the risks they undertook during this period.

Black, Jensen, and Schole's presentation of the security market lines for periods from 1932 to 1965, reproduced in Figures 27–3A through 27–3C, provides further evidence of the discrepancy between the theoretical and actual relationships between risk and return. Although the empirical relationships appear linear, the slope of the line in some periods runs counter to what would be expected. Specifically, the negatively sloped security market lines are inconsistent with the notion that investors are rewarded for risk.

Figures 27–3A through 27–3C also illustrate that the reward that the market provides risk-takers (measured by the slope of the security market line) varies significantly from year to year.

FIGURE 27–2: Average monthly return versus systematic risk for four 105-month subperiods in the interval January 1931–December 1965

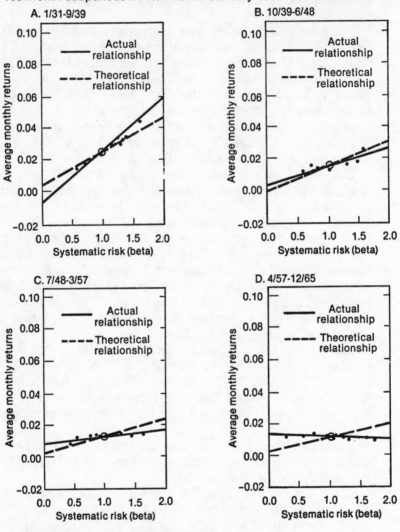

Source: Black, Jensen, and Scholes [26].

Clearly, accurate forecasts of the intercept and slope of this line in future periods could enable an investor to reap substantial profits. Unfortunately, Fama and MacBeth [77] have found that the time sequence of security market lines conforms to a random-walk model. This means that the intercept and slope of future lines cannot be forecast from the pattern of historical changes in these variables.

FIGURE 27–3A: Average monthly returns versus systematic risk for six successive two-year periods from 1932 to 1943.

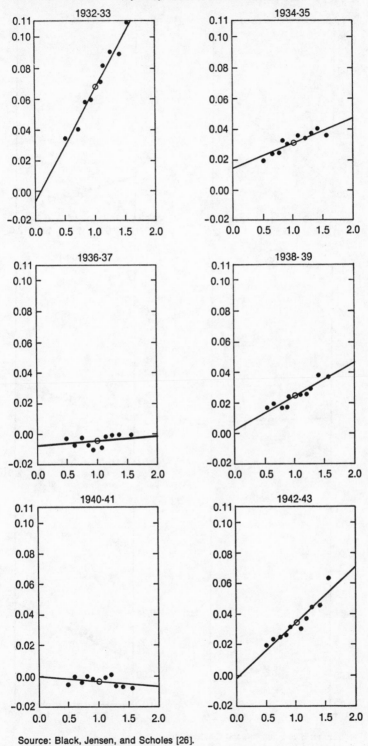

Source: Black, Jensen, and Scholes [26].

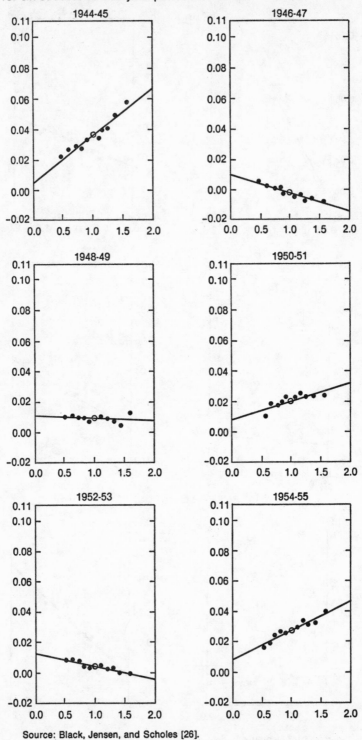

FIGURE 27–3B: Average monthly returns versus systematic risk for six successive two-year periods from 1944 to 1955

Source: Black, Jensen, and Scholes [26].

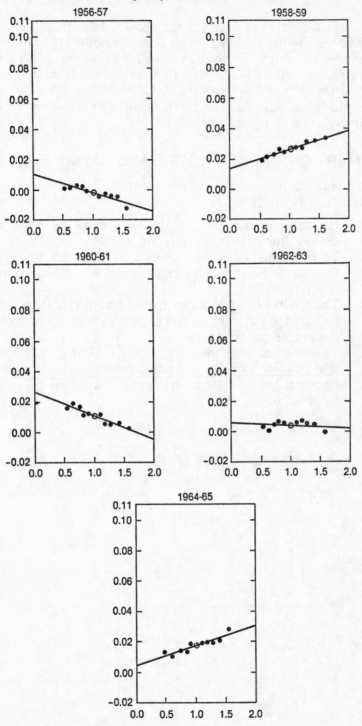

FIGURE 27–3C: Average monthly returns versus systematic risk for five successive two-year periods from 1956 to 1965.

Source: Black, Jensen, and Scholes [26].

In an attempt to describe the observed relationship between risk and return, Black, Jensen, and Scholes [26] suggested a model in which the returns on a zero-beta portfolio are basically, substituted for the riskless rate of interest in the Sharpe-Lintner-Treynor-Mossin CAPM. This model accurately reproduces, but provides no theoretical explanation for empirically observed phenomena.

SUMMARY OF MARKET MODEL AND CAPM TESTS

The conclusions that can be drawn from these empirical tests are as follows:

1. On the average, and in the long run, investors are rewarded for bearing systematic risk.
2. The average relationship between risk and return is linear.
3. On the average, nonsystematic risk is not related to security returns.
4. The CAPM (which states that the zero-risk intercept will be equal to the riskless rate of return) is not consistent with the empirical findings.
5. The joint market model and the CAPM (which predicts that the slope of the security market line will be positive) have not been substantiated by the empirical evidence [see Jensen, 26, pp. 36–7].

Chapter 28

Extensions to the capital asset pricing model

A number of extensions to the basic CAPM have been proposed which seek to explain the empirically observed relationship between risk and return. Michael Brennan [37] and Fischer Black [23] have shown, for example, that the simplifying assumption of riskless borrowing and lending could explain the discrepancies between the theoretical and the observed results.

Other extensions have been formulated by William Fouse at Wells Fargo Investment Advisors. Fouse uses a security valuation model (discussed in Chapter 31) and analysts' estimates of systematic risk to construct ex ante (before the fact) estimates of security market lines. Figure 28–1A represents Wells Fargo's security market lines as plotted on June 30, 1970 and June 30, 1972, respectively. The security market line on June 30, 1970 indicated a market environment in which investors were well rewarded for assuming risks. Two years later, however, on June 30, 1972, the ex ante security market line portrayed an expected relationship under which taking on incremental amounts of risk did not carry the promise of commensurate increases in return.

Figure 28–1B shows the Wells Fargo ex ante security market lines on December 31, 1974 and June 30, 1975. At year-end 1974, market participants were very pessimistic (the Dow Jones Industrials Average closed at 616), and there was widespread aversion to accepting market-related risk. Accordingly, those few people who were willing to assume market risk were rewarded by relatively large expected incremental returns. Within six months, the market, as measured by the Dow Jones Industrial Average, had moved up 263 points to 879. These

FIGURE 28-1: Wells Fargo ex ante security market lines

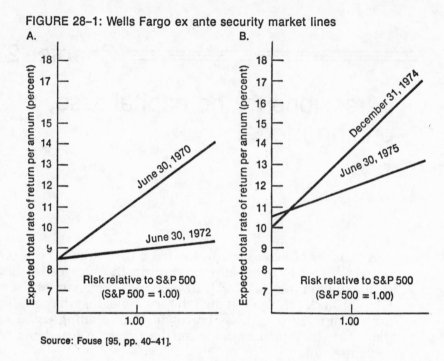

Source: Fouse [95, pp. 40-41].

higher prices are reflected in the lower expected returns for the June 30, 1975 ex ante security market line. Thus, in comparison to the market environment of December 31, 1974, an incremental market risk undertaken on June 30, 1975 carried significantly less promise of incremental returns.

LIQUIDITY MARKET LINE

While market liquidity is not explicitly described by capital market theory, it is conceptually consistent with it. Basically, capital market theory states that investors must be paid to assume risk. It follows, then, that the lower the market liquidity of a stock (i.e., the higher the risk), the higher is the expected return that will be demanded by the marketplace.

Using a liquidity ratio which measures the dollar value of trading required to elicit a 1 percent price variation, Wells Fargo has divided the stocks it analyzes into five liquidity sectors. Figure 28-2 shows the security market lines, called *liquidity* market lines, for each liquidity sector. The family of liquidity lines in Figure 28-2 shows that on December 31,

FIGURE 28–2: Wells Fargo liquidity market lines

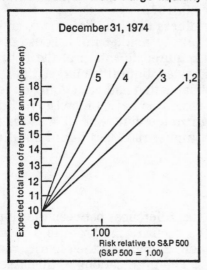

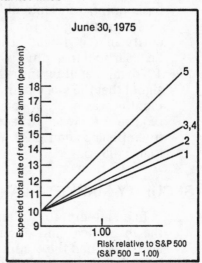

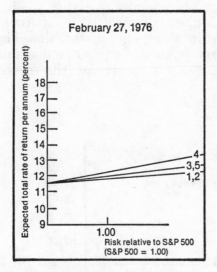

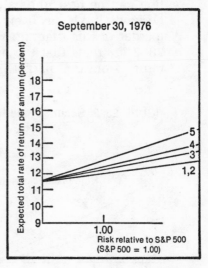

Source: Fouse [96, p. 43].

1974, for a beta of 1.0, there was a 440 basis point[1] spread in expected return between liquidity market lines 1 and 5. This spread had diminished to 230 basis points by June 30, 1975 and narrowed still further to only 50 basis points on February

---

[1] One hundred basis points is equal to 1 percentage point. Hence, 440 basis points is equal to 4.40 percent.

27, 1976. The liquidity "fan" then reopened to a spread of 190 basis points on September 30, 1976.

Commenting on the usefulness of Wells Fargo's ex ante security market lines and liquidity market lines, Fouse stated: "no particular genius was required to interpret the February 1976 market line and associated liquidity market lines as a signal that the stock market game that had been going on for 15 months was over, or soon would be over. Likewise, it did not require prescience to recognize the winter of 1974 as the time to emphasize equities, and higher risk, less liquid equities at that." [96, p. 45]

SECURITY MARKET PLANE

In an attempt to explain the differences between the slope of the theoretical and observed security market line, Fouse has also examined the assumption, underlying the security market line, that there are no taxes. The implications of this assumption can be best understood by examining Figure 28–3. The horizontal axis has been deliberately reversed to facilitate the merger of this diagram with the security market line. Figure 28–3 assumes that the average total expected annual rate of return from the market portfolio is 15 percent (shown on the

FIGURE 28–3: Security yield line

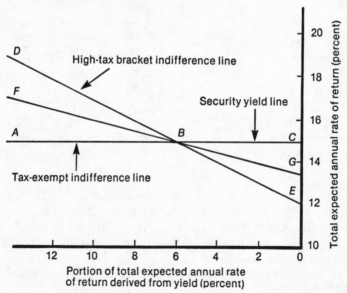

vertical scale), with 6 percent (shown on the horizontal scale), of the total return assumed to be derived from yield and the remaining 9 percent (not shown) derived from capital appreciation. The line *ABC* in Figure 28–3 is the indifference line for a tax-exempt investor. This means that as long as the total expected rate of return is constant at 15 percent, a tax-exempt investor does not care what proportion of the total return is derived from yield.

This is not the case, however, for a tax-paying investor whose yield income is taxed at double the rate levied on capital appreciation. Thus, moving from the assumed average expected yield of the market portfolio (6 percent), most tax-paying investors would be worse off if they received the same total expected return of 15 percent—but with the yield component accounting for a larger proportion of the total return.

Compare, for example, an investment in which all of the expected return is derived from yield with an investment where all of the expected return consists of capital appreciation. If an investor paid twice the taxes on return derived from yield, the aftertax return would be half that obtained from capital appreciation.

The high-tax bracket indifference line *DBE* in Figure 28–3 illustrates that if 50 percent of the yield is taxed away (and, to simplify the illustration, the nonyield portion goes untaxed), an investor will be indifferent to any combination of yield and total expected return along line *DBE*. That is, if all yields are halved by taxes, a 12 percent total return with zero yield leaves 12 percent. Similarly, an 18 percent total return with a 12 percent yield portion that is reduced by half provides an aftertax return of 12 percent.

With an estimate of point *B*—the intersection of the total expected annual rate of return for a universe of stocks and the portion of the total expected return derived from yield—plus a forecast of the slope of the tax indifference line derived from specific tax rates—a specific indifference line can be drawn for any individual.

More importantly, if tax-paying investors demand greater returns from more heavily taxed high-yield stocks, as this implies, high-yield stocks would have to offer investors higher than average total returns. Similarly, under the market's pricing mechanism, a stock with a small portion of its total return consisting of yield could attract sufficient purchasers at a lower than average total return. The relationship between the estimated total return and that portion of total return derived

FIGURE 28-4: Construction of a security market plane

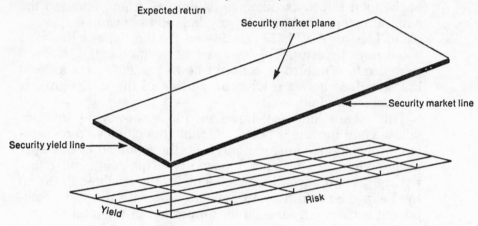

from yield can be portrayed by a *security yield line* such as line *FBG* in Figure 28-3.

The "yield" dimension is not recognized in the risk versus expected return relationship described by the security market line. This shortcoming can be eliminated, however, by expanding the two-dimensional security market line into a three-dimensional *security market plane*.

Figure 28-4 illustrates the features of a security market plane. The two dimensions defining a security market line are risk and total expected return. The addition of a security yield line—the relationship between the yield portion and the total expected return—as the third dimension creates a security market plane.

Chapter 29

Prediction and translation

If current prices in the major investment markets reflect both publicly disseminated and privately held information, these markets can be regarded as efficient. In turn, if major capital markets are efficient, the only predictable portions of the differences between security prices are those which arise from differences in systematic risk. In such a completely efficient market environment, the task of portfolio management would be solely to select an appropriate risk class and then achieve maximum diversification as inexpensively as possible. Further, if the market is truly efficient, actively managed portfolios will perform no better than randomly selected portfolios with the same amount of risk—a conclusion that is supported by empirical studies of performance.

Aside from the lack of evidence that some investors can achieve consistently above-average performance, there is enough evidence of inefficiency that the market must be characterized as "almost" efficient. Even with a limited amount of inefficiency, however, studies of historical performance provide no evidence that these inefficiencies are being translated into profitable investment strategies.

To probe this paradox, it is useful to think of performance in two stages: prediction and translation. Specifically,

1. Can some investors make better than average predictions?
2. If they can, can these better than average predictions be translated into better than average risk-adjusted performance?

The distinction between "prediction" and "translation" is valuable for two reasons. First, it might well be that certain investors have superior predictive ability but that their translation process from thought to action is so ineffective that they

217

achieve no better than average performance. Second, if the translation process is assumed to be perfect, it is possible, through computer simulations, to determine what amount of *predictive ability* is required to attain a given amount of above-average *performance.*

PREDICTIONS VERSUS RESULTS

Keith Ambachtsheer, who heads Canavest, Inc., has studied both prediction and translation. To study predictive ability, Ambachtsheer asked analysts to rank their predictions in order of *relative* expected price movements. Then, using a ranking scheme from 1 to 5 (where 5 is the largest gain), he compared the ex ante (before the fact) forecasts with the ex post (after the fact) results by the procedure illustrated in Tables 29–1 and 29–2.

TABLE 29–1: Perfectly correlated predictions and results

			↓ Results ↓					
			Relative performance categories					
			1	2	3	4	5	
→ Predictions →	Relative performance categories	1	10					10
		2		20				20
		3			40			40
		4				20		20
		5					10	10
			10	20	40	20	10	

Total predictions in each category

Total results in each category

The horizontal rows of Table 29–1 show the ex ante *predictions.* The vertical columns of the table show the ex post *results.* Because predictions and results are perfectly correlated in this case, of the ten before the fact predictions in rating category 1, all ten after the fact results are also in rating category 1. Similarly, each of the other predictions corresponds exactly to the results.

Note that the "average" relative performance category 3 contains the largest number of predictions. The reason for this is that most stocks are assumed to be average performers. Relatively fewer predictions concern stocks which are expected to perform significantly better or worse, than the average. Similarly, the results can be expected to cluster around the average, with relatively fewer especially good or bad performers tallied in the extreme categories.

Table 29–2 portrays quite a different relationship between predictions and results. Here the predictions are the same: 10

TABLE 29–2: Uncorrelated predictions and results

			↓	Results		↓		
			Relative performance categories					
			1	2	3	4	5	
Predictions → 4	Relative performance categories	1	1	2	4	2	1	10
		2	2	4	8	4	2	20
		3	4	8	16	8	4	40
		4	2	4	8	4	2	20
		5	1	2	4	2	1	10
			10	20	40	20	10	

Total predictions in each category

Total results in each category

in the first category, 20 in the second, and so on. The results, however, are different. Only one of the ten predictions in relative performance category 1 was accurate. More importantly, since 10 percent of all results were in relative performance category 1, 10 percent of the predictions would be expected to fall there purely by chance. Thus, the pattern portrayed in Table 29–2 is lacking in any correlation between prediction and results.

When data are arrayed in this form, it is relatively easy to calculate the correlations between the predicted relative performance catagories and actual results. Ambachtsheer has labeled the correlation coefficients calculated from such tables as "information coefficients," or ICs.

Table 29–3 illustrates a comparison of *predictions* made on

TABLE 29–3: Comparison of predictions against results

	Relative performance categories — Results 9–1–78					Number of securities	After the fact average relative performance category	Actual percentage change
Predictions (12–1–77) / Relative performance categories	1	2	3	4	5			
1	0	4	1	0	0	5	2.2	−1.8
2	3	5	13	1	0	22	2.5	6.5
3	2	10	40	18	4	74	3.2	21.5
4	0	3	19	12	1	35	3.3	27.9
5	0	0	1	4	0	5	3.8	41.0
Number of securities	5	22	74	35	5			
Before the fact average relative performance category	2.4	2.5	3.1	3.5	3.2			
Actual percentage change	−13.9	−3.8	10.9	48.7	109.1			

Predictions

Results

December 1, 1977 (the horizontal rows) with the *results* of those predictions as of September 1, 1978 (the vertical columns). It was estimated as of December 1, 1977 that 5 securities would fall in relative performance category 1, 22 in category 2, 74 in category 3, 35 in category 4, and 5 in category 5. (Category 1 represents the worst relative performers and category 5 the best.) To facilitate comparison of the forecasted ratings, the results are categorized according to the same frequency. That is, the 5 worst performing stocks are placed in result category 1, the 22 next best performers in result category 2, 74 in category 3, and so on.

The first row of Table 29–3 shows that of the five stocks that were predicted to have the worst relative performance (category 1), after the fact four stocks fell in category 2, and one stock was in category 3. Thus, the average after the fact relative performance rating (category) for stocks predicted to be in relative performance category 1 was 2.2. In terms of actual performance, the first row of the extreme right-hand column indicates that the average performance of stocks with before the fact relative performance ratings of 1 turned out to be −1.8 percent over the period.

Moving down the "actual percentage change" column, notice that the changes increase with each of the successively higher rated groups—ranging from −1.8 percent for the predicted worst performers to +41.0 percent for the predicted best performers. Clearly stocks predicted to be in the worst relative performance category 1 turned out to be the worst performers. Also, the stocks predicted to fall in the best relative performance category 5 turned out to be the strongest performers.

Similarly, the column labeled "after the fact average relative performance category" reveals a positive relationship between the predicted and actual ratings. While the relationship is not perfect, stocks predicted to be in the lower relative performance categories were, after the fact, in lower average relative performance categories. The same tendency prevailed for stocks predicted to be in the higher relative performance categories.

The first column of "results" in Table 29–3 shows that the five worst performing stocks (in after the fact performance category 1) had an average before the fact relative performance rating of 2.4. Moving across the row labeled "before the fact average performance category," the numbers tend to increase. This is further evidence of a positive relationship between the predicted and actual results.

Basically, the percentage change column at the far right indicates how the imperfect forecasting would have translated into actual performance. The percentage change column at the bottom of the table indicates what could have been attained from perfect forecasting. Thus, the five worst performing stocks were actually down 13.9 percent. The five stocks that were predicted to be the worst performers were down an average of 1.8 percent. Hence, while not perfect, the predictions illustrated in Table 29–3 have quite good discriminatory ability.

To simplify analysis of the kind of information presented in Table 29–3, the relationship can, as mentioned earlier, be reduced to a single number—the so-called information coefficient (IC). The IC for Table 29–3 is 0.42. While the positive relationship between predictions and results in Table 29–3 is relatively easy to see, it should be emphasized that this is an extremely high IC value. ICs most often range between 0.10 and 0.20 (see Ambachtsheer [4, 5, 6]).

CAN PREDICTIONS OF MODEST QUALITY BE USED PROFITABLY?

Using a computer simulation to make an unerring translation from prediction to action, Stewart Hodges and Richard Brealey [122] found that with an IC of 0.15—the level Ambachtsheer found to be average—an investment manager could, over the long run, outperform an index fund by about 1.5 percent per year. This assumed that forecast revisions and appropriate portfolio revisions took place only once annually. Using a "live" study of 16 forecasting groups (as opposed to a computer simulation) and six-month holding periods, Ambachtsheer also found similar evidence that a modest amount of forecasting ability (i.e., ICs of 0.15) could be used to outperform a market index fund [4].

Basically, the IC argument presented by Ambachtsheer is that a prediction ranked "good" is one that forecasters expect to perform one standard deviation better than the mean. Given Ambachtsheer's assumption that the standard deviation of return for a stock portfolio is around 18 percent, if the IC (i.e., the correlation between the forecaster's expectations and reality) is 0.15, that rate of prediction success multiplied by the prediction will yield the potential success from perfect translation. Thus, if forecasters have a 0.15 success rate (IC) in predicting stocks which will appreciate 18 percent (one standard deviation), their potential success is 0.15 × 18%, or 2.7 percent—before transaction costs.

COMPOSITE FORECASTING

James Farrell and Keith Ambachtsheer [84] have reasoned that two or more separate sources of information can be combined to form a composite IC. By their formulation, if two independent sources of information each have ICs of 0.15, the combined IC would be 0.21.[1]

To illustrate composite forecasting, Farrell and Ambachtsheer developed a composite IC from two well-known valuation services: Value Line and Wells Fargo. Basically, the Value Line valuation approach is based on relative price and earnings estimates, resulting in a one through 5 ranking scheme (where one is best). The Wells Fargo valuation approach is based on a dividend discount model (to be discussed in Chapter 31) which ranks stocks from highest to lowest on the basis of expected risk-adjusted return.

Table 29–4 shows the comparative ICs for the two advisers over six, six-month periods. In addition to the differences portrayed, statistical tests showed that there was close to zero correlation between the two forecasts. Given this statistical independence between the two sets of forecasts, the two were combined, with the Wells Fargo information given twice the weight of the Value Line information. The IC for the combined information (as shown in Table 29–4) averaged 0.152.

TABLE 29–4: Six-month information coefficients

	9/73–3/74	3/74–9/74	9/74–3/75	3/75–9/75	9/75–3/76	3/76–9/76	Mean	Standard deviation
Wells Fargo	0.12	0.16	0.01	0.13	0.08	0.31	0.135	0.100
Value Line	0.17	0.04	−0.09	0.16	0.11	0.01	0.067	0.100
Combined	0.17	0.18	0.00	0.16	0.10	0.30	0.152	0.099

Source: Farrell and Ambachtsheer [84].

Next, by setting down careful guidelines, Farrell and Ambachtsheer constructed simulated portfolios from the September 1973 ICs which appear in Table 29–4 and rebalanced each portfolio every six months over the succeeding three-year period. Table 29–5 shows the performance of the three simulated portfolio strategies against both the S&P 500 and the

$$^1IC_{12} = \sqrt{IC_1^2 + IC_2^2}$$

TABLE 29–5: Performance results of three simulated portfolio strategies against the S&P 500 and the Becker performance data for pension funds

	9/73 to 9/76 annualized	Performance results					
		3/76 to 9/76	9/75 to 3/76	3/75 to 9/75	9/74 to 3/75	3/74 to 9/74	9/73 to 3/74
Top Becker Fund	11.9%	—	—	—	—	—	—
Combined: Wells Fargo and Value Line	9.3	7.1	27.4	4.8	43.7	−29.6	− 9.7
Wells Fargo	8.3	8.2	25.2	4.2	42.0	−29.0	−10.8
Value Line	4.8	4.9	27.8	5.4	34.1	−32.1	−10.5
S&P 500 Index	3.3	4.4	25.0	2.7	34.5	−30.8	−11.7
"Universe"	1.8	5.6	19.6	2.3	34.7	−32.2	−10.5
20th percentile Becker Funds	0.8	5.3	26.2	3.1	44.2	−32.2	−14.1
50th percentile Becker Funds	− 2.9	2.5	22.3	−0.3	39.2	−35.2	−17.2
80th percentile Becker Funds	− 5.6	0.8	18.9	−3.4	35.2	−38.4	−20.5
Bottom Becker Fund	−16.1	—	—	—	—	—	—

Source: Farrell and Ambachtsheer [84].

Becker performance data for pension funds. Note that the three simulated portfolios outperformed the S&P 500 and all would have ranked high in the upper 20th percentile of the Becker funds over the period.

It should be noted that the returns on the simulated portfolios were adjusted for transaction costs and management fees. The S&P 500 reflects neither, of course, while the Becker figures exclude management fees. Also, it should be noted that the performance of an index of the universe of stocks from which the simulated portfolios were drawn underperformed the S&P 500. This indicates that the superior performance of the simulated portfolios was based on selection and not an especially favorable universe.

ACTIVE VERSUS PASSIVE MANAGEMENT

Very few people like to be considered average. For most investment managers, being average is just not good enough. But the truth of the matter is that, by any measure, half are below average and half are above average. Over the long haul, common stocks have provided an average compound annual rate of return of nearly 10 percent (excluding commissions and taxes). This is a better record than bonds, savings accounts, and most tangible commodities have shown. Also, common stocks traded on national exchanges are readily transferable. Hence, for some investors, an "average" performance might be a reasonable objective.

For those who consciously decide to seek average performance, MPT has confirmed a very easy way to achieve it: merely spread holdings over many issues and hold them for long periods. For those who opt for this "passive" investment strategy, it is comforting to know that their average results will be *better than half of those "active" investors who try to beat the averages!*

For those who opt for "active" strategies, the concept of ICs can be very useful. *Passive management* is based on a strategy of controlling risk through diversification and providing a fair, risk-adjusted, rate of return. *Active management* is intended to "beat the market." The focal point of the concept of ICs is that *active management can only be justified when an organization*

1. Possesses a measurable degree of predictive ability, and
2. Translates its forecasting ability into investment actions that more than offset the costs associated with the portfolio rebalancing process.

Chapter 30

Valuation theory

A source of popular confusion about MPT should be clarified at this point. MPT holds that estimates of future risk and expected return are the key ingredients in the investment decision process. Accordingly, the task, or even more strongly, the responsibility, of the security analyst is to derive such estimates of future risk and expected return. This does not imply, however, that all users of MPT technology will come out with the same, or even approximately the same, results. Nor does this imply that the role of the security analyst is diminished as a consequence.

While much has been learned about the ways to arrive at estimates of future risk and expected return, it should be emphasized that these are still individually derived forecasts. Different analysts have different preferences for different kinds of information. Further, by analyzing information in different ways, they arrive at independent estimates. As always, analysts are free to exercise their personal prerogatives in making these forecasts.

Accordingly, the application of MPT does not diminish the role of the security analyst. Quite to the contrary, the estimates provided by the security analysts are at the core of the investment decision process. The role of the security analysts has, however, changed dramatically. Before MPT, the job of many security analysts was reduced to (a) providing estimates of near-term earnings, (b) estimating a future price-earnings ratio, and (c) multiplying the estimated earnings by the estimated price-earnings ratio to determine an estimated price. This valuation would be the basis for a purchase or sale recommendation on a stock.

This kind of pre-MPT analysis has two major shortcomings. First, the critically important dimension of risk is omitted.

Second, the variability of price-earnings ratios (illustrated earlier in Figure 7–1) often eclipses the earnings component. Not surprisingly, this kind of analysis prompted the famous economist, John Maynard Keynes, to write

> A conventional valuation which is established as the outcome of the mass psychology . . . is liable to change violently as the result of a sudden fluctuation of opinion due to factors which do not really make much difference to the prospective yield; since there will be no strong roots of conviction to hold it steady. . . .
>
> . . . It might have been supposed that competition between expert professionals, possessing judgment and knowledge beyond that of the average private investor, would correct the vagaries of the ignorant individual left to himself. It happens, however, that . . . [most professional investors] are, in fact, largely concerned, not with making superior long-term forecasts of the probable yield of an investment over its whole life, but with foreseeing changes in the conventional basis of valuation a short time ahead of the general public. They are concerned, not with what an investment is really worth, . . . but what the market will value it at, under the influence of mass psychology, three months or 6 years hence.
>
> . . . The actual, private object of most skilled investment today is "to beat the gun," as the Americans so well expressed it, to outwit the crowd, and pass the bad, or depreciating half-crown to the other fellow.
>
> This battle of wits to anticipate the basis of conventional valuation a few months hence, rather than the prospective yield of an investment over a long term of years, does not even require gulls amongst the public to feed the maws of the professional;—it can be played by professionals amongst themselves. . . . [Professional investing] is, so to speak, a game . . . of Old Maid, of Musical Chairs—a pastime in which he is victor who . . . passes the Old Maid to his neighbour before the game is over, who secures the chair for himself when the music stops. [148, pp. 154–56]

VALUATION APPROACHES

There are two basic approaches to common stock valuation. The *traditional approach* outlined earlier, involves (a) estimating a stock's earnings per share (EPS) for the next year or so, (b) estimating the price-earnings ratio that is expected to prevail when the estimated earnings are reported, and (c) multiplying the estimated future earnings per share by the estimated price-earnings ratio to obtain the estimated future price.[1] While most people who use this approach stop here, the estimated dividend flow can be incorporated into the analysis to obtain an estimate of the rate of return for the forecast period.

There are serious questions over the usefulness of any of the myriad forms of this analytical approach. First, it omits any explicit estimate of risk. Second, the considerable evidence in support of the semistrong form of the efficient market hypothesis (discussed in Part One) leads to the resounding conclusion that no information of real value can be derived from such analysis!

Approaching the problem of security valuation from a different perspective, *classical value theory*—the basis for security valuation within the context of MPT—focuses on the *true*, or *intrinsic*, value of an asset. Specifically, classical value theory holds that the value of a financial asset is the discounted sum of all future income flows that will be received by the owner of the asset.

The seminal notion that the *intrinsic value* of an asset is derived from the discounted present value of the asset's future stream of "cash" flows was first advanced by Irving Fisher [87] at Yale around the turn of the century. Later, John Burr Williams described what might be called the pure theory in his classic 1938 book *The Theory of Investment Value.* [286] More recently, Nicholas Molodovsky [195], the late editor of the *Financial Analysts Journal*, crusaded for more widespread use of the technique.

The application of intrinsic value theory to the valuation of common stocks is relatively easy. It merely involves calculating and then summing the present values of the future payments anticipated by the holder of the stock.

PRESENT VALUE

The concept of *present value* is best understood by referring to some examples. Suppose you were considering the purchase of a contract under which you would receive a guaranteed payment of $1,000 one year from today. How much would you currently pay for a guaranteed $1,000 one year from today? The answer to this question depends on the "price of money"—that is, the interest rate that you expect to prevail during the period.

---

[1] Mathematical purists should note that the product of two expected values will not equal the expected value of the product if there is a correlation between the two original estimates.

TABLE 30–1: Present value of $1

Years into the future	Discount rate				
	5.0%	6.0%	7.0%	8.0%	9.0%
1.........	0.952 381	0.943 396	0.934 579	0.925 926	0.917 431
2.........	0.907 030	0.889 996	0.873 439	0.857 339	0.841 680
3.........	0.863 838	0.839 619	0.816 298	0.793 832	0.772 183
4.........	0.822 703	0.792 094	0.762 895	0.735 030	0.708 425
5.........	0.783 526	0.747 258	0.712 986	0.680 583	0.649 931
6.........	0.746 215	0.704 961	0.666 342	0.630 170	0.596 267
7.........	0.710 681	0.665 057	0.622 750	0.583 490	0.547 034
8.........	0.676 839	0.627 412	0.582 009	0.540 269	0.501 866
9.........	0.644 609	0.591 899	0.543 934	0.500 249	0.460 428
10.........	0.613 913	0.558 395	0.508 349	0.463 194	0.422 411
11.........	0.584 679	0.526 788	0.475 093	0.428 883	0.387 533
12.........	0.556 837	0.496 969	0.444 012	0.397 114	0.355 535
13.........	0.530 321	0.468 839	0.414 964	0.367 698	0.326 179
14.........	0.505 068	0.442 301	0.387 817	0.340 461	0.299 246
15.........	0.481 017	0.417 265	0.362 446	0.315 242	0.274 538
16.........	0.458 112	0.393 646	0.338 735	0.291 891	0.251 870
17.........	0.436 297	0.371 364	0.316 574	0.270 269	0.231 073
18.........	0.415 521	0.350 344	0.295 864	0.250 249	0.211 994
19.........	0.395 734	0.330 513	0.276 508	0.231 712	0.194 490
20.........	0.376 890	0.311 805	0.258 419	0.214 548	0.178 431
21.........	0.358 942	0.294 155	0.241 513	0.198 656	0.163 698
22.........	0.341 850	0.277 505	0.225 713	0.183 941	0.150 182
23.........	0.325 571	0.261 797	0.210 947	0.170 315	0.137 781
24.........	0.310 068	0.246 979	0.197 147	0.157 699	0.126 405
25.........	0.295 303	0.232 999	0.184 249	0.146 018	0.115 968
26.........	0.281 241	0.219 810	0.172 196	0.135 202	0.106 393
27.........	0.267 848	0.207 368	0.160 930	0.125 187	0.097 608
28.........	0.255 094	0.195 630	0.150 402	0.115 914	0.089 548
29.........	0.242 946	0.184 557	0.140 563	0.107 328	0.082 155
30.........	0.231 377	0.174 110	0.131 367	0.099 377	0.075 371
31.........	0.220 360	0.164 255	0.122 773	0.092 016	0.069 148
32.........	0.209 866	0.154 957	0.114 741	0.085 200	0.063 438
33.........	0.199 873	0.146 186	0.107 235	0.078 889	0.058 200
34.........	0.190 355	0.137 912	0.100 219	0.073 045	0.053 395
35.........	0.181 290	0.130 105	0.093 663	0.067 635	0.048 986
36.........	0.172 657	0.122 740	0.087 536	0.062 625	0.044 941
37.........	0.164 436	0.115 793	0.081 809	0.057 986	0.041 231
38.........	0.156 605	0.109 239	0.076 457	0.053 691	0.037 826
39.........	0.149 148	0.103 056	0.071 455	0.049 713	0.034 703
40.........	0.142 046	0.097 222	0.066 780	0.046 031	0.031 838
41.........	0.135 282	0.091 719	0.062 412	00.42 621	0.029 209
42.........	0.128 840	0.086 527	0.058 329	0.039 464	0.026 797
43.........	0.122 704	0.081 630	0.054 513	0.036 541	0.024 584
44.........	0.116 861	0.077 009	0.050 946	0.033 834	0.022 555
45.........	0.111 297	0.072 650	0.047 614	0.031 328	0.020 692
46.........	0.105 997	0.068 538	0.044 499	0.029 007	0.018 984
47.........	0.100 949	0.064 658	0.041 588	0.026 859	0.017 416
48.........	0.096 142	0.060 998	0.038 867	0.024 869	0.015 978
49.........	0.091 564	0.057 546	0.036 324	0.023 027	0.014 659
50.........	0.087 204	0.054 288	0.033 948	0.021 321	0.013 449
60.........	0.053 536	0.030 314	0.017 257	0.009 876	0.005 681
70.........	0.032 866	0.016 927	0.008 773	0.004 574	0.002 400
80.........	0.020 177	0.009 452	0.004 460	0.002 119	0.001 014
90.........	0.012 387	0.005 278	0.002 267	0.000 981	0.000 428
100.........	0.007 605	0.002 947	0.001 152	0.000 455	0.000 181

The arithmetic of converting a known future value—in this illustration $1,000—into an equivalent present value is called *discounting*. The first line of Table 30–1 shows the present value of $1, one year from today, discounted at selected interest rates. Assume, for example, that the going interest rate for a riskless investment which will be held exactly one year is 8 percent. Given this assumption, we can use Table 30–1 to derive the equivalent present value of a contract under which we would be guaranteed $1,000 one year from today. Specifically, the Table 30–1 value at the intersection of line one (corresponding to one year into the future) and column four (corresponding to an 8 percent discount rate) is 0.925926—the space between the two numbers in the table having been added only for reading simplicity. This means that if you invested $0.925926 today and received an 8 percent annual rate of return, your investment would appreciate to $1.00 one year from now (i.e., the original investment of $0.925926 plus the 8 percent return, or 0.074074, equals $1.00). Conversely, and more in keeping with financial jargon, you could say that "the present value of $1.00, discounted at 8 percent for one year, is $0.925926."

The present value of any amount can be readily obtained from multiplying the *discount factor* in Table 30–1 by the amount in question. Thus, to determine the answer to the initial question—the present value of $1,000 discounted at 8 percent for one year—we merely need to multiply $1,000 by the *discount factor* in Table 30–1 to obtain the answer of $925.93. That is, given an interest rate of 8 percent, the discount factor of 0.925926 from Table 30–1 times $1,000 indicates that $925.93 today is equivalent to $1,000 one year from today.

We can extend this kind of analysis, using the discount factors from Table 30–1, to determine the present value of any future stream of payments. How much, for example, is a bond worth which one year from today will pay $50, two years from today will pay another $50, and three years from today will pay a final $50 plus $1,000?

The calculation of the present value of such a bond is shown in Table 30–2. Using the discount factors from Table 30–2 and an assumed annual discount (interest) rate of 8 percent, we can determine that the present value of $50 one year from today is $46.30. Similarly, using the discount factor for two years, we can determine that the present value of $50 two years from today is $42.87. Finally, based on the discount factor for three years, we can determine that the present value of the final

TABLE 30-2: Present value of a bond (based on an 8.0 percent annual discount rate)

Payment date	Amount	×	Discount factor	=	Present value
One year from today	$50		0.925926		$ 46.30
Two years from today	$50		0.857339		42.87
Three years from today	$1,050		0.793832		833.52
Total present value					$922.69

payment of $1,050 is $833.52. Summing each of these present values, we arrive at an aggregate present value of $922.69.

An important advantage of this type of valuation is that the analyst can use any combination of assumptions about different spot and forward interest rates. (*Spot prices* and *spot rates* refer to prices or rates for the *current time period*. *Forward rates*, or *forward prices*, on the other hand, refer to rates, or prices, that apply to *future contract periods*.) The relationship between the prevailing spot rate and various forward rates is shown by both the shape and the level of the current *yield curve*.

YIELD CURVES

Yield curves provide a visual representation of the current *term structure of interest rates*. Quite simply, the term structure of interest rates refers to the relationship (i.e., the "structure") of the different rates of return that are currently available on interest-bearing investments that are made for different periods of time (or, if you prefer, different "terms"). Generally, moving further into the future, higher rates of return will be required to compensate investors for the increased risk that is associated with longer term investments. Fortunately, however, life in the real world of investing is much more exciting than one might posit for the "general" case. Thus, at any moment in time both the shape and the level of the yield curve (reflecting the current term structure of interest rates) are important elements in security valuation.

Figures 30-1, 30-2, and 30-3 show the characteristic shape of the yield curve under three "classic" interest rate scenarios. The use of specific numbers in these figures has been avoided in order to concentrate on the alternative "shapes." The vertical scale of the yield curve denotes increasing interest rates (in

FIGURE 30–1: Rising yield curve

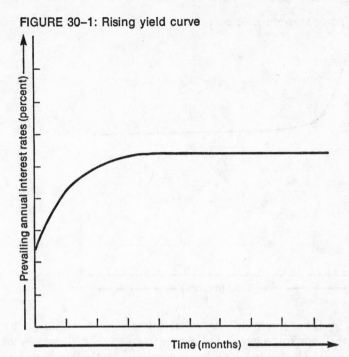

percentages) and the horizontal scale denotes increasing time (in months).

Basically, the shape of the yield curve depends on the marketplace's assessment of the future course of short-term rates. Figure 30–1 shows the so-called *rising yield curve*. This curve,

FIGURE 30–2: Flat yield curve

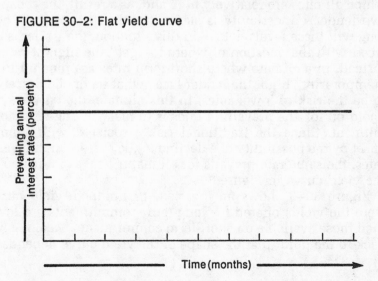

FIGURE 30–3: Inverted yield curve

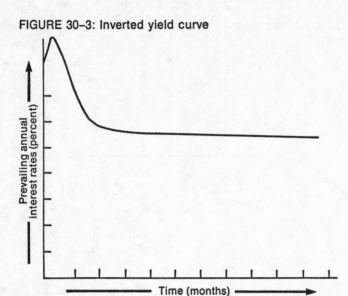

depicting the "normal," or most common, situation, shows
that long-term rates exceed short-term rates. Yield curves with
this general shape tend to be associated with the belief that
short-term interest rates will remain low. In this climate, bor-
rowers are willing to pay higher rates for long-term funds and
lenders will demand higher rates for long-term obligations
than for short-term obligations.

Figure 30–2 shows a relatively *flat yield curve*. The interest
rate scenario accompanying a flat yield curve would be one in
which all rates are relatively high and, as a result, the prospective lender's uncertainty is slanted in the direction of "how
long will these levels hold?" In this situation, the lender is not
faced with the question of where to "get" the highest return.
Instead, in a climate where short-term rates are thought to be
"temporarily" high, the lender faces what he or she perceives
to be the risk of lower rates. In this climate, the only way to
"hold on to" the prevailing rates is to make a long-term commitment. Since the traditional risk associated with time is
offset by the possibility of a decline in the current high level of
rates, the same rate prevails for all maturities, as indicated by
the yield curve in Figure 30–2.

Figure 30–3 shows an *inverted*, or humped, *yield curve*.
Here the yields offered for long-term commitments are lower
than those available on short-term commitments. Again, going
back to the point that the shape of the yield curve depends on

the market's assessment of the future for short-term rates, a downward sloping curve means that the high short-term rates are being viewed as transitory. As an example, suppose that the return on one-month government securities is 10 percent and the yield on two-year government securities is 9 percent. The downward sloping yield curve which would depict this situation really indicates that, at this moment, the "market" believes the 10 percent short-term rate will not prevail in this climate. In fact, an equitable two-year return—in the face of the "temporary" 10 percent on one-month loans—is only 9 percent.

Yield curves are important because they offer a perspective on the rates that are available for various holding periods. In addition, they underline the importance of building estimates of forward interest rates into investment analysis.

The dramatic changes that can occur in yield curves in a period as short as one year are illustrated in Figure 30–4. In December 1977, the yield curve was a classic "rising" shape.

FIGURE 30–4: Government securities yield curves (yield to maturity— Treasury bills, notes and bonds)

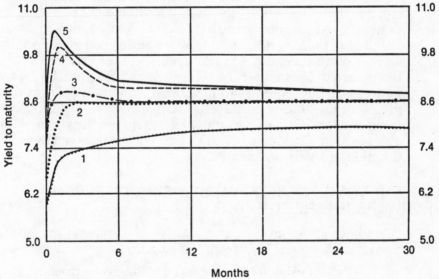

1 December 16, 1977
2 June 16, 1978
3 September 20, 1978
4 November 20, 1978
5 December 21, 1978

Source: Merrill Lynch, *Capital Market Monitor*, December 26, 1978, p. 5.

Six months later, the curve was the same basic shape, but three-month obligations had risen more than 100 basis points (100 basis points equal 1 percentage point). By December 1978, the curve was a classic "inverted," or "humped," shape.

YIELD TO MATURITY

It is important to clarify the difference between forward interest rates and yield to maturity figures. *Forward interest rates*, on the one hand, refer to the current prevailing rates for contracts in specific future, or "forward," time periods. The notion of a forward interest rate is important because it allows us to enter into a contract today that is based on the interest rate that one assumes will prevail during any future (forward) separately segmented time period. *Yield to maturity*, on the other hand, represents the average annualized rate of return that will prevail over the entire multi-period duration of an investment.

Because the yield to maturity figure reduces the returns on different kinds of investments of different durations to a single average interest rate, it is the most commonly used measure of return for bonds. It is a useful number, but it is important to realize that the yield to maturity figure has a serious drawback—it assumes a constant rate of return over the entire duration of the investment. This shortcoming can be especially serious when there are wide differences in forward rates (i.e., the different rates currently being charged for specific future periods, such as "next year"). Another important point is that yield curves do not portray the term structure of "forward" interest rates. Yield curves plot yield to maturity, which is the average annualized rate of return that will be received over the duration of the investment.

CALCULATING PRESENT VALUE USING DIFFERENT FORWARD INTEREST RATES

We have seen that the present value of a known future payment can be determined from the equation:

Present value = Discount factor × Future payment

The equation for the above discount factor is

(year 1)   (year 2)   (year 3) $\cdots$ (year n)

$$\left(\frac{1}{1+r}\right) \qquad \left(\frac{1}{1+r}\right) \qquad \left(\frac{1}{1+r}\right) \qquad \left(\frac{1}{1+r}\right)$$

where r is the interest rate in each year for any number of years. If we make the assumption that r is constant from year to year, we can easily compute the discount factors that appear in Table 30–1. Take, for example, the problem of determining the discount factor for five years at 9 percent. It is simply

$$\left(\frac{1}{1.09}\right)\left(\frac{1}{1.09}\right)\left(\frac{1}{1.09}\right)\left(\frac{1}{1.09}\right)\left(\frac{1}{1.09}\right) = 0.649931$$

the value that appears in Table 30–1.

While the above analysis is appealing because of its simplicity, it is unreasonable to assume that interest rates will remain the same for the next five years. Thus, while we might believe that the "average" rate for the next three years will be 9 percent, we might estimate that the year-to-year rates will be 11 percent, 10 percent, 9 percent, 8 percent, and 7 percent. These assumptions can be used to determine the appropriate discount rate by merely changing r, the year-by-year interest rate, in the above equation. Specifically,

$$\left(\frac{1}{1.11}\right)\left(\frac{1}{1.10}\right)\left(\frac{1}{1.09}\right)\left(\frac{1}{1.08}\right)\left(\frac{1}{1.07}\right) = 0.65205$$

Assuming that we were calculating the present value of $100,000 five years hence, under these two procedures (i.e., using an average discount rate and using specific year-by-year rates) the comparative values would be:

$65,020.50 based on year-by-year forecasts
versus
$64,993.10 based on the average value

Obviously, the two procedures yield strikingly similar results and, as a result, little advantage is gained from explicit estimates of year-to-year changes. This has important implications for the construction of valuation models.

Chapter 31

Valuation models

For a riskless asset (i.e., a noncallable default-free bond such as a short-term government security), information on the structure of forward interest rates can be used to discount the cash flows produced. The aggregate present value of these discounted cash flows will equal the present value of the bond. The valuation of risky assets, such as common stocks, requires two changes in this approach:

1. Since there is some possibility that scheduled payments will not be made, *the analysis must be based on "expected" cash flow.*
2. Since the risk is, by definition, greater than that for holding a riskless asset, *the "expected" cash flow must be discounted on the basis of a higher forward structure of interest rates (i.e., one that reflects the additional risk).*

Once the above changes are incorporated into the analysis, the technique of appropriately discounting, and then summing, the expected cash flows can be used to value common stocks. However, before proceeding with an example of this valuation procedure, two points need to be emphasized:

1. In this analysis, only *cash* that is received by the investor is used in the valuation process.
2. Since many streams of future dividends can reasonably be expected to continue "forever," the analysis must deal with the discounted present value of an *infinite series of dividend payments.*

Each of these points deserves some elaboration.

DIVIDENDS NOT EARNINGS

The consideration only of dividends, makes a clear decision not to analyze company earnings. While this is perplexing to some people, the relevance of dividends versus earnings as a source of value, and in turn, a basis for analysis, is, in the words of William Sharpe, "a repeated but somewhat pointless controversy." [252, p. 302] The rationale for calculating the intrinsic value of a share of common stock from its dividends, instead of earnings per share, is that the only value that is ever *received* by the stockholder, is the dividend. From this perspective, earnings are important only in so much as they provide dividends.

The validity of dividend-based stock valuation can be better appreciated on considering what can be done with a firm's *earnings*. Basically, aftertax earnings can be used for financing

1.   Net new investments in plant and equipment.
2.   Purchases of outstanding shares of the company's common stock.
3.   Dividend distributions to shareholders.

It is important to realize that management's decision to invest (or not to invest) in new plant and equipment does not depend on company earnings. Corporate managers make new investment decisions, just like everyone else, on the merits of the proposed project. That is, net new investments are made because the expected returns on these investments are forecast to be in excess of those on available alternatives with similar risks. Also, once management concludes that an investment should be made (again, based on its expected risk and reward), the project can be financed in a variety of ways—only one of which is through retained earnings.

Setting aside the second possible use of earnings—to purchase outstanding shares of the company's common stock—the rationale for basing valuation models on future dividend streams can be better understood by reference to Figure 31–1.

Figure 31–1 illustrates that earnings can be used to increase a firm's assets. Net new investments create assets which can be combined with other resources, such as labor, to produce future earnings. Typically, in a company's early years—while it has internal investment opportunities, such as expansion to meet the demands of a growing market—earnings are channeled into net new investment.

What is confusing about the notion of a dividend discount model is that while a company might not pay dividends, it clearly has "value." The validity of the dividend discount model can best be illustrated by an example. Imagine a company which expects annual earnings of $1 per share far into

FIGURE 31-1: Disposition of earnings—two of the choices

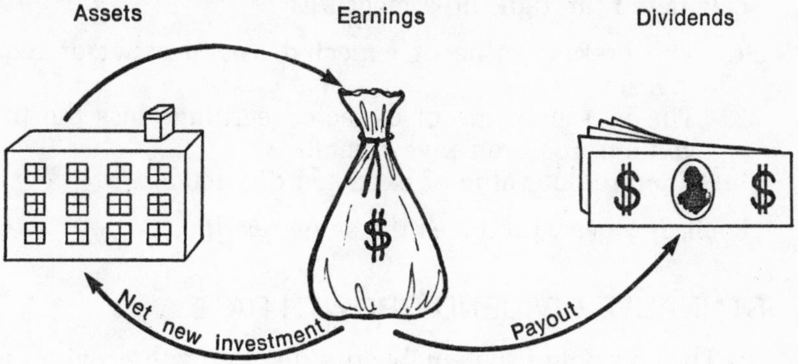

the future. Suppose, further, that in order to sustain this constant flow of expected earnings, the net new investment in plant and equipment will have to be increased at the rate of $1 per share per year. In this rather farfetched example, since an amount equal to each year's earnings must be continually channeled into net new investments, there is never any hope of a sustainable payout and, hence, no value.

Nor can a firm increase the value of its shares simply by increasing the payout ratio (the portion of earnings that is paid out as dividends). Astute analysts would "flag" such dividend increases as detracting from the amount which would otherwise be channeled into net new investments and which, in turn, would increase the expected growth in earnings per share.

This overly simplified example brings out two important points:

1. For any nondividend-paying stock, the market presumption is that "eventually" earnings are going to outpace the company's need for additional plant and equipment. When this happens, earnings will exceed the funds that are channeled into net new investments creating the capacity to pay *dividends.*

2. Focusing one's attention on the present value of a forecasted stream of earnings can be misleading. The variable of interest is the present value of expected earnings *net of any investment that is required to produce the earnings.* And, as can be noted from Figure 31-1, earnings less net new investments equal *dividends.*

According to valuation theory, the value of an equity can be calculated through three measures:

1. The present value of expected earnings net of required investment.
2. The present value of expected earnings less the present value of required investment.
3. The present value of expected dividends.

Each, however, produces the same result!

SUSTAINABLE DIVIDEND GROWTH RATE

The concept of sustainable dividend growth provides a useful understanding of the relationship between a company's return on equity, reinvestment rate, dividend payout ratio, and dividend growth rate. The *reinvestment rate* is the percentage of return that is retained by the company for reinvestment. Typically, the amount that is not reinvested is paid out in dividends. This amount is referred to as the *dividend payout ratio.*

Theoretically, a company's *sustainable dividend growth rate* is its return on equity times its reinvestment rate. This is best understood by referring to Table 31–1. The first line of

TABLE 31–1: Concept of sustainable dividend growth

Equity pool	Return on equity	Return	Rein-vest-ment rate	Rein-vestment amount	Dividend amount	Dividend growth rate
$10,000.00	12%	$1,200.00	60%	$720.00	$480.00	—
10,720.00	12	1,286.40	60	771.89	514.56	7.2%
11,491.84	12	1,379.02	60	827.41	551.61	7.2

this table shows a 12 percent return on an initial equity pool of $10,000 and a 60 percent reinvestment rate. In this situation, 60 percent of the first period's return ($720) is carried forward to the second period, and 40 percent of the return ($480) is paid out as dividends. Notice, however, that if the return on equity and reinvestment ratio remain constant in the subsequent periods, dividends will grow by the return on equity (12 percent) times the reinvestment rate (60 percent), or 7.2 percent per period.

DISCOUNTING INFINITE INCOME STREAMS

The second point that requires elaboration concerns the problem of determining the present value of an *infinite stream of expected dividends*. While this might appear to present an insurmountable difficulty, the fact is that the present value of increasingly more distant dividends becomes progressively less important. This is best illustrated by reference to Table 31–2.

Table 31–2 shows the present value of $1 for annual discount rates ranging from 10 percent to 14 percent for future periods up to 100 years. (Table 30–1 showed the same information for annual discount rates ranging from 5 percent to 9 percent.) The table value for $1 can also be thought of as the decimal equivalents for the discounted present value of any amount. Using the 12 percent discount rate as an example, notice how rapidly the present value of a future stream of dividends declines further out into the future.

Specifically, using a 12 percent discount factor, Table 31–2 shows that a payment to be received in five years has a present value that is worth only $0.57 (or 57 percent), of that future payment. Similarly (with a 12 percent discount rate), a payment that will be received in ten years has a present value worth only 32 percent of the future payment. Going even further into the future to, say 25 years (using the 12 percent discount rate), the present value of such a payment is only about 6 percent of the future payment.

From a slightly different perspective, consider the present value of an annual annuity of $1. Using the 12 percent discount rate in Table 31–2, note that the present value of $1 in one year is 89 cents and the present value of $1 in 20 years is $0.10. This means that even if the discount factor did not fall further beyond the 20th year, the annuity's contribution to present value from the 20th to the 29th year would be roughly the same as the contribution derived from the 1st year. In reality, however, by the 30th year, the present value of the dollar has decreased to $0.03. Even if this discount factor did not fall (which of course it does), the annuity over the next 30 years would make roughly the same contribution to the present value as next year's dollar.

Thus, while the valuation of common stocks based on an infinite stream of future dividends might at first appear to pose an unmanageable problem, the fact that the present values become progressively smaller further into the future (unless

TABLE 31-2: Present value of $1

Years in the future	Discount rate				
	10.0%	11.0%	12.0%	13.0%	14.0%
1.........	0.909 091	0.900 901	0.892 857	0.884 956	0.877 193
2.........	0.826 446	0.811 622	0.797 194	0.783 147	0.769 468
3.........	0.751 315	0.731 191	0.711 780	0.693 050	0.674 972
4.........	0.683 013	0.658 731	0.635 518	0.613 319	0.592 080
5.........	0.620 921	0.593 451	0.567 427	0.542 760	0.519 369
6.........	0.564 474	0.534 641	0.506 631	0.480 319	0.455 587
7.........	0.513 158	0.481 658	0.452 349	0.425 061	0.399 637
8.........	0.466 507	0.433 926	0.403 883	0.376 160	0.350 559
9.........	0.424 098	0.390 925	0.360 610	0.332 885	0.307 508
10.........	0.385 543	0.352 184	0.321 973	0.294 588	0.269 744
11.........	0.350 494	0.317 283	0.287 476	0.260 698	0.236 617
12.........	0.318 631	0.285 841	0.256 675	0.230 706	0.207 559
13.........	0.289 664	0.257 514	0.229 174	0.204 165	0.182 069
14.........	0.263 331	0.231 995	0.204 620	0.180 677	0.159 710
15.........	0.239 392	0.209 004	0.182 696	0.159 891	0.140 096
16.........	0.217 629	0.188 292	0.163 122	0.141 496	0.122 892
17.........	0.197 845	0.169 633	0.145 644	0.125 218	0.107 800
18.........	0.179 859	0.152 822	0.130 040	0.110 812	0.094 561
19.........	0.163 508	0.137 678	0.116 107	0.098 064	0.082 948
20.........	0.148 644	0.124 034	0.103 667	0.086 782	0.072 762
21.........	0.135 131	0.111 742	0.092 560	0.076 798	0.063 826
22.........	0.122 846	0.100 669	0.082 643	0.067 963	0.055 988
23.........	0.111 678	0.090 693	0.073 788	0.060 144	0.049 112
24.........	0.101 626	0.081 705	0.065 882	0.053 225	0.043 081
25.........	0.092 296	0.073 608	0.058 823	0.047 102	0.037 790
26.........	0.083 905	0.066 314	0.052 521	0.041 683	0.033 149
27.........	0.076 278	0.059 742	0.046 894	0.036 888	0.029 078
28.........	0.069 343	0.053 822	0.041 869	0.032 644	0.025 507
29.........	0.063 039	0.048 488	0.037 383	0.028 889	0.022 375
30.........	0.057 309	0.043 683	0.033 378	0.025 565	0.019 627
31.........	0.052 099	0.039 354	0.029 802	0.022 624	0.017 217
32.........	0.047 362	0.035 454	0.026 609	0.020 021	0.015 102
33.........	0.043 057	0.031 940	0.023 758	0.017 718	0.013 248
34.........	0.039 143	0.028 775	0.021 212	0.015 680	0.011 621
35.........	0.035 584	0.025 924	0.018 940	0.013 876	0.010 194
36.........	0.032 349	0.023 355	0.016 910	0.012 279	0.008 942
37.........	0.029 408	0.021 040	0.015 098	0.010 867	0.007 844
38.........	0.026 735	0.018 955	0.013 481	0.009 617	0.006 880
39.........	0.024 304	0.017 077	0.012 036	0.008 510	0.006 035
40.........	0.022 095	0.015 384	0.010 747	0.007 531	0.005 294
41.........	0.020 086	0.013 860	0.009 595	0.006 665	0.004 644
42.........	0.018 260	0.012 486	0.008 567	0.005 898	0.004 074
43.........	0.016 600	0.011 249	0.007 649	0.005 219	0.003 573
44.........	0.015 091	0.010 134	0.006 830	0.004 619	0.003 135
45.........	0.013 719	0.009 130	0.006 098	0.004 088	0.002 750
46.........	0.012 472	0.008 225	0.005 445	0.003 617	0.002 412
47.........	0.011 338	0.007 410	0.004 861	0.003 201	0.002 116
48.........	0.010 307	0.006 676	0.004 340	0.002 833	0.001 856
49.........	0.009 370	0.006 014	0.003 875	0.002 507	0.001 628
50.........	0.008 519	0.005 418	0.003 460	0.002 219	0.001 428
60.........	0.003 284	0.001 908	0.001 114	0.000 654	0.000 385
70.........	0.001 266	0.000 672	0.000 359	0.000 193	0.000 104
80.........	0.000 488	0.000 237	0.000 115	0.000 057	0.000 028
90.........	0.000 188	0.000 083	0.000 037	0.000 017	0.000 008
100.........	0.000 073	0.000 029	0.000 012	0.000 005	0.000 002

the growth in dividend payments matches or exceeds the discount rate) resolves the potential difficulty.

Using this approach the value of a share of common stock is the sum of the *discounted* present value of the estimated future stream of *dividends*. Specifically, "estimated future dividend" replaces "1" in the numerator of the discounting formula discussed in Chapter 30. Thus, the present value of next year's dividend is

$$\frac{\text{Next year's dividend}}{1 + r}$$

where r is the discount, or interest, rate. Similarly, the present value of the dividend expected the year after next is

$$\frac{\text{Second-year dividend}}{(1 + r)(1 + r)}$$

Based on general algebraic notation, where d_1 is next year's expected dividend, d_2 is the expected dividend two years hence, and so on, the present value of a common stock becomes

$$\begin{array}{l}\text{Present} \\ \text{value}\end{array} = \frac{d_1}{1 + r} + \frac{d_2}{(1 + r)^2} + \frac{d_3}{(1 + r)^3} + \cdots \begin{array}{l}\text{and so on} \\ \text{indefinitely}\end{array}$$

In summary, classical valuation theory states that

| PRESENT VALUE | can be derived from the | DISCOUNT RATE | and | DIVIDEND STREAM |

Notice that in the foregoing "equation," a discount rate and a dividend stream is used to arrive at a present value. Using some algebraic manipulation, however, the "equation" can be rewritten so that the

| IMPLICIT DISCOUNT RATE | can be derived from the | PRESENT VALUE | and | DIVIDEND STREAM |

Using this transformed equation, with estimates of (a) present value and (b) the future dividend stream, it is possible to calculate the stock's *implicit discount rate*—the expected rate of total return that equates the current price with the forecasted dividend stream.

Basically, the implicit discount rate for a stock is the same as the yield to maturity for a bond. Given a security's price and its dividend stream, implicit discount rate, or *implied return*, is calculated as if it was a bond with an infinite stream of coupon payments. The resultant figure, the *implicit discount rate*, is considered by MPT proponents such as William Fouse, of Wells Fargo Investment Advisors, to be *"the single most important piece of information to have about a common stock"* (italics added). [96, p. 40]

Two things are required to calculate a security's implied return—the present value of the security and a long-term estimate of the security's dividend stream. Obviously, the present value (the current market price) is readily available. A forecast of the long-term dividend stream is usually developed from analyst's inputs to a dividend growth model.

DIVIDEND GROWTH MODELS

Dividend growth models provide an analytical framework for determining the value of a share of stock from estimated growth rates in the components of value—earnings and payout ratios. Most dividend growth models divide the future into three stages: (a) a time period that is within the analyst's forecast horizon, (b) a variable-length normalizing period, and (c) an infinitely long period of normal growth.

Basically, the period within the analyst's forecast horizon is defined as an "explicit" growth stage. For the explicit forecast period, analysts provide year-by-year estimates of expected dividends and earnings. For the variable length normalizing period, analysts estimate (a) the length of the "normalizing" period, (b) the transitional earnings growth rate, (c) the transitional dividend payout ratio, and (d) the "pattern" of change in the earnings growth rate during the normalizing period. The most distant stage, beyond the analyst's forecast horizon and the "normalizing" period, is assumed to be an infinitely long period during which the growth of the company is equal to that of the economy. These stages are illustrated in Figure 31–2.

Several observations about growth models are relevant here. First, as illustrated in Table 31–2, the present value of progressively more distant dividends rapidly decreases to the point of insignificance. Thus, forecast errors in more distant time periods have a minimal impact on expected rates of return. Second, dividend growth models are used for the relative valuation of a universe of securities. In this valuation process, near-

FIGURE 31–2: Growth model forecast periods

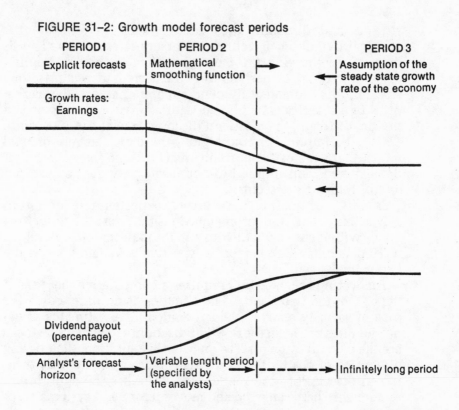

term estimates, at which superior security analysts should be able to demonstrate their forecasting abilities, are the most important. Similarly, since all dividends are assumed to grow at the same rate in the most distant forecast period, the assumptions in this period do not alter the relative valuations.

Finally, it should not be construed that this kind of forecasting requires an infinite forecasting horizon. Today's market price reflects today's consensus expectation. Tomorrow's market prices will reflect tomorrow's consensus expectations. Thus, today's forecasts need to predict tomorrow's consensus—not a perpetual forecast!

THE LINK BETWEEN MPT AND VALUATION THEORY

Classical investment value theory defines the value of an investment as the discounted present value of the future stream of payments derived from ownership. The *dividend discount model* shows how estimates of future dividend streams and discount rates can be used to translate the classical definition of value into practical estimates. This is done by rearranging the value equation so that an implicit discount rate can be derived from the current market price of a stock and its estimated dividend stream. That is, if the market price of a security is combined with estimates of its expected dividend stream, the dividend discount model can be used to derive the *implicit discount rate*—the expected rate of total return that equates the current price with the forecasted dividend stream. This implicit discount rate provides an *expected rate of return for a security.*

In MPT, estimating a security's expected rate of return solves only half the problem. Consider, for example, two bonds with identical maturities and the expected rates of return of 10 percent and 12 percent, respectively. Which bond is the better investment?

Answering this question requires a comparative measure of the risk of the two bonds. The situation is no different in the case of security analysis. Given comparative estimates of expected rates of return (or implicit discount rates), which stocks are the best investments? To answer this question, the missing dimension of risk must be provided. This can be done by turning to the CAPM—the model that describes the equilibrium relationship between expected rate of return and systematic, or market-related, risk. This model holds that an appropriate discount rate for any asset can be derived from two factors: (a) the risk-free rate of return and (b) an additional, or premium, return that is commensurate with the asset's risk.

Determining the first factor—the risk-free rate of return—is relatively easy. It is merely the return that can be earned without incurring risk. Conceptually, the risk-free rate of return is the rate for the pure rental of money plus an inflation hedge. The risk-free rate of return is only part of the equation, however. For an estimate of the other component—the risk premium—we can turn to capital market theory. This theory holds that the risk premium of each stock is a linear function of systematic risk, or beta.

The link between MPT and valuation theory is shown in Figure 31–3. That is, valuation theory says that the value of an asset depends on the expected future stream of dividends and an appropriate discount rate. In turn, the CAPM says that the discount rate depends on the risk-free rate of return and the risk premium. Since the risk-free rate is easily determined, the missing element is quantification of the appropriate risk pre-

FIGURE 31–3: The link between MPT and valuation theory

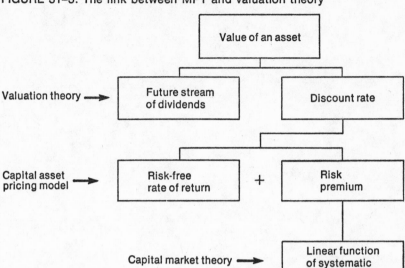

mium. Capital market theory holds, however, that the risk premium is a linear function (i.e., it can be represented by a straight line) of systematic risk.

A forward-looking estimate of systematic risk is an ex ante estimate of beta. Thus, with estimates of the future stream of dividends, the risk-free rate of return, and beta, the equilibrium expected rate of return of any asset can be determined. Herein lies the enormous significance of beta in security valuation.

Much progress has been made in improving the forecast reliability of beta coefficients by introducing company fundamentals into the analysis. Accordingly, before turning to the subject of betas, and their prediction, it will be useful to focus on the comparative analysis of company fundamentals.

Chapter 32

Company fundamentals

It would be difficult to find two identical companies. Clearly, Ford is different from General Motors; IBM is different from Control Data, and so on. But *how* do these companies differ? And how do these differences translate into differing risk and return expectations?

To answer the first question—how companies differ—a comparative analysis of company fundamentals is required. Generally speaking, *fundamentals* encompass all of the accounting-related data which appear on a company's financial statements. Techniques which facilitate this kind of comparative analysis are presented in this chapter.

Specifically, the goal here is to (a) clarify some often confusing accounting terms, (b) suggest a convenient technique that can be used for balance sheet and income statement comparisons, and (c) illustrate a system of ratios which link data on the balance sheet and the income statement. The graphic techniques presented here were largely developed by my long-time colleague, Chris Mader—holder of the Anvil Award for Teaching Excellence at the Wharton School of Finance.

BALANCE SHEET

Within the accounting profession, different terms are used to describe the same thing. Each of the following terms, for example, refers to the same document:

Balance sheet
Statement of financial condition
Position statement
Statement of net worth
Statement of assets, liabilities, and owners' equity

The balance sheet (as it is most commonly known) is the basic financial statement for a firm. It shows, on the left-hand side of the page, what the company owns (valued at acquisition cost plus installation minus accumulated depreciation) and, on the other side of the page, the sources of the funds that were used to acquire those assets.

By definition, the total amounts represented on each side of a balance sheet are numerically equal—they balance. Specifically, the equation for a balance sheet is

(Left side)   (Right side)
Assets   = Liabilities + owners' equity
(What is owned)   (How it was funded)

An asset is something of sustained value that is owned by the company. The value of an asset (as it appears on the balance sheet) is cost plus installation minus accumulated depreciation. It is important to note that this definition and valuation convention can result in a very misleading picture of a company. Consider, for example, all of the things that are of value to a company but are not "owned" (and, hence, cannot be called "assets"). Obviously, management and employees are not "owned." In an accounting sense, people are resources which are leased or rented. And since leased resources are not "owned," they do not appear on the balance sheet. Thus, for example, the value of IBM's highly trained technical and sales personnel is not reflected on the company's balance sheet.

Another way in which balance sheets can be misleading stems from the convention of valuing assets at cost plus installation. Consider, for example, the current market value of real estate purchased 15 years ago. (Only since March 23, 1976, has the Securities and Exchange Commission's Rule 3–17, Regulation SX required firms with over $100 million in sales to provide unaudited estimates of the value of their assets at *replacement cost.*)

The final thing to remember about a balance sheet is that it is a static picture of an enterprise "as of the close of business on a particular day." Clearly, if you know that you are going to have your picture taken on December 31, you will do whatever you can to look your best on that day.

In spite of the definitional problems, the balance sheet can be useful in the comparative analysis of companies. A technique which will facilitate this comparison is to represent the two sides of the balance sheet as two equally tall columns of money. Graphically, these can be thought of as two tall buildings, such as New York's World Trade Towers. This columnar representation is shown in Figure 32–1.

Next, it is useful to think of the data to be analyzed in terms of percentages—not the typically incomprehensible absolute

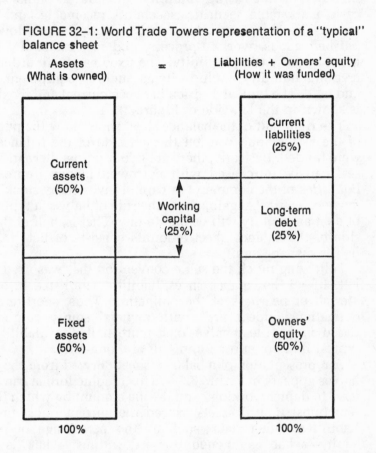

FIGURE 32–1: World Trade Towers representation of a "typical" balance sheet

numbers that appear on the balance sheets of large companies. From this perspective, the balance sheet for a "typical" manufacturing company can be drawn by the "rule of halves." That is, beginning on the asset (left) half of the page, all assets are listed in order of decreasing liquidity. Thus, the *current assets* (those most likely to be converted into cash during an operating cycle) are shown first, followed by the fixed assets. Fixed assets are those things of long-term usefulness to the firm which are not likely to be converted to cash, or consumed, within the next operating cycle. Based on the rule of halves, a typical manufacturing company would have half current and half fixed assets.

Within each of the broad categories of current and fixed, assets are listed in order of decreasing liquidity. Current assets, in order of decreasing liquidity, include accounts such as cash, marketable securities, accounts receivable, and inventories. The inventory category is, in turn, broken down into finished goods, work-in-process, and raw materials, also in order of decreasing liquidity. The fixed assets, in order of decreasing liquidity, include items such as equipment, plant, and land. The typical division between current and fixed assets is shown in the left side of Figure 32–1.

The right half of the balance sheet shows how the purchases of the assets appearing on the left side of the balance sheet were funded. Basically, there are two funding alternatives. Assets can be purchased with borrowed money (representing *liabilities* of the company) or capital invested by stockholders (*owners' equity*). Again, using the rule of halves, a typical mix of debt and equity will be one-to-one. That is, half of the right side of the balance sheet amounts consists of liabilities and half is owners' equity.

Following much the same convention that was used on the left side of the balance sheet, liabilities are listed in order of "term" or nearness of the obligation. Thus, short-term debt obligations appear first, with owners' equity coming last. Based on the rule of halves once more, half of the liabilities of a typical firm are current and half are long-term.

A representation of a balance sheet derived from the rule of halves appears in Figure 32–1. This graphic format can also be used to depict working capital—the amount by which the current (most liquid) assets exceed the current (most pressing) liabilities. Other data, such as the percentage of owners' equity—what is owned (assets) minus what is owed (liabilities)—can also readily be derived from this kind of graphic presentation.

Figure 32–2 uses the World Trade Tower approach to contrast the December 31, 1978 balance sheets of two automobile manufacturers—General Motors and Ford Motor Company. While General Motors ($30.6 billion in assets) is larger than Ford ($22 billion in assets), the step-by-step comparison of each balance sheet category is now very easy. The tower comparison reveals, for example, that General Motors's assets were more liquid. General Motors had 59 percent of its assets in the

FIGURE 32–2: Comparative balance sheets

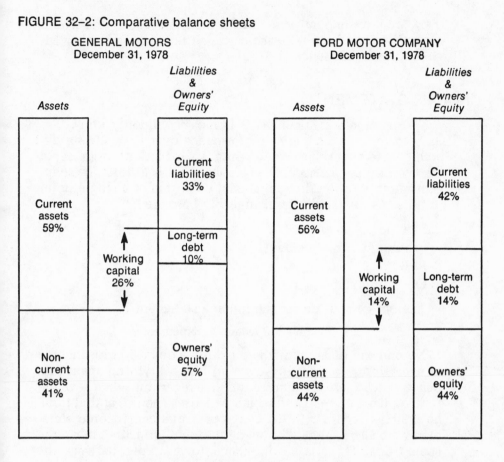

current category compared to 56 percent for Ford. The fact that General Motor's working capital accounts for 26 percent of its assets, versus Ford's 14 percent, shows that money is tighter at Ford.

Debt represents 43 percent of General Motors' liabilities and equity, against 56 percent for Ford. Thus, in terms of three comparisons—(a) asset liquidity, (b) working capital, and (c) the debt to equity ratio—General Motors has the stronger balance sheet. Clearly, on the basis of these fundamentals, General Motors is more attractive. Knowing nothing else, but assuming a reasonably efficient market, one would be surprised to find both General Motors and Ford priced equally. In fact, if they were, it might reasonably be concluded that General Motors was undervalued (or Ford was overvalued, or both). But, alas, there are few such surprises in the market—just as one would expect General Motors' price-earnings ratio on December 31, 1978 was almost twice Ford's.

INCOME STATEMENT

The income statement (as it is most commonly known) is used to report managerial performance over time. It is a *dynamic* statement reflecting the progress (or lack of progress) of the firm. By comparison, the balance sheet is a *static*, or snapshot, picture of the firm's financial condition at a single point in time. Terms used interchangeably here are

Income statement
Profit and loss statement
P&L
Operating statement

The basic equation for the income statement is

$$\text{Income} = \text{Revenue} - \text{Expenses}$$

No one can disagree with so simple a definition for income as everything brought in (revenue) less everything spent (expenses). Yet, there are many subtleties regarding *when* revenue is recognized as such and *which* expenses should, at that time, be matched against it. To compound matters, income statements are also replete with many different terms that mean the same thing. There is no difference, for example, between the following:

Revenues
Sales
Turnover (in Europe)
Gross income
"The top line"

Similarly, there is no difference between

Income
Profit
Earnings
Net income
"The bottom line"

The income statements of different companies can also be

compared using the World Trade Tower approach. It merely requires the algebraic rearrangement of the basic equation from

$$\text{Income} = \text{Revenue} - \text{Expenses}$$

to

$$\text{Revenue} = \text{Expenses} + \text{Income}$$

In this format, we can convert any company's numerical percentages and represent each side of the equation as easily comparable "towers," as shown in Figure 32–3.

FIGURE 32–3: World Trade Tower representation of a "typical" income statement

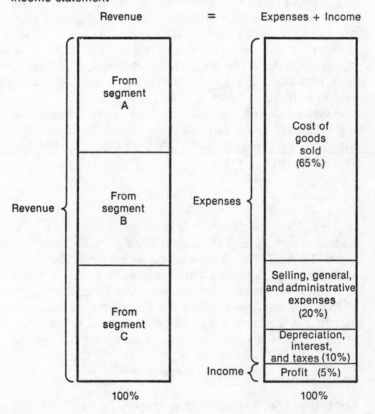

Under the segment accounting rules now in effect (for audited companies), whenever 10 percent or more of a company's revenues are from a given line of business (such as a sales division or a rental segment), the revenues from that segment must be reported separately. Thus, the revenue (left-hand) column is merely a graphic representation of the percentages of the company's revenue that are derived from each major segment of its business. Similarly, the expenses and income (right) column, breaks out the percentages of the company's expenses by various categories. And, last but not least, the bottom of the right-hand column shows the amount that is left after expenses are subtracted from revenues—net aftertax profit, or income.

FINANCIAL ANALYSIS

Financial analysis is the study of the interrelationship between an enterprise's financial structure (balance sheet) and its operating results (income statement). Basically, the task is to determine how efficiently a company employs its assets and how it has chosen to finance the acquisition and carrying costs of those assets. The key system of ratios employed in this analysis is explained below.

Asset turnover. Asset turnover (sometimes called operating leverage) is the ratio of sales per dollar of assets employed during the year. It is calculated by dividing net sales by the average assets. Thus,

$$\text{Asset turnover} = \frac{\text{Sales}}{\text{Assets}}$$

In fiscal 1978 (ended June 30), for example, Tandy Corporation had an asset turnover ratio of 2.06. This means that during fiscal 1978, Tandy Corporation generated $2.06 in sales for each (average) dollar's worth of assets that it owned.

Return on sales. Return on sales (sometimes abbreviated ROS and sometimes called the operating margin, or net profit margin) is the percentage of profit earned on sales. It is calculated by dividing net income, or earnings, by net sales. Thus,

$$\text{Return on sales} = \frac{\text{Earnings}}{\text{Sales}}$$

Continuing with the same example, in fiscal 1978 the Tandy Corporation had a return on sales of 6.2 percent. This means that the Tandy Corporation earned 6.2 cents in net (aftertax) profit for each dollar of sales.

Return on assets. Return on assets (sometimes abbreviated ROA) is the percentage of net profit earned on total assets. It is the product of asset turnover and return on sales:

$$\text{Asset turnover} \times \text{Return on sales} = \text{Return on assets}$$

$$\frac{\text{Sales}}{\text{Assets}} \quad \times \quad \frac{\text{Earnings}}{\text{Sales}} \quad = \quad \frac{\text{Earnings}}{\text{Assets}}$$

Note that when the fraction representing "asset turnover" is multiplied by the fraction representing "return on sales," the "sales" terms in the two fractions cancel each other. Thus, return on assets can be calculated either by multiplying asset turnover by return on sales or by merely dividing earnings by assets. The Tandy Corporation had a return on assets of 12.8 percent in fiscal 1978—12.8 cents for each dollar of assets.

Financial leverage. Financial leverage is the measure of how many dollars of assets are held in relation to each dollar of stockholders' equity—in other words, how much of a company's asset base is financed with stockholders' equity and how much with borrowed funds. It is calculated by dividing average assets by average stockholders' equity. Thus,

$$\text{Financial leverage} = \frac{\text{Assets}}{\text{Equity}}$$

During fiscal 1978, the leverage ratio for Tandy Corporation was 3.39, indicating that the company employed $3.39 of assets for each dollar of stockholders' equity.

Return on equity. Return on equity (sometimes abbreviated ROE)—a key measure of the profitability of an equity investment—is the net income earned by a company expressed as a percentage return on the stockholders' investment. Its relationship to return on assets and financial leverage is as follows:

$$\text{Return on assets} \times \text{Financial leverage} = \text{Return on equity}$$

$$\frac{\text{Earnings}}{\text{Assets}} \quad \times \quad \frac{\text{Assets}}{\text{Equity}} \quad = \quad \frac{\text{Earnings}}{\text{Equity}}$$

Note that when the fraction representing "return on assets" is multiplied by the fraction representing "financial leverage," the "asset" terms in each fraction are canceled out. Thus, return on equity can be calculated either by multiplying return on assets by the financial leverage ratio or merely by dividing earnings by equity. For fiscal 1978, the Tandy Corporation had a whopping aftertax return on equity of 43.6 percent—the highest in the firm's history and unequaled by any other major retailer or electronics and computer company.[1]

---

[1] For further analysis of these data, the interested reader is referred to the Tandy Corporation annual report. It may be obtained without charge by writing Tandy Corporation, Shareholder Relations, 1800 One Tandy Center, P.O. Box 17180, Fort Worth, Texas 76102; or by telephone (817) 390–3091.

We can gain much insight into the Tandy Corporation by arraying the *system* of financial ratios which produces return on equity in the format shown in Table 32–1.

The sources, data, and relationships expressed by this system of ratios can be summarized as shown below:

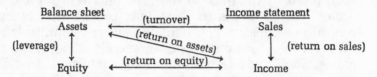

Thus, leverage provides a measure of the balance sheet relationship between the assets and equity. Turnover, return on assets, and return on equity define relationships between key items on the balance sheet and income statement. Finally, return on sales provides a measure of the relationship between sales and income on the income statement.

Given these relationships and the data presented in Table 32–1, the interrelationships which produced Tandy's final return on equity figure can be probed. Moving from left to right across the 1978 line, it is apparent that asset turnover (sales/assets) is down slightly from fiscal 1977. Reference to the balance sheet shows that total assets increased over the year from $475 million to $553 million—for an average of $514 million for fiscal 1978. Reference to the income statement shows that sales rose from $953 million in fiscal 1977 to $1,065 million in fiscal 1978. Thus, both assets and sales showed year-to-year increases, but sales per average dollar of assets employed (measured by the *asset turnover* ratio) declined.

Moving to the next column, it is evident that *return on sales* (income/sales) has also decreased. Since income is the difference between sales and expenses, the expense items on the income statement can be scrutinized for an explanation of the drop in the return on sales figure. The expense figures show that part of the decline in return on sales stems from a year-to-year doubling of interest expense—from roughly $15 million to $30 million. Further probing reveals that the bulk of this incremental interest expense reflects an increase in debt issued to repurchase the company's common stock. The rationale behind this financing decision was that the profit margins of the company were running in excess of the interest costs on the new debt. Thus, the repurchase of shares with borrowed funds was expected to enhance the return on equity.

The fourth column of Table 32–1 shows a significant increase in *financial leverage* during fiscal 1978, following the

TABLE 32–1: Illustrative system of key financial ratios for the Tandy Corporation

	Asset turnover (operating leverage) $\dfrac{Sales}{Average\ assets}$		Return on sales (net margin) $\dfrac{Net\ income}{Sales}$		Return on assets $\dfrac{Net\ income}{Average\ assets}$		Financial leverage $\dfrac{Average\ assets}{Average\ equity}$		Return on equity $\dfrac{Net\ income}{Average\ equity}$
1972	1.39	×	3.9%	=	5.4%	×	1.61	=	8.7%
1973	1.34	×	4.4	=	5.9	×	2.06	=	12.2
1974	1.47	×	3.6	=	5.3	×	2.41	=	12.8
1975	1.71	×	5.1	=	8.7	×	2.53	=	22.0
1976	2.04	×	8.7	=	17.7	×	2.18	=	38.6
1977	2.16	×	7.3	=	15.8	×	2.37	=	37.2
1978	2.06	×	6.2	=	12.8	×	3.39	=	43.4

Source: Tandy Corporation's June 30, 1978 Annual Report.

stock repurchase program. The result, in the final column, is a return on equity of 43.4 percent.

With the financial data on Tandy Corporation arrayed in the format of Table 32–1, it is possible to "go beyond" return on equity by disecting the system of financial ratios that produce it. The asset turnover column reveals, for example, that the amount of sales generated per dollar of assets has remained fairly constant since fiscal 1976. By comparison, the company's return on sales has fallen since 1976. The product of the first two ratios, return on assets, has similarly fallen since 1976. The information in the next column, shows that Tandy increased its financial leverage. Finally, the product of return on assets and financial leverage produces return on equity.

Clearly, the objective here is not to comment on the investment merits of Tandy Corporation, but rather to provide some insight into how the fundamental risk and return characteristics of a company can change over time. Importantly, MPT has addressed the subject of how changes in an investment's fundamentals can alter its potential risks and returns. Barr Rosenberg's pioneering work in this area is discussed in the next chapter.

Chapter 33

Prediction of beta

Systematic risk, measured by beta coefficients, is the risk which cannot be eliminated by diversification. Thus, beta prediction—the only estimate of risk in a well-diversified portfolio—has a pivotal role in MPT.

EX POST BETAS

Ex post or backward-looking, betas are best understood by imagining an experiment in which pairs of market and security returns are plotted, with the market return on the horizontal axis and the security's return on the vertical axis. The slope of a regression line fitted through these points measures the degree to which market returns, on average, have been associated with the security's returns.

Caution needs to be exercised in interpreting an historical beta. First, it cannot be assumed that the true beta is fixed over time. Quite the contrary, there is reason to expect that beta does change. Second, historical beta is merely an estimate of the "true" underlying beta. During any historical period, the observed combinations of market and security returns that are used to calculate a historical beta represent the "true" beta, plus or minus random factors which are unique to a security. Third, historical betas should not obscure the fact that while historical betas are useful when interpreting historical performance, prediction requires betas that are ex ante, forward-looking, estimates.

BETA DOES NOT DESCRIBE A CAUSAL RELATIONSHIP

Much of the confusion surrounding beta can be avoided by remembering that beta does not describe a causal relationship. A certain level of market return does not result in a certain

263

level of security return. Instead, both market and security returns depend on a third variable—the economy. Economic events cause systematic changes in both security and market prices.

Properly viewed, beta reflects the fact that both market and security returns depend on common events. Thus, the most logical way to forecast beta is to quantify the relationship between market and security returns and these factors. What, for example, is the relationship between changes in the expected rate of inflation and the returns of both individual securities and the market? Compared to the market, which securities are sensitive to inflation and which are not?

BETA FORECASTING AND SECURITY ANALYSIS

Approached from this perspective, beta forecasting is strikingly similar to security analysis. Conventional security analysis recognizes two components of return: (a) that arising from events which bear particularly on the company in question and (b) the component resulting from events which affect the economy, or the market, as a whole. The sum of these two components is the total expected return.

The lack of certainty surrounding the events which solely impact a company is the specific risk. However, since the events specific to individual firms tend to cancel out through diversification, on the average, specific returns do not add to market return. Consequently, the uncertainty which is not specific to individual companies—the nonspecific risk— accounts for almost all of a portfolio's risk. This nonspecific risk—that inherent in the economy and shared by other companies—cannot be diversified away. Nonetheless, the nonspecific risk can be estimated from a prediction of the amount of economy-related uncertainty surrounding the security return—in other words, beta.

Traditionally, of the two components of risk and return, security analysis has emphasized the specific, company-related, factor. The age-old quest for misvalued securities has tended to focus on events which are specific to individual firms. Yet, most of the risk and return in a portfolio are linked to the market. In turn, the market component of risk and return for a security is derived from the economic events which impact on many stocks. It follows that one of the most fruitful areas of research has dealt with the extension of fundamental security analysis that is concerned with the relationship between a security's return and nonspecific, economywide events—so-called *fundamental betas.*

ROSENBERG'S FUNDAMENTAL BETAS

Barr Rosenberg has pioneered in the prediction of fundamental betas through *relative response coefficients.* Basically, a relative response coefficient is the ratio of the expected response of a security to the expected response of the market if both the security and the market are impacted by the same event. For example, if the event is inflation, those stocks which react to inflation in the same way as the market will have a high relative response coefficient for this event. Similarly, stocks that are not as sensitive to inflation as the market will have a low relative response coefficient for inflation.

Suppose, that an investor is interested in studying the impact of future energy and inflation developments on the market and on two stocks. Assume that there is an equal likelihood that future events in each of these areas will turn out to have favorable, unchanged, or unfavorable implications. This situation, plus the "relative response" which each event-outcome combination is expected to elicit, are depicted in Table 33–1.

TABLE 33–1: Contributions to return for hypothetical
event-outcome sequences

		Percentage contribution to return		
Event	*Outcome*	*Market*	*Stock A*	*Stock B*
Energy.........	Favorable	+6	+4	+8
	Unchanged	0	0	0
	Unfavorable	−6	−4	−8
Inflation	Favorable	+3	+6	0
	Unchanged	0	0	0
	Unfavorable	−3	−6	0

Source: Rosenberg and Guy [227].

Stock A is expected to respond two thirds as much as the market to an energy-related event, while stock B is anticipated to react one third more strongly than the market. To an inflation event, stock A is expected to respond twice as much as the market, while stock B is not expected to show any reaction to inflation events.

The relationships portrayed in Table 33–1 can be used to contrast the expected values and variances of returns on securities with those of the market when both are impacted by the same macroeconomic events. In this illustration, the expected (average) impact of these two events on market return is zero, and the variance is 30 percent.[1] The variance of future market returns can be separated into the variances generated by each of the two events. In this illustration, energy uncertainties cause 24 percentage points of the variance in market returns. Similarly, the variance caused by inflation uncertainty amounts to 6 percent.

DETERMINATION OF BETA

In general terms, a security's beta is determined by

1. The proportional contributions of various categories of economic events to market variance.
2. The relative response of security returns to these same events—the relative response coefficients.

More specifically, the beta for any security is the weighted average of its relative response coefficients, each weighted by the proportion of total variance in market returns due to that event.[2]

In the example in Table 33–1, energy is the greatest source of uncertainty (variance). Thus, in the calculation of beta, energy uncertainty receives proportionately more emphasis. In terms of response to the two economic events, stock B is expected to be volatile in a changing energy situation. It is not

---

[1] To assist the reader who wishes to pursue this subject in more detail, the numerical example used here is identical to that used by Rosenberg and Guy. The interested reader can find the procedure used to calculate this variance (as well as other information) in [227, pp. 63–4].

[2] In technical terms

$$B_{im} = \sum_{j=1}^{J} \left(\frac{V_j}{\sum_{j=1}^{J} V_j} \right) \gamma_{ji}$$

where

B_{im} = Beta for security i.
V_j = Contribution of the economywide event j to the market variance in any period.
γ_{ji} = Ratio of the response of security i and the market to event j—the relative response coefficient.

surprising, therefore, that the betas for stocks A and B are 0.9 and 1.1, respectively.[3]

BETAS VARY OVER TIME

The importance of the foregoing discussion of the composition of beta is that a security's beta will change when

1. The variance contributed by the various categories of economic events changes.
2. The response coefficients change.

Also, to the degree that these changes can be predicted or explained, beta can be predicted or explained.

The preceding chapter on company fundamentals discussed the capital structures of firms. Clearly, as a firm becomes more or less leveraged (i.e., the proportion of debt in its capitalization structure increases or decreases, respectively), its relative response coefficient to virtually all economic events will increase or decrease. As a result, its beta will also rise or fall (after Rosenberg and Guy [227]).

HISTORICAL VERSUS FUTURE BETA VALUES

It is important to remember that the "true" beta is never observed. Before the fact, ex ante, predictions of the true value can be derived from properly weighted relative response coefficients. With after the fact data on the historical relationship between risk and return, it is possible to develop a regression line which serves as an estimate of the underlying true beta value that produced these results. In practice, both ex ante and ex post betas have specific uses.

The choice of historical or future beta values depends on the proposed application. When the beta is to be used for ex post performance evaluation, the coefficient is used to estimate the portion of total return which was derived from market and nonmarket components. In this case, since there is no need to be concerned with forward-looking, ex ante, estimates for individual securities, backward-looking, ex post, betas are appropriate.

The process of calculating backward-looking betas is conceptualized in Figure 33–1. After the relationship between his-

---

[3] Again, the interested reader will find an explanation of the calculation of these numbers in [227].

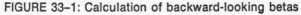

FIGURE 33–1: Calculation of backward-looking betas

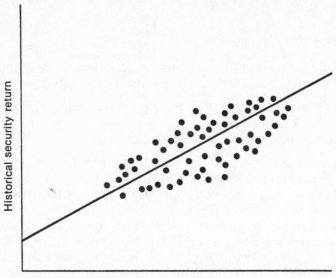

Historical market return

torical pairs of market and security returns has been plotted, a regression line, or "least squares" line of best fit, is calculated. In mathematical terms, such lines are plotted so as to minimize the sum of the squared distances between them and the points of observation, hence, the term "least squares" regression estimate. The slope of the least squares regression line is the ex post beta coefficient.

Sample ex post betas and other historical information are shown in the sample page drawn from a *Merrill Lynch Market Sensitivity Report,* reproduced as Table 33–2. During the historical period covered by the report (60 months), Allis Chalmers had a *beta* of 0.94—indicating that it was not as sensitive to the market as the average stock in the S&P 500 Index. Allis Chalmer's *alpha* was 2.13 during the same period—indicating a positive nonmarket-related return of 213 basis points. The R-squared of 0.27 indicates that during the period studied, 27 percent of the variance in Allis Chalmer's price was attributable to the market.

The *residual standard deviation* is a summary measure of the distances from the plotted points to the regression line. The residual standard deviation is an ex post measure of the security's specific, or nonmarket, risk that was present during the

TABLE 33–2: Merrill Lynch Market Sensitivity Report: 2/27/79 (for the first 30 stocks—alphabetical by ticker symbol— in the S&P 500 Index)

Ticker symbol	Security name	Price (1–31–79)	Beta	Alpha	R-squared	Residual standard deviation	Standard error: Beta	Standard error: Alpha
ACF	ACF INDUSTRIES, INC.	30.38	1.06	-0.27	0.47	5.83	0.15	0.75
AMF	AMF, INC.	17.50	1.22	-0.04	0.41	8.13	0.21	1.05
ARA	ARA SERVICES, INC.	41.00	1.15	-0.44	0.46	6.70	0.17	0.87
ASA	ASA LTD.	25.38	0.74	-0.19	0.05	11.54	0.29	1.49
ABT	ABBOTT LABORATORIES	33.50	1.17	1.72	0.55	5.79	0.15	0.75
AMT	ACME CLEVELAND CORP.	20.25	0.85	0.90	0.16	8.58	0.22	1.11
AET	AETNA LIFE & CASUALTY	42.25	1.16	0.63	0.39	7.92	0.20	1.02
AHN	AHMANSON, H.F. & CO.	22.50	1.35	1.43	0.31	11.35	0.29	1.47
ANK	AKZONA INC.	13.13	0.91	-0.46	0.19	8.83	0.22	1.14
ACV	ALBERTO CULVER CO.	8.00	1.00	0.04	0.20	9.89	0.25	1.28
AL	ALCAN ALUMINUM LTD.	36.38	0.79	0.31	0.16	7.51	0.19	0.97
ACD	ALLIED CHEMICAL CORP.	30.00	1.13	-0.52	0.48	6.35	0.16	0.82
ALS	ALLIED STORES CORP.	22.63	1.11	1.42	0.35	7.97	0.20	1.03
AH	ALLIS-CHALMERS CORP.	30.75	0.94	2.13	0.27	7.50	0.19	0.97
APC	ALPHA PORTLAND INDS.	16.63	0.88	0.44	0.15	9.73	0.25	1.26
AA	ALUMINUM CO. OF AMERICA	51.13	0.80	0.30	0.18	7.44	0.19	0.96
AGM	AMALGAMATED SUGAR CO.	17.00	0.54	-0.24	0.01	8.72	0.22	1.13
AMX	AMAX, INC.	51.13	0.96	0.23	0.31	7.14	0.18	0.92
AMR	AMERICAN AIRLINES	11.88	1.39	0.95	0.33	11.42	0.29	1.48
AT	AMERICAN BRANDS	50.25	0.83	0.51	0.55	3.43	0.09	0.44
ABC	AMERICAN BROADCASTING	35.38	1.21	1.69	0.33	9.34	0.24	1.21
AC	AMERICAN CAN CO.	36.63	0.68	0.49	0.27	4.24	0.11	0.55
ACY	AMERICAN CYANAMID CO.	25.38	1.04	0.37	0.55	4.94	0.13	0.64
AEP	AMERICAN ELEC POWER	22.75	0.81	-0.13	0.29	5.58	0.14	0.72
AXP	AMERICAN EXPRESS CO.	29.50	1.49	-0.41	0.64	6.68	0.17	0.86
AGI	AMERICAN GENERAL INS.	27.38	1.21	1.21	0.49	6.87	0.17	0.89
AHP	AMERICAN HOME PRODUCTS	27.50	1.09	-0.48	0.44	6.51	0.17	0.84
AHS	AMER HOSPITAL SUPPLY	25.88	1.54	-0.26	0.58	7.77	0.20	1.00
AMI	AMERICAN MEDICAL INT'L.	28.50	1.59	3.45	0.45	10.47	0.27	1.35
AMO	AMERICAN MOTORS CORP.	6.13	0.84	-0.56	0.07	12.81	0.33	1.65

period. The greater a particular stock's residual standard deviation, the greater is the effect of company-related events on the price of the stock. Given that the data are monthly and that roughly two thirds of the deviations fall within plus or minus one standard deviation, Allis Chalmer's residual standard deviation of 7.50 indicates that in roughly two out of every three months, Allis Chalmer's price was within plus or minus 7.50 percent (750 basis points) of the price estimated by the beta of the regression line and the level of the market at the time. In analyzing this number, remember that for a single stock the market accounts for only about 30 percent of total uncertainty. That is, for the average stock, the monthly R-squared—the portion of the total variance attributed to the market—is around 30 percent. With the remaining 70 percent of the monthly risk, on the average, coming from nonmarket sources, it is not surprising to find ex post monthly residual standard deviations of the magnitude of those in Table 33–2.

The regression procedure used to calculate alpha and beta (shown conceptually in Figure 33–1) relies on sampling to estimate the "true" underlying values. It follows that the greater the number of cases included in the sample, the smaller any errors between the "sample estimated" and the "true" value will be. The *standard error of estimate* provides an estimate of the probable extent of this kind of error. Thus, Allis Chalmer's standard error of beta of 0.19 indicates that there is a 68 percent chance (i.e., plus or minus one standard deviation) that the "true" beta is within ±0.19 of the estimated value. Similarly, the standard error of alpha of 0.97 indicates that there is a 68 percent chance that the "true" alpha is within 97 basis points of the estimated alpha.

ADJUSTED BETAS

There is much evidence (see Blume [31]) that over time, deviant betas regress to normal. Accordingly, many services which provide historical betas (such as the report in Table 33–2), "adjust" for this regression tendency, so that the historical figures will more closely approximate the "true" forward-looking beta.

USE OF BETA FOR PORTFOLIO SELECTION

To quote Rosenberg and Guy, ". . . an accurate prediction of beta is the most important single element in predicting the future behavior of a portfolio." [227, p. 65] That is, in the portfolio context, the relevant risk of a security lies in its impact on the risk of a portfolio. Further, the risk of a well-diversified portfolio is almost exclusively linked to the sensitivity of its component securities to future market moves. For this purpose, backward-looking betas are inappropriate.

Instead, it is necessary to (a) consider the *sources* of such future moves, (b) project the security's *reaction* to such sources, and (c) assign *probabilities* to the likelihood of each possible occurrence. This process, in turn, requires a thorough understanding of (a) the economics of the relevant industry, (b) both operating leverage and financial leverage of the company (see the discussion in Chapter 32), and of (c) other fundamental factors with meaningful relative response coefficients.

As mentioned earlier, Barr Rosenberg has pioneered in developing fundamentally derived betas that have been shown to be more accurate than historically derived estimates. To calculate fundamentally based predictions of beta and residual risk, Rosenberg uses the following categories of information:

1. *Market variability.* This index measures the impact of certain factors on the relationship between the market variability of returns and security returns. Such factors include:
   a. Historical beta.
   b. Historical standard deviation of residual return.
   c. Share turnover rate.
   d. Trading volume divided by the standard deviation of return.
   e. Average monthly price range.
2. *Earnings variability.* This index measures the variability of earnings. (Needless to say, earnings variability contributes to risk.) Among the descriptors used here are:
   a. Variability (coefficient of variation) of annual earnings per share.
   b. Typical proportion of earnings that are extraordinary items.
   c. Variability (coefficient of variation) of cash flow.
   d. Earnings covariability with total corporate earnings.
   e. The "Beaver" beta: regression coefficient between normalized earnings-price ratio of the firm and normalized earnings-price ratio of the economy.
   f. A measure of the absence of earnings diversification across industries.

g. Reported foreign operating income as a percentage of total operating income.

3. *Low valuation and "unsuccess."* This index is designed to measure the variability of returns (risk) inherent in consistently low-market-valuation stocks with dismal operating records. These factors include:

a. Growth in earnings per share.
b. Delta earnings: a measure of proportional changes in adjusted earnings per share.
c. "Relative strength" rate of return.
d. Indicator of very low current earnings.
e. Ratio of book value of equity per share to stock price.
f. Applicable federal tax rate.
g. Average proportional cut in dividends.
h. Return on equity.

4. *Immaturity and smallness.* This index differentiates between the older and larger firms—which have accumulated substantial fixed assets and have a more secure economic position and a lower degree of risk—and the small, younger, and riskier firms. Among the descriptors in this index are:

a. Logarithm of total assets.
b. Capitalization: market value of common equity.
c. Market share.
d. Ratio of net plant to gross plant.
e. Ratio of gross plant to common equity.
f. Ratio of estimated net plant in current dollars to common equity.
g. Number of prior years of available monthly prices.
h. Earnings history.

5. *Growth orientation.* This index measures the risk associated with the so-called high-multiple stocks. Among the descriptors used are:

a. A measure of normal payout.
b. Dividend yield.
c. Asset growth rate.
d. Variability of capital structure.
e. Earnings-price ratio.

6. *Financial structure.* This index measures financial risk by incorporating leverage (long-term debt and equity as a percentage of book value), coverage of fixed charges, the ratio of debt to total assets, liquidity, and net monetary debt. In general, the more highly leveraged a financial structure, the greater is the risk to the common stockholders. These factors include:

      a. Book leverage: book value (long-term debt plus preferred equity) divided by market book value (common equity).

      b. Market leverage: book value (long-term debt plus preferred equity) plus market value (common equity) divided by market value (common equity).

      c. Ratio of total debt to assets.

      d. Estimated probability of noncoverage of fixed charges, using a trend value for current operating income.

      e. Ratio of typical cash flow to current liabilities.

      f. Liquidity of current financial position.

      g. Potential dilution.

      h. Proportional adjustment to earnings for inflation.

      i. Tax liability adjustment to net monetary debt.

7. *Other characteristics.* In addition to these six risk indexes, Rosenberg uses special variables for each industry group to account for risk that is typical of the industry itself and cannot be explained by the preceding six indexes. These include factors such as:

      a. NYSE listing.

      b. Commodities exchange listing.

      c. Raw material ownership.

      d. Producers goods manufacturers.

      e. Retailers.

      f. Wholesalers.

      g. Coefficient of variation of quarterly earnings about trend.

      h. Ratio of plant to total sales.

      i. Estimated probability that operating income may fall below fixed charges.

      j. Ratio of intangibles to market value (or equity).

      k. S&P quality rating and indicator for its existence.

      l. Operating leverage.

      m. Variability of operating income.

      n. Growth rate of operating income.

      o. Operating profit margin.

      p. Mean retained earnings per dollar of assets.

      q. Rate of growth of total sales.

      r. Estimate of nonsustainable growth.

      s. Marketability (annual trading volume).

      t. Negative returns in the past.

      u. Variability of proportional earnings growth rate.

      v. Variability of earnings-price ratio.

      w. Rate of return on investment.

      x. Growth valuation adjustments.

EXTRAMARKET COVARIANCE

Basically, Rosenberg's research provides a more refined decomposition of risk and return. The simple decomposition of return (and risk) is

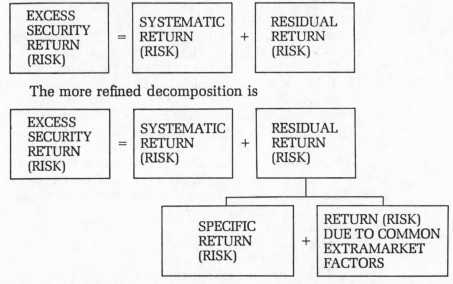

The more refined decomposition is

As discussed earlier, systematic risk is the degree to which security returns are related to market moves. The measure of systematic risk is beta. Systematic return, equal to the security beta times the market excess return (the excess of market return over the risk-free rate) is the component of return arising from systematic risk. The residual return is merely any remaining return that cannot be explained by the systematic return. The residual risk can, however, be further broken down into specific risk and extramarket covariance.

Specific risk is the uncertainty in the return that arises from events that are specific to the firm. Specific risk is unrelated to events that impact on other firms and is sometimes referred to as the "unique" risk or "independent" risk of the company (see Rosenberg et al. [233, p. 88]).

Extramarket covariance is the remaining component of residual risk. It is manifested as a tendency of related assets to move together in a way that is independent of the market as a whole. The term "covariance" refers to the tendency of stock prices to move together, or "covary." The term "extramarket" means that these comovements are not related to the movements of the market as a whole. Extramarket covariance can be thought of as the middle ground between systematic and specific risk. Systematic risk impacts all firms. Specific risk impacts only one firm. Extramarket covariance impacts a homogeneous group of firms, such as those belonging to a certain industry or those with large capitalizations.

For individual stocks specific risk is most important, accounting for about 50 percent of the total risk, with the remainder about equally divided between systematic risk and extramarket covariance. For a well-diversified portfolio, systematic risk is likely to be 80 or 90 percent of the total risk.

For portfolios with concentrations of stocks in certain industry groups, or classes of stocks such as interest-sensitive stocks, extramarket covariance is very important. Thus, the construction of prudent, well-reasoned portfolios requires the prediction of all three aspects of risk—systematic, specific, and extramarket. It is noteworthy in this regard that the Rosenberg prediction scheme derives estimates of both market returns and extramarket covariances from a single underlying model. (The interested reader will find a general explanation of this procedure in Rosenberg and Guy [227] and a detailed explanation in Rosenberg [233]).

EMPIRICAL TESTS OF FUNDAMENTAL BETAS

Rosenberg and Marathe [229] have compared the forecasting accuracy of the so-called fundamental betas with the predictive power of historically derived and regression-adjusted betas (vis-à-vis the Merrill Lynch procedure) over 230 months with an average of 1,200 firms studied in each month. Using historically derived and regression-adjusted values as a benchmark, Rosenberg and Marathe compared the predictive power of each of their various prediction rules. These comparisons are summarized in Table 33–3.

Based only on their market variability descriptors, there were significant increases in predictive power (when compared with the historically derived and regression-adjusted values). Specifically, the use of their market variability descriptors added 57 percent to the predictive power for beta and 22 percent to the predictive power for the residual standard deviation. What is most striking, however, is that by using only fundamental information—with no market variability descriptors whatsoever—Rosenberg and Marathe obtained 45 percent and 10 percent improvements in the predictive power of beta and the residual standard deviation, respectively.

TABLE 33–3: A comparison of the forecasting accuracy of historically
derived betas and Rosenberg and Marathe's fundamentally derived betas

	Predictive power	
Values derived from	Beta (percent)	Residual standard deviation (percent)
Historically derived and regression adjusted	100%	100%
Using only market variability descriptors	157	122
Using only fundamental descriptors	145	110
Using the complete prediction rule	186	132

Source: Rosenberg and Marathe [229, p. 134].

When both market variability information and fundamental
information were combined into their complete decision rule,
the results were little short of remarkable. There was an 86
percent improvement in the predictive power for beta and a 32
percent increase in the predictive power for the residual standard deviation. Thus, the so-called fundamental betas provide
the linch pin between theory and application.

Chapter 34

Inflation and valuation

The most provocative financial article to appear in the last decade was published in 1979 by Franco Modigliani and Richard Cohn. In this article, Modigliani, a world-famous financial theorist, alleges that ". . . because of inflation-induced errors, investors have systematically undervalued the stock market by 50 percent." [192, p. 24] Since the Modigliani-Cohn position is destined to stir much debate, the basic points of their arguments are summarized in this chapter.

MODIGLIANI AND COHN'S THESIS

Theoretically, equity investments represent claims against physical assets whose real (inflation-adjusted) returns should be unaffected by inflation. Moreover, many equity investments represent claims against levered assets (those partially funded by debt). In inflationary times, these debts have the advantage that they are repaid with devalued currencies.

In reality, however, equities have not provided the much-sought hedge against inflation. In nominal (noninflation-adjusted) terms, the market indices have not progressed since the upward inflationary spiral started in the late 1960s. In real (inflation-adjusted) terms, the major market indices have declined by almost half over the same period.

The explanation for the dismal performance of the equity investments over the last 15 years must, by definition, rest with the investor perception that real (inflation-adjusted) earnings have decreased and/or the fact that investors demand a higher earnings capitalization rate.

As discussed in Chapter 7, a common valuation procedure concentrates on the "multiple" that the market places on a company's earnings. The reciprocal of the earnings multiple is

the *earnings capitalization rate*. Thus, a company that is
priced at an earnings multiple of five has an earnings capitalization rate of 20 percent ($^1/_5$). Similarly, a company that is
prices at an earnings multiple of 20 has an earnings capitalization rate of 5 percent ($^1/_{20}$).

The earnings capitalization rate is the rate of return demanded by the marketplace for capital. As illustrated in the
preceding examples, earnings multiples are inversely related
to earnings capitalization rates. Thus, earnings multiples are
depressed if investors demand higher rates of return for the
use of their capital.

By this formulation, the market price of a stock is equal to its
earnings divided by its earnings capitalization rate. It follows,
therefore, that the price of a stock will fall when either earnings decrease or capitalization rates increase.

Using this formulation, most analysts place the responsibility for the market's dismal performance since the late 1960s on
the inflation-adjusted earnings component. Citing such evidence as the fact that adjusted earnings of industrial corporations *declined* from $38.2 billion in 1967 to $30.2 in 1977, this
conclusion seems warranted.

Modigliani and Cohn disagree. While they contend that it is
proper to adjust earnings downward, they contend that
analysts should factor in the *beneficial* effect that inflation has
on the company's debts.

An outstanding explanation of how inflation reduces reported earnings—even though true earnings are unaffected—is
provided by Stanford Rose's interpretation of Modigliani and
Cohn's work.

> . . . Suppose the rate of inflation is zero, and a company with
> earnings before taxes and interest charges of $100 borrows
> $1,000 from a bank for a one-year period. Since there is no
> inflation, the company pays the real rate of interest—say, 3
> percent. So pretax profits equal $100 minus $30 in interest, or
> $70.
>
> Now assume that the inflation rate suddenly jumps to 8 per-
> cent. If the company's loan is a variable-rate obligation, the
> bank immediately raises its interest charge to 11 percent—3
> percent plus the 8 percent inflation premium. Interest charges
> thereupon rise from $30 to $110.
>
> In an accounting sense, the company's $70 profit has tem-
> porarily turned into a $10 loss. In a real sense, however, noth-
> ing whatever has happened to profits. At the end of the year, the
> company pays the bank back the $1,000. But since inflation has
> eroded the value of this repayment by 8 percent, its "real"

worth is $80 less, or only $920. If that $80 were added back into company profits, these would remain at the original $70. Unfortunately, according to generally accepted accounting principles, corporations must sock earnings for interest expenses, but they cannot adjust them upward for repayments made in depreciated dollars (or for the higher nominal values of assets bought with the loan proceeds). So the profits of industrial corporations seem to be much lower than they actually are.

Consider some data for 1977, which is the most recent year for which true corporate profits can be estimated. The debt owed by the average industrial corporation in that year amounted to about five times its annual profits. But the real burden of that debt obviously fell by the 1977 rate of inflation, or by about 7 percent. In order to measure corporate profits accurately, it is therefore necessary to raise reported earnings by approximately 35 percent—the rate of inflation times the amount of outstanding net debt. Since the Department of Commerce estimates that understated depreciation and phony inventory gains reduced 1977 reported profits by about a third, the required adjustments just about cancel out.

The widely publicized notion that true corporate profits decline sharply during a period of high inflation turns out to be a myth. [222, p. 139]

In all, Modigliani and Cohn explored three possible explanations for the apparent contradiction between the theoretical ability of equities to hedge against inflation, and the reality that they have not. First, they examined the possibility that inflation-adjusted profits may actually have deteriorated. Second, they examined the possibility that inflation has boosted required capitalization rates (the rates of return demanded by equity investors in exchange for the use of their capital). Third, they examined the possibility that "in the presence of unaccustomed and fluctuating inflation . . . [investors] price equities in ways that fail to reflect their true economic value." [192, p. 25]

CORPORATE PROFITABILITY AND THE LEVEL OF THE MARKET

To analyze the real (inflation-adjusted) profitability of corporate capital Modigliani and Cohn studied two measures of return on capital: corporate value added and return on replacement cost. To measure corporate value added they calculated total return as "the sum of interest plus after-tax profits adjusted to eliminate the effect of paper gains on inventories and to reflect depreciation on a replacement, rather than an historical cost basis." [192, p. 25] Except for the mid-60s bulge, Modigliani and Cohn found this series to be basically "trend-less . . . [and] from 1975 on, . . . [to be] not significantly different from, and certainly not lower than, that prevailing from the beginning of the 1950s through the first half of the 1960s." [192, p. 25] Similarly, they found historical returns on replacement costs (the ratio of the total return used in the first series to the estimated replacement cost) to be "roughly flat with a bulge in the mid-60s." [192, p. 25]

On the basis of this evidence, Modigliani and Cohn con-clude that, despite inflation, corporate profits have not de-clined over the last decade. In reconciling this conclusion with the popular view that inflation has eroded profits, Modigliani and Cohn emphasized two important points. First, the mid-1960s represented a period of unprecedented returns on capi-tal and should not be used as a reference point. Second, earn-ings per share—a readily available and popular measure of return—underestimate true corporate profits.

Modigliani and Cohn also addressed the popular claim that inflated profits precipitate inflated taxes on the real (inflation adjusted) profits. They correctly point out, however, that this claim "fails to recognize . . . that stockholders are not taxed on that part of their return that consists of depreciation of debt. In other words, they are allowed to deduct their entire interest expense even though the portion of it corresponding to the inflation premium is really a return on capital. Because of this the share of pretax operating income paid in taxes declines with the rate of inflation." [192, p. 27]

Thus, our tax system erroneously taxes inflated profits while, at the same time, erroneously reducing the inflated prof-its by classifying a portion of return of capital as an interest expense. For the market as whole (although not necessarily for individual firms) these effects tend to cancel out, leading Mo-digliani and Cohn to conclude that the failure of equities to provide a hedge against inflation cannot be traced to taxation or a deterioration in corporate profitability.

As a second possible explanation for the failure of equity investments to provide the theoretical hedge against inflation, Modigliani and Cohn evaluated the possibility that the earn-ings capitalization rate demanded by the marketplace should be systematically raised as inflation increases (i.e., the price-earnings ratios should be systematically lowered).

Theoretically, an equity's nominal (noninflation-adjusted)

growth fully reflects the rate of inflation. If the price earnings ratio remains constant, say at 5, a 10 percent earnings increase will translate into a 10 percent price increase. Conversely, if earnings growth parallels the rate of inflation, the only way market values will not pace the rate of inflation is if the market applies a lower earnings multiple to the inflated earnings.

Basically, in an inflationary environment, interest rates rise by the rate of inflation (to compensate lenders for the erosion of the real purchasing power of their claims). This means that there are two equivalent ways to determine the value of a firm in the world of inflation: (1) to capitalize real (inflation-adjusted) profits at the real capitalization rate, or (2) discount the stream of nominal (not inflation-adjusted) earnings at an appropriate nominal discount rate. In Modigliani and Cohn's words "if either valuation is done correctly, the real value of the firm will be found to be unaffected by inflation." [192, p. 29]

Again, quoting from Rose

> Instead of discounting future earnings by the real rate of interest—2 or 3 percent, plus an appropriate risk premium—investment advisers have been discounting them by 7 or 8 percent, plus the risk premium. Thus, a mistake in evaluating the numerator of the stock-valuation ratio gives rise to another, and even more serious, mistake in evaluating the denominator, the capitalization rate . . . [and, as a result] . . . stock values have been scissored by rapid changes in both numerators and denominators. [222, p. 140]

The magnitude of this "scissoring" effect is enormous. According to Modigliani and Cohn, "each percentage point of inflation typically reduces market value by a staggering 13 percent relative to what it would be if valued rationally . . . [and as a result of the failure of the investment community to recognize the errors in traditional valuation] as of year-end 1977 . . . the actual market value [of the S&P index] was only 46 percent of its correct value." [192, p. 33]

Chapter 35

Conclusion

Modern portfolio theory-based applications include:

1. Security valuation.
2. Portfolio optimization.
3. Asset allocation.
4. Performance measurement.

Basically, MPT holds that there is a forecastable relationship between risk and return. Moving from this premise, MPT first asserts that by discarding the traditional approaches to security analysis, it is possible accurately to forecast expected return, as well as the key risk relationships that are inherent in expected returns. After first using MPT techniques to derive estimates both of expected returns and risk relationships for individual investments, MPT can then be used to construct portfolios which uniquely balance an investor's willingness to assume risks with the investor's desire for larger and larger returns. The third area to which MPT has been applied is asset allocation—basically analyzing investment alternatives to determine the combination of available assets that best matches investor preferences.

The first three applications include varying elements of classification, estimation, and control of risk. The fourth, and final, application uses MPT compatible techniques for the continuous assessment of investment performance against the MPT-derived estimates.

While many people perceive "their" favorite security (or, securities) as somehow "unique," there is no evidence to support the hypothesis that in toto, organized securities markets operate in this fashion. [237, p. 198] The reality is that organized securities markets operate in a very organized way.

The gap between theory and practice which long characterized the investment profession is rapidly disappearing. As a result, people are becoming less naïve. Today, there is a growing awareness that if one investment manager consistently outperforms the risk-adjusted averages, others must consistently underperform the same average. Logically, as the "losers" in what Keynes called the "game of investing" become aware of their underperformance, they will change managers. In their selection of a new manager, they will choose either a firm that can provide the fair rate of return inherent in a "passive" strategy, or one of the consistent "winners." In either case, however, the population of naïve investors that any consistent "winners" must depend upon for their above-average returns will shrink.

Beyond the new words like quants (those who apply quantitative investment techniques), super-quants, pseudo-quants, and even turncoat-quants (those who purportedly understand MPT but make a living out of lobbying against it), prudence is no longer defined as performance. *Prudence is a methodology that allows investors to classify, estimate, and control risk and return.*

Bibliography

1. Alexander, Sidney S. "Price Movements in Speculative Markets: Trends or Random Walks," *Industrial Management Review*, vol. 2, no. 2 (May 1961), pp. 7–26. Reprinted (and expanded) in Paul H. Cootner, ed., *The Random Character of Stock Market Prices*. Cambridge, Mass.: M.I.T. Press, 1964, pp. 199–218 and 338–372.

2. Altman, E., B. Jacquillat, and M. Levasseur. "La Stabilité tu Coefficient Beta," *Analyse Financière*, no. 16, 1st Trimestre (1974), pp. 43–54.

3. Andersen, Theodore A. "Trends in Profit Sensitivity," *Journal of Finance*, vol. 28, no. 4 (December 1963), pp. 637–46. Reprinted in James Lorie and Richard Brealey, ed., *Modern Developments in Investment Management: A Book of Readings*. 2d ed. Hinsdale, Ill.: Dryden Press, 1978, pp. 659–68.

4. Ambachtsheer, Keith P. "Profit Potential in an 'Almost Efficient' Market," *Journal of Portfolio Management*, vol. 1, no. 1 (Fall 1974), pp. 84–87.

5. _____. "Can Selectivity Pay in an Efficient Market?" *Journal of Portfolio Management*, vol. 2, no. 4 (Summer 1976), pp. 19–22.

6. _____. "Where Are the Customers' Alphas?" *Journal of Portfolio Management*, vol. 4, no. 1 (Fall 1977), pp. 52–56.

7. Arditti, Fred D. "Risk and the Required Return on Equity," *Journal of Finance*, vol. 22, no. 1 (March 1967), pp. 19–36.

8. Babcock, Guildord C. "The Concept of Sustainable Growth," *Financial Analysts Journal*, vol. 26, no. 3 (May–June 1970), pp. 108–44.

9. _____. "The Trend and Stability of Earnings per Share." *Proceedings of the Seminar on the Analysis of Security Prices*, University of Chicago, November 1970.

10. Bachelier, Louis. *Théorie de la Speculation*. Paris: Gauthier–Villars, 1900. Translation by A. James Boness, reprinted in Paul H. Cootner, ed., *The Random Character of Stock Market Prices*. Cambridge, Mass.: M.I.T. Press, 1964, pp. 17–78.

11. Ball, Philip, and John W. Kennelly. "The Informational Content of Quarterly Earnings. An Extension and Some Further Evidence," *Journal of Business*, vol. 45, no. 3 (July 1972), pp. 403–15.

285

12. Ball, Ray, and Philip Brown. "An Empirical Evaluation of Accounting Income Numbers," *Journal of Accounting Research*, vol. 6, no. 2 (Autumn 1968), pp. 159–78. Reprinted in James Lorie and Richard Brealey, ed., *Modern Developments in Investment Management: A Book of Readings*. 2d ed. Hinsdale, Ill.: Dryden Press, 1978, pp. 559–78.

13. Ball, Ray, and Ross Watts. "Some Time Properties of Accounting Incomes," *Journal of Finance*, vol. 27, no. 3 (June 1972), pp. 663–82.

14. Barker, C. Austin. "Effective Stock Splits," *Harvard Business Review*, vol. 34, no. 1 (January–February 1956), pp. 101–06.

15. _____. "Stock Splits in a Bull Market," *Harvard Business Review*, vol. 35, no. 3 (May–June 1957), pp. 72–79. Reprinted in E. Bruce Fredrikson, ed., *Frontiers of Investment Analysis*. Scranton, Pa.: International Textbook Co., 1965, pp. 540–51.

16. Bauman, W. Scott. "Performance Objectives of Investors." Occasional Paper No. 2. Financial Analysts Research Foundation, 1975.

17. _____. "Evaluation of the Portfolio Management System." Occasional Paper No. 3. Financial Analysts Research Foundation, 1975.

18. Beaver, William H. "Financial Ratios as Predictors of Failure," *Journal of Accounting Research*, Autumn supplement 1966, pp. 71–111.

19. _____. "Market Prices, Financial Ratios and the Prediction of Failure," *Journal of Accounting Research*, vol. 6, no. 2 (Autumn 1968), pp. 179–92.

20. Beaver, William, and James Manegold. "The Association between Market-Determined and Accounting-Determined Measures of Systematic Risk: Some Further Evidence," *Journal of Financial and Quantitative Analysis*, vol. 10, no. 2 (June 1975), pp. 231–84.

21. Beaver, William, Paul Kettler, and Myron Scholes. "The Association between Market Determined and Accounting Determined Risk Measures," *Accounting Review*, vol. 45, no. 11 (October 1970), pp. 654–82.

22. Bergstrom, Gary L. "A New Route to Higher Returns and Lower Risks," *Journal of Portfolio Management*, vol. 2, no. 1 (Fall 1975), pp. 30–38.

23. Black, Fischer. "Capital Market Equilibrium with Restricted Borrowing," *Journal of Business*, vol. 45, no. 3 (July 1972), pp. 444–55.

24. _____. "Yes, Virginia, There Is Hope: Tests of the Value Line Ranking System," *Financial Analysts Journal*, vol. 29, no. 5 (September–October 1973), pp. 10–14.

25. _____. "The Investment Policy Spectrum: Individuals, Endowment Funds and Pension Funds," *Financial Analysts Journal*, vol. 32, no. 1 (January–February 1976), pp. 23–31. Reprinted in James Lorie and Richard Brealey, ed., *Modern Developments in Investment Management: A Book of Readings*. 2d ed. Hinsdale, Ill.: Dryden Press, 1978, pp. 397–405.

26. Black, Fischer, Michael C. Jensen, and Myron Scholes. "The Capital Asset Pricing Model: Some Empirical Tests," in Michael C. Jensen,

ed., *Studies in the Theory of Capital Markets.* New York: Praeger Publishers, Inc., 1972.

27. Black, Fischer, and Myron Scholes. "The Effects of Dividend Yield and Dividend Policy on Common Stock Prices and Returns," *Journal of Financial Economics,* vol. 1, no. 1 (May 1974), pp. 1–22.

28. Blume, Marshall E. "The Assessment of Portfolio Performance—An Application to Portfolio Theory." Unpublished Ph.D. dissertation. University of Chicago, 1968.

29. _____. "Portfolio Theory: A Step towards Its Practical Application," *Journal of Business,* vol. 43, no. 2 (April 1970), pp. 152–73.

30. _____. "On the Assessment of Risk," *Journal of Finance,* vol. 26, no. 1 (March 1972), pp. 1–10. Reprinted in James Lorie and Richard Brealey, ed., *Modern Developments in Investment Management: A Book of Readings.* 2d ed. Hinsdale, Ill.: Dryden Press, 1978, pp. 432–41.

31. _____. "Betas and Their Regression Tendencies," *Journal of Finance,* vol. 30, no. 3 (June 1975), pp. 785–96.

32. Blume, Marshall E., and Irwin Friend. "Risk, Investment Strategy, and Long-run Rates of Return," *Review of Economics and Statistics,* vol. 61, no. 3 (August 1974), pp. 259–69.

33. Bower, Dorothy H., and Richard S. Bower. "Test of a Stock Valuation Model, *Journal of Finance,* vol. 25, no. 5 (May 1970), pp. 483–92.

34. Brealey, Richard A. *An Introduction to Risk and Return from Common Stock Prices.* Cambridge, Mass.: M.I.T. Press, 1969.

35. _____. *Security Prices in a Competitive Market.* Cambridge, Mass.: M.I.T. Press, 1971.

36. Breen, William. "Low Price-Earnings Ratios and Industry Relatives," *Financial Analysts Journal,* vol. 25, no. 4 (July–August 1969), pp. 125–27.

37. Brennan, Michael J. "Capital Market Equilibrium with Divergent Borrowing and Lending Rates," *Journal of Financial and Quantitative Analysis,* vol. 6, no. 4 (December 1971), pp. 1197–1205.

38. Brown, Philip, and Ray Ball. "An Empirical Evaluation of Accounting Income Numbers," *Journal of Accounting Research,* vol. 6, no. 3 (Autumn 1968), pp. 159–78.

39. Brown, Philip, and Victor Niederhoffer. "The Predictive Content of Quarterly Earnings," *Journal of Business,* vol. 41, no. 4 (October 1968), pp. 488–97.

40. Buffett, Warren E. "How Inflation Swindles and Equity Investor," *Fortune,* vol. 95, no. 5 (May 1977), pp. 250–67.

41. Cagan, Phillip. "Common Stock Values and Inflation—The Historical Record of Many Countries," National Bureau of Economic Research, Report No. 13, March 1974.

42. Cohen, A. W. *The Chartcraft Method of Point and Figure Trading.* Larchmont, N.Y.: Chartcraft, Inc., 1963.

43. _____. *Technical Indicator Analysis by Point and Figure Technique.* Larchmont, N.Y.: Chartcraft, Inc., 1963.

44. Cohen, Jerome B., Edward D. Zinbarg, and Arthur Zeikel. *Investment Analysis and Portfolio Management.* Homewood, Ill.: Richard D. Irwin, Inc., 1973.

45. Cohen, Kalman J., and Jerry A. Pogue. "An Empirical Evaluation of Alternative Portfolio Selection Models," *Journal of Business*, vol. 40, no. 2 (April 1967), pp. 166–93.

46. _____. "Some Comments concerning Mutual Fund versus Random Portfolio Performance," *Journal of Business*, vol. 41, no. 2 (April 1968), pp. 180–90.

47. Colker, S. S. "An Analysis of Security Recommendations by Brokerage Houses," *Quarterly Review of Economics and Business*, vol. 3, no. 2 (Summer 1963), pp. 19–28.

48. Cootner, Paul H. "Stock Prices: Random vs. Systematic Changes." *Industrial Management Review*, vol. 3, no. 2 (Spring 1962), pp. 24–45. Reprinted in Paul H. Cootner, ed., *The Random Character of Stock Market Prices.* Cambridge, Mass.: M.I.T. Press, 1964. Reprinted in E. Bruce Fredrikson, ed., *Frontiers of Investment Analysis.* Scranton, Pa.: International Textbook Co., 1965, pp. 489–510.

49. _____. "Stock Market Indexes: Fallacies and Illusions," *Commercial and Financial Chronicle*, vol. 204, no. 6616 (September 29, 1966), pp. 18–19. Reprinted in James Lorie and Richard Brealey, ed., *Modern Developments in Investment Management: A Book of Readings.* 2d ed. Hinsdale, Ill.: Dryden Press, 1978, pp. 94–100.

50. Cootner, Paul H., ed. *The Random Character of Stock Market Prices.* Cambridge, Mass.: M.I.T. Press, 1964.

51. Copeland, R. M., and R. J. Marioni. "Executives' Forecasts of Earnings per Share vs. Forecasts of Naïve Models," *Journal of Business*, vol. 45, no. 4 (October 1972), pp. 497–512.

52. Cowles, Alfred. "Can Stock Market Forecasters Forecast?" *Econometrica*, vol. 1, no. 3 (July 1933), pp. 309–24.

53. _____. "A Revision of Previous Conclusions Regarding Stock Price Behavior," *Econometrica*, vol. 28, no. 4 (October 1960), pp. 909–15. Reprinted in Paul H. Cootner, ed., *The Random Character of Stock Market Prices.* Cambridge, Mass.: M.I.T. Press, 1964, pp. 132–38.

54. Cowles, Alfred, and Herbert F. Jones. "Some À Posteriori Probabilities in Stock Market Action," *Econometrica*, vol. 5, no. 3 (July 1937), pp. 280–94.

55. Cragg, J. G., and Burton G. Malkiel. "The Consensus and Accuracy of Some Predictions of the Growth of Corporate Earnings," *Journal of Finance*, vol. 23, no. 1 (March 1968), pp. 67–84.

56. Crowell, Richard. "Earnings Expectations, Security Valuation and the Cost of Equity Capital." Unpublished Ph.D. dissertation, Massachusetts Institute of Technology, 1967.

57. Cushing, Barry. "The Effects of Accounting Policy Decision on Trends in Reported Corporate Earnings per Share." Ph.D. dissertation, Michigan State University, 1969.

58. Darling, P. G. "The Influence of Expectations and Liquidity on Dividend Policy," *Journal of Political Economy*, vol. 65, no. 3 (June 1957), pp. 209–24.

59. Darvas, Nicholas. *How I Made $2,000,000 in the Stock Market.* Larchmont, N.Y.: American Research Council, 1960.

60. Douglas, George W. "Risk in the Equity Market: An Empirical Appraisal of Market Efficiency." Unpublished Ph.D. dissertation, Yale University, 1967.

61. Durand, David. "Growth Stocks and the Petersburg Paradox," *Journal of Finance*, vol. 12, no. 3 (September 1957), pp. 348–63. Reprinted in James Lorie and Richard Brealey, ed., *Modern Developments in Investment Management: A Book of Readings.* 2d ed. Hinsdale, Ill.: Dryden Press, 1978, pp. 492–507.

62. Edwards, Robert D., and John Magee. *Technical Analysis of Stock Trends.* 4th ed. Springfield, Mass.: John Magee, 1962.

63. Elton, Edwin J., and Martin J. Gruber. "Marginal Stockbroker Tax Rates and the Clientele Effect," *Review of Economics and Statistics*, vol. 52, no. 1 (February 1970), pp. 68–74.

64. ———. "Improving Forecasting through the Design of Homogeneous Groups," *Journal of Business*, vol. 44, no. 4 (October, 1971), pp. 432–50.

65. Elton, Edwin J., Martin J. Gruber, and Manfred W. Padberg. "Optimal Portfolios from Simple Ranking Devices," *Journal of Portfolio Management*, vol. 4, no. 3 (Spring 1978), pp. 15–18.

66. Evans, John L. "Diversification and the Reduction of Dispersion: An Empirical Analysis." Unpublished Ph.D. dissertation, University of Washington, 1968.

67. Evans, John L., and Stephen H. Archer. "Diversification and the Reduction of Dispersion: An Empirical Analysis." *Journal of Finance*, vol. 23, no. 12 (December 1968), pp. 761–67.

68. Fama, Eugene F. "The Behavior of Stock Market Prices," *Journal of Business*, vol. 38, no. 1 (January 1965), pp. 34–105.

69. ———. "Risk, Return and Equilibrium: Some Clarifying Comments," *Journal of Finance*, vol. 23, no. 3 (March 1968), pp. 29–40.

70. ———. "Efficient Capital Markets: A Review of Theory and Empirical Work," *Journal of Finance*, vol. 25, no. 2 (May 1970), pp. 383–417. Reprinted in James Lorie and Richard Brealey, ed., *Modern Developments in Investment Management: A Book of Readings.* 2d ed. Hinsdale, Ill.: Dryden Press, 1978, pp. 109–53.

71. ———. "Risk, Return and Equilibrium," *Journal of Political Economy*, vol. 79, no. 1 (January–February 1971), pp. 30–55.

72. ———. "Components of Investment Performance," *Journal of Finance*, vol. 27, no. 5 (June 1972), pp. 551–67. Reprinted in James Lorie and Richard Brealey, ed., *Modern Developments in Investment Management: A Book of Readings.* 2d ed. Hinsdale, Ill.: Dryden Press, 1978, pp. 448–65.

73. ———. "A Note on the Market Model and the Two Parameter

Model," *Journal of Finance*, vol. 28, no. 5 (December 1973), pp. 1181–86.

74. _____. "The Empirical Relationship between the Dividend and Investment Decisions of Firms," *American Economic Review*, vol. 44, no. 3 (June 1974), pp. 304–18.

75. Fama, Eugene F., and H. Babiak. "Dividend Policy: An Empirical Analysis," *Journal of the American Statistical Association*, vol. 63, no. 12 (December 1968), pp. 1132–61.

76. Fama, Eugene F., and Marshall E. Blume. "Filter Rules and Stock Market Trading," *Journal of Business*, vol. 39, no. 1, pt. 2 (January 1966), pp. 226–41.

77. Fama, Eugene F., and James D. MacBeth. "Risk, Return, and Equilibrium: Empirical Tests," *Journal of Political Economy*, vol. 81, no. 3 (May–June 1973), pp. 607–36.

78. Fama, Eugene F., Lawrence Fisher, and Michael C. Jensen. "The Adjustment of Stock Prices to New Information," *International Economic Review*, vol. 10, no. 1 (February 1969), pp. 1–21. Reprinted in James Lorie and Richard Brealey, ed., *Modern Developments in Investment Management: A Book of Readings*. 2d ed. Hinsdale, Ill.: Dryden Press, 1978, pp. 177–97.

79. Fama, Eugene F., Lawrence Fisher, Michael C. Jensen, and Richard Roll. "The Adjustment of Stock Prices to New Information," *International Economic Review*, vol. 10, no. 2 (February 1969), pp. 1–21.

80. Farrar, Donald Eugene. *The Investment Decision under Uncertainty*. Englewood Cliffs, N.J.: Prentice-Hall, Inc., 1962.

81. Farrell, James L., Jr. "Analyzing Covariation of Return to Develop Homogeneous Stock Groupings," *Journal of Business*, vol. 47, no. 2 (April 1974), pp. 186–207.

82. _____. "Homogeneous Stock Groupings: Implications for Portfolio Management," *Financial Analysts Journal*, vol. 31, no. 3 (May–June 1975), pp. 50–62.

83. _____. "The Multi-Index Model and Practical Portfolio Analysis." Occasional Paper No. 4. Financial Analysts Research Foundation, 1976.

84. Farrell, James, and Keith Ambachtsheer. "Can Active Management Add Value?" Unpublished paper, 1979.

85. Ferber, Robert. "Short-run Effects on Stock Market Services on Stock Prices," *Journal of Finance*, vol. 13, no. 1 (March 1958), pp. 80–95.

86. Ferguson, Robert. "Active Portfolio Management," *Financial Analysts Journal*, vol. 31, no. 3 (May–June 1975), pp. 63–72.

87. Fisher, Irving. *The Rate of Interest*. American Economic Association, 1907.

88. Fisher, Lawrence. "Determinants of Risk Premiums on Corporate Bonds," *Journal of Political Economy*, vol. 67, no. 3 (June 1959), pp. 217–37. Reprinted in James Lorie and Richard Brealey, ed., *Modern Developments in Investment Management: A Book of Readings*. 2d ed. Hinsdale, Ill.: Dryden Press, 1978, pp. 727–47.

89. _____. "Outcomes for 'Random' Investments in Common Stocks Listed on the New York Stock Exchange," *Journal of Business*, vol. 3, no. 4 (April 1965), pp. 149–61.

90. _____. "Using Modern Portfolio Theory to Maintain an Efficiently Diversified Portfolio," *Financial Analysts Journal*, vol. 31, no. 3 (May–June 1975), pp. 73–85.

91. Fisher, Lawrence, and James H. Lorie. "Rates of Return on Investments in Common Stocks," *Journal of Business*, vol. 37, no. 1 (January 1964), pp. 1–21. Reprinted (in part) in E. Bruce Fredrikson, ed., *Frontiers of Investment Analysis*. Scranton. Pa.: International Textbook Co., 1965, pp. 159–76.

92. _____. "Rates of Return on Investments in Common Stocks: The Year-by-Year Record, 1926–1965," *Journal of Business*, vol. 41, no. 3 (July 1968), pp. 291–316. Reprinted in James Lorie, and Richard Brealey, ed., *Modern Developments in Investment Management: A Book of Readings*. 2d ed. Hinsdale, Ill.: Dryden Press, 1978, pp. 16–41.

93. _____. "Some Studies of Variability of Returns on Investment in Common Stocks," *Journal of Business*, vol. 43, no. 2 (April 1970), pp. 99–134. Reprinted in James Lorie and Richard Brealey, ed., *Modern Developments in Investment Management: A Book of Readings*. 2d ed. Hinsdale, Ill.: Dryden Press, 1978, pp. 42–77.

94. _____. *A Half Century of Returns on Stocks and Bonds*. Chicago: University of Chicago, Graduate School of Business, 1977. Reprinted (in part) in James Lorie and Richard Brealey, ed., *Modern Developments in Investment Management: A Book of Readings*. 2d ed. Hinsdale, Ill.: Dryden Press, 1978, pp. 78–93.

95. Fouse, William L. "Risk and Liquidity: The Keys to Stock Price Behavior," *Financial Analysts Journal*, vol. 32, no. 3 (May–June 1976), pp. 35–45.

96. _____. "Risk and Liquidity Revisited," *Financial Analysts Journal*, vol. 33, no. 1 (January–February 1977), pp. 40–5.

97. Fouse, William F., William W. Jahnke, and Barr Rosenberg. "Is Beta Phlogiston?" *Financial Analysts Journal*, vol. 30, no. 1 (January–February 1974), pp. 70–80.

98. Francis, Jack Clark. "Do Some Stocks Consistently Lead or Lag the Market?" Working Paper No. 5-12. Rodney L. White Center for Financial Research, University of Pennsylvania, n.d.

99. Friedman, Milton, and Anna J. Schwartz. *Monetary History of the United States, 1867–1960*. Princeton, N.J.: Princeton University Press, 1963.

100. Friend, Irwin, et al. *A Study of Mutual Funds*. Prepared for the Securities and Exchange Commission by the Securities Research Unit, Wharton School of Finance and Commerce, University of Pennsylvania. Washington, D.C.: U.S. Government Printing Office, 1962.

101. Friend, Irwin, and Marshall Blume. "Risk and the Long-Run Rate of Return on NYSE Common Stocks." Working Paper No. 18-72, The Wharton School of Finance and Commerce, Rodney L. White Center for Financial Research, 1972.

102. Friend, Irwin, and Douglas Vickers. "Portfolio Selection and Investment Performance," *Journal of Finance*, vol. 20, no. 2 (September 1965), pp. 391–415.

103. Friend, Irwin, Marshall Blume, and Jean Crockett. *Mutual Funds and Other Institutional Investors: A New Perspective.* New York: McGraw-Hill Book Company, 1970.

104. Friend, Irwin, James Longstreet, Ervin Miller, and Arleigh Hess. *Investment Banking and the New Issues Market.* New York: New York World Publishing Company, 1967.

105. Furst, R. W. "Does Listing Increase the Market Price of Common Stock?" *Journal of Business*, vol. 43, no. 4 (April 1970), pp. 174–80.

106. Gaumnitz, Jack E. "Investment Diversification under Uncertainty: An Examination of the Number of Securities in a Diversified Portfolio." Unpublished Ph.D. dissertation, Stanford University, 1967.

107. Gaviria, Nestor G. "Inflation and Capital Asset Market Prices: Theory and Tests." Unpublished Ph.D. dissertation, Graduate School of Business, Stanford University, 1973.

108. Godfrey, Michael D., Clive W. J. Granger, and Oskar Morgenstern. "The Random-Walk Hypothesis of Stock Market Behavior." *Kyklos*, vol. 17, fasc. 1 (1964), pp. 1–30.

109. Graham, Benjamin, David L. Dodd, and Sidney Cottle. *Security Analysis.* 4th ed. New York: McGraw-Hill Book Company, 1951.

110. Granger, Clive W. J. "What the Random-Walk Model Does Not Say," *Financial Analysts Journal*, vol. 26, no. 3 (May–June 1970), pp. 91–93.

111. Granger, Clive W. J., and Oskar Morgenstern. "Spectral Analysis of New York Stock Market Prices," *Kyklos*, vol. 16 (1963), pp. 1–27. Reprinted in Paul H. Cootner, ed., *The Random Character of Stock Market Prices*, Cambridge, Mass.: M.I.T. Press, 1964.

112. Grayson, C. Jackson. "Decisions under Uncertainty: Drilling Decisions by Oil and Gas Operators," Division of Research, Harvard Business School, 1960. Chapter 10, "Utility," reprinted in James Lorie and Richard Brealey, ed., *Modern Developments in Investment Management: A Book of Readings.* 2d ed. Hinsdale, Ill.: Dryden Press, 1978. pp. 275–309.

113. Green, David, Jr., and Joel Segall. "Brickbats and Straw Men: A Reply to Brown and Niederhoffer," *Journal of Business*, vol. 41, no. 4 (October 1968), pp. 498–502.

114. ———. "The Predictive Power of First Quarter Earnings Reports," *Journal of Business*, vol. 40, no. 1 (January 1967), pp. 44–55.

115. ———. "Return of Straw Man," *Journal of Business*, vol. 43, no. 1 (January 1970), pp. 63–65.

116. Hagin, Robert L. "An Empirical Evaluation of Selected Hypotheses Related to Price Changes in the Stock Market." Unpublished Ph.D. dissertation, University of California (Los Angeles), 1966.

117. Hagin, Robert L. (with Chris Mader). *The New Science of Investing.* Homewood, Ill.: Dow Jones-Irwin, Inc., 1973.

118. Hakansson, Nils H. "Capital Growth and the Mean-Variance Approach to Portfolio Selection," *Journal of Financial and Quantitative Analysis*, vol. 6, no. 1 (January 1971), pp. 517–58.

119. Hanna, M. "Short Interest: Bullish or Bearish?—Comment," *Journal of Finance*, vol. 23, no. 6 (June 1968), pp. 520–23.

120. Hausman, Warren H. "A Note on the Value Line Contest: A Test of the Predictability of Stock-Price Changes," *Journal of Business*, vol. 42, no. 3 (July 1969), pp. 317–20.

121. Hausman, Warren H., R. R. West, and J. A. Largay. "Stock Splits, Price Changes, and Trading Profits: A Synthesis," *Journal of Business*, vol. 44, no. 1 (January 1971), pp. 69–77.

122. Hodges, Stewert D., and Richard A. Brealey. "Portfolio Selection in a Dynamic and Uncertain World," *Financial Analysts Journal*, vol. 29, no. 2 (March–April 1973), pp. 50–65. Reprinted in James Lorie and Richard Brealey, ed., *Modern Developments in Investment Management: A Book of Readings*. 2d ed. Hinsdale, Ill.: Dryden Press, 1978, pp. 348–63.

123. Homa, Kenneth E., and Dwight M. Jaffee. "The Supply of Money and Common Stock Prices," *Journal of Finance*, vol. 26, no. 5 (December 1971), pp. 1045–66.

124. Horrigan, James. "The Determination of Long-Term Credit Standing with Financial Ratios," *Journal of Accounting Research*, Autumn supplement 1966, pp. 44–62.

125. Houthakker, Hendrik S. "Systematic and Random Elements in Short-Term Price Movements," *American Economic Review*, vol. 51, no. 2 (May 1961), pp. 164–72.

126. Ibbotson, Roger G. "Price Performance of Common Stock New Issues," *Journal of Financial Economics*, vol. 2, no. 3 (September 1975), pp. 235–72.

127. Ibbotson, Roger G., and Rex A. Sinquefield. *Stocks, Bonds, Bills and Inflation: The Past (1926–1976) and the Future (1977–2000)*. Charlottesville, Va.: Financial Analysts Research Foundation, 1977.

128. ———. "Stocks, Bonds, Bills and Inflation: Year-by-Year Historical Returns (1926–74)," *Journal of Business*, vol. 49, no. 1 (January 1976), pp. 11–47.

129. Jaffe, Jeffrey F. "Special Information and Insider Trading," *Journal of Business*, vol. 47, no. 3 (July 1974), p. 410–29.

130. James, F. E., Jr. "Monthly Moving Averages—An Effective Investment Tool?" *Journal of Financial and Quantitative Analysis*, vol. 3, no. 3 (September 1968), pp. 315–26.

131. Jensen, Michael C. "Random Walks: Reality or Myth—Comment," *Financial Analysts Journal*, vol. 23, no. 6 (November–December 1967), pp. 77–85.

132. ——— "The Performance of Mutual Funds in the Period 1945–64," *Journal of Finance*, vol. 23, no. 2 (May 1968), pp. 389–416. Reprinted in James Lorie and Richard Brealey, ed., *Modern Developments in Investment Management: A Book of Readings*. 2d ed. Hinsdale, Ill.: Dryden Press, 1978, pp. 231–58.

133. _____. "Risk, the Pricing of Capital Assets, and the Evaluation of Investment Portfolios," *Journal of Business*, vol. 42, no. 4 (April 1969), pp. 167–247.

134. _____. "Capital Markets: Theory and Evidence," *Bell Journal of Economics and Management Science*, vol. 3, no. 2 (Autumn 1972), pp. 357–98.

135. _____. "Tests of Capital Market Theory and Implications of the Evidence." Research Paper No. 1. Financial Analysts Research Foundation, 1975.

136. Jensen, Michael C., ed. *Studies in the Theory of Capital Markets.* New York: Praeger Publishers, 1972.

137. Jensen, Michael C., and George A. Benington. "Random Walks and Technical Theories: Some Additional Evidence," *Journal of Finance*, vol. 25, no. 2 (May 1970), pp. 469–81.

138. _____. "Random Walks and Technical Theories: Some Additional Evidence," *Journal of Finance*, vol. 25, no. 2 (May 1970), pp. 469–81. Reprinted in James Lorie and Richard Brealey, ed., *Modern Developments in Investment Management: A Book of Readings.* 2d ed. Hinsdale, Ill.: Dryden Press, 1978, pp. 164–76.

139. Jiler, William L. *How Charts Can Help You in the Stock Market.* New York: Commodity Research Publication Corp., 1962. Reprinted (in part) in Bill Alder, ed., *The Wall Street Reader.* New York: The World Publishing Co., 1970, pp. 15–23.

140. Joy, O. Maurice, Robert H. Litzenberger, and Richard W. McEnally. "The Adjustment of Stock Prices to Announcements of Unanticipated Changes in Quarterly Earnings," *Journal of Accounting Research*, vol. 15, no. 2 (Autumn 1977), pp. 207–25.

141. Kaish, S. "Odd-Lot Profit and Loss Performance," *Financial Analysts Journal*, vol. 25, no. 9 (September–October 1969), pp. 83–92.

142. Kaplan, Robert S., and Richard Roll. "Investor Evaluation of Accounting Information: Some Empirical Evidence," *Journal of Business*, vol. 45, no. 2 (April 1972), pp. 225–57.

143. Kaplan, Robert S., and Roman L. Weil. "Risk and the Value Line Contest," *Financial Analysts Journal*, vol. 29, no. 4 (July–August 1973), pp. 56–62.

144. Kendall, Maurice George. *The Advanced Theory of Statistics.* London: Griffin, 1943.

145. _____. "The Analysis of Economic Time Series—Part I: Prices," *Journal of the Royal Statistical Society,* Series A (General), vol. 116, pt. 1 (1953), pp. 11–25. Reprinted in Paul H. Cootner, ed., *The Random Character of Stock Market Prices,* Cambridge, Mass.: M.I.T. Press, 1964, pp. 85–99.

146. Kewley, T. J., and R. A. Stevenson. "The Odd-Lot Theory as Revealed by Purchase and Sales Statistics for Individual Stocks," *Financial Analysts Journal*, vol. 23, no. 5 (September–October 1967), pp. 103–06.

147. _____. "The Odd-Lot Theory for Individual Stocks: A Reply," *Fi-*

nancial Analysts Journal, vol. 25, no. 1 (January–February 1969), pp. 99–104.

148. Keynes, John Maynard. *The General Theory of Employment Interest and Money.* London: Macmillan and Company, 1936.

149. King, Benjamin F. "The Latent Statistical Structure of Security Price Changes." Unpublished Ph.D. dissertation, University of Chicago, 1964.

150. _____. "Market and Industry Factors in Stock Price Behavior," *Journal of Business,* vol. 39, no. 1, pt. 2 (January 1966), pp. 139–90.

151. Kisor, Manown, Jr., and Van A. Messner. "The Filter Approach and Earnings Forecasts," *Financial Analysts Journal,* vol. 25, no. 1 (January 1969), pp. 109–15.

152. Kisor, Manown, Jr., and Victor Niederhoffer. "Odd-Lot Short Sales Ratio: It Signals a Market Rise." *Barron's* September 1, 1969, p. 8.

153. Klein, D. J. "The Odd-Lot Stock Trading Theory." Ph.D. dissertation Michigan State University, 1964.

154. Klemkosky, Robert C., and John D. Martin. "The Effect of Market Risk on Portfolio Diversification," *Journal of Finance,* vol. 30, no. 1 (March 1975), pp. 147–54.

155. Kraus, Alan, and Hans Stoll. "Price Impacts of Block Trading on the New York Stock Exchange," *Journal of Finance,* vol. 27, no. 3 (June 1972), pp. 569–88.

156. Latané, Henry Allen, and Donald L. Tuttle. "An Analysis of Common Stock Price Ratios," *Southern Economic Journal,* vol. 33, no. 1 (January 1967), pp. 343–54.

157. Lessard, Donald F. "World, Country and Industry Relationships in Equity Returns: Implications for Risk, Reduction through International Diversification," *Financial Analysts Journal,* vol. 32, no. 1 (January–February 1976), pp. 31–38.

158. Levitz, Gerald D. "Market Risk and the Management of Institutional Equity Portfolios," *Financial Analysts Journal,* vol. 30, no. 1 (January–February 1974), pp. 53ff.

159. Levy, Haim. "Equilibrium in an Imperfect Market: A Constraint on the Number of Securities in the Portfolio," *American Economic Review,* vol. 68, no. 4 (September 1978), pp. 643–58.

160. Levy, Robert A. "An Evaluation of Selected Applications of Stock Market Timing Techniques, Trading Tactics and Trend Analysis." Unpublished Ph.D. dissertation, The American University, Washington, D.C., 1966.

161. _____. "Random Walks: Reality or Myth," *Financial Analysts Journal,* vol. 23, no. 6 (November–December 1967), pp. 129–32.

162. _____. "Random Walks: Reality or Myth—Reply," *Financial Analysts Journal,* vol. 23, no. 1 (January–February 1968), pp. 129–32.

163. _____. "On the Short-Term Stationarity of Beta Coefficients," *Financial Analysts Journal,* vol. 27, no. 6 (November–December 1971), pp. 55–62.

164. _____. "A Note on the Safety of Low P/E Stocks," *Financial Analysts Journal*, vol. 29, no. 1 (January–February 1973), p. 57.

165. Lintner, John. "Distribution of Incomes of Corporation among Dividends, Retained Earnings and Taxes," *American Economic Review*, vol. 46, no. 5 (May 1956), pp. 97–113.

166. _____. "Dividends, Earnings, Leverage, Stock Prices and the Supply of Capital to Corporations," *Review of Economics and Statistics*, vol. 44, no. 8 (August 1962), pp. 243–69.

167. _____. "The Valuation of Risk Assets and the Selection of Risky Investments in Stock Portfolios and Capital Budgets," *Review of Economics and Statistics*, vol. 47, no. 2 (February 1965), pp. 13–37.

168. _____. "Security Prices, Risk, and Maximal Gains from Diversification," *Journal of Finance*, vol. 20, no. 12 (December 1965), pp. 587–615.

169. _____. "Inflation and Security Returns," *Journal of Finance*, vol. 30, no. 2 (May 1975), pp. 259–80.

170. _____. "Inflation and Common Stock Prices in a Cyclical Context," National Bureau of Economic Research, 53rd Annual Report, September 1973. Reprinted in James Lorie and Richard Brealey, ed., *Modern Developments in Investment Management: A Book of Readings*. 2d ed. Hinsdale, Ill.: Dryden Press, 1978, pp. 669–82.

171. Lintner, John, and Robert Glauber. "Higgledy Piggledy Growth in America." Unpublished paper prepared for the Seminar on the Analysis of Security Prices, University of Chicago, May 1967. Reprinted in James Lorie and Richard Brealey, ed., *Modern Developments in Investment Management: A Book of Readings*. 2d ed., Hinsdale, Ill.: Dryden Press, 1978, pp. 594–611.

172. Logue, Dennis Emhardt. "An Empirical Appraisal of the Market for First Public Offerings of Common Stock." Unpublished Ph.D. dissertation, Cornell University, 1971.

173. Lorie, James, and Richard Brealey, ed. *Modern Developments in Investment Management: A Book of Readings*. 2d ed. Hinsdale, Ill.: Dryden Press, 1978.

174. Lorie, James H., and Mary T. Hamilton. *The Stock Market: Theories and Evidence*. Homewood, Ill.: Richard D. Irwin, Inc., 1974.

175. Lorie, James H., and Victor Niederhoffer. "Predictive and Statistical Properties of Insider Trading," *Journal of Law and Economics*, vol. 11, no. 4 (April 1968), pp. 35–53.

176. McDonald, John G. "Objectives and Performance of Mutual Funds, 1960–1969," *Journal of Financial and Quantitative Analysis*, vol. 9, no. 3 (June 1974), pp. 311–44.

177. McDonald, John G., and A. K. Fisher. "New Issue Stock Price Behavior," *Journal of Finance*, vol. 27, no. 1 (March 1972), pp. 97–102.

178. McKibben, Walt. "Econometric Forecasting of Common Stock Investment Returns: A New Methodology Using Fundamental Operating Date," *Journal of Finance*, vol. 27, no. 5 (May 1972), pp. 371–80.

179. Malkiel, Burton G. "Equity Yields, Growth, and the Structure of

Share Prices," *American Economic Review,* vol. 53, no. 12 (December 1963), pp. 1004–30.

180. Malkiel, Burton G., and John G. Cragg. "Expectations and the Structure of Share Prices," *American Economic Review,* vol. 40, no. 4 (September 1970), pp. 601–17.

181. Malkiel, Burton G., and Richard E. Quandt. *Strategies and Rational Decisions in the Securities Options Market.* Cambridge, Mass.: M.I.T. Press, 1969.

182. Mandelbrot, Benoit. "The Variation of Certain Speculative Prices," *Journal of Business,* vol. 36, no. 4 (October 1962), pp. 394–419. Reprinted in Paul H. Cootner, ed., *The Random Character of Stock Market Prices,* Cambridge, Mass.: M.I.T. Press, 1964, pp. 307–37.

183. _____. "Forecasts of Future Prices, Unbiased Markets, and 'Martingale' Models," *Journal of Business,* vol. 39, no. 1, pt. 2 (January, 1966), pp. 242–55.

184. _____. "The Variation of Some Other Speculative Prices," *Journal of Business,* vol. 40, no. 4 (October 1967), pp. 393–413.

185. Markowitz, Harry M. "Portfolio Selection." *Journal of Finance,* vol. 7, no. 1 (March 1952), pp. 77–91. Reprinted in E. Bruce Fredrikson, ed., *Frontiers of Investment Analysis.* Scranton, Pa.: International Textbook Co., 1965, pp. 353–66, and Reprinted in James Lorie and Richard Brealey, ed., *Modern Developments in Investment Management: A Book of Readings.* 2d ed., Hinsdale, Ill.: Dryden Press, 1978, pp. 310–24.

186. _____. *Portfolio Selection: Efficient Diversification of Investments.* New York: John Wiley & Sons, Inc., 1959.

187. May, A. Wilfred. "Current Popular Delusions about the Stock Split and Stock Dividend," *The Commercial and Financial Chronicle,* vol. 184, no. 5586 (November 15, 1956), p. 5.

188. _____. "On Stock Market Forecasting and Timing," *The Commercial and Financial Chronicle,* vol. 186, no. 5690 (Thursday, November 14, 1957), p. 5. Reprinted in Richard E. Ball, ed., *Readings in Investments,* Boston: Allyn and Bacon, Inc., pp. 380–92.

189. Mayor, T. H. "Short Trading Activities and the Price of Equities: Some Simulation and Regression Results," *Journal of Financial and Quantitative Analysis,* vol. 3, no. 9 (September 1968), pp. 283–98.

190. Merjos, A. "New Listings and Their Price Behavior," *Journal of Finance,* vol. 25, no. 9 (September 1970), pp. 783–94.

191. Miller, Merton H., and Franco Modigliani. "Dividend Policy, Growth, and the Valuation of Shares," *Journal of Business,* vol. 34, no. 4 (October 1961), pp. 411–33. Reprinted in James Lorie and Richard Brealey, ed., *Modern Developments in Investment Management: A Book of Readings.* 2d ed. Hinsdale, Il.: Dryden Press, 1978, pp. 508–30.

192. Modigliani, Franco, and Richard A. Cohn. Inflation, Rational Valuation and the Market," *Financial Analysts Journal,* vol. 35, no. 2 (March–April 1979), pp. 24–44.

193. Modigliani, Franco, and Merton Miller. "The Cost of Capital, Corporate Finance, and the Theory of Investment," *American Economic Review*, vol. 48, no. 3 (June 1958), pp. 261–97.

194. Modigliani, Franco, and Gerald Pogue. "An Introduction to Risk and Return," *Financial Analysts Journal*, vol. 30, no. 2 (March–April 1974), p. 68.

195. Molodovsky, Nicholas. *Investment Values in a Dynamic World: Collected Papers of Nicholas Molodovsky*. Homewood, Ill.: Richard D. Irwin, Inc., 1974.

196. Moore, Arnold B. "A Statistical Analysis of Common Stock Prices." Unpublished Ph.D. dissertation, University of Chicago, 1962.

197. Mossin, Jan. "Equilibrium in a Capital Asset Market," *Econometrica*, vol. 34, no. 10 (October 1966), pp. 768–83.

198. ———. *Theory of Financial Markets*. Englewood Cliffs, N.J.: Prentice-Hall, Inc., 1973.

199. Murphy, Joseph E., Jr. "Relative Growth of Earnings per Share—Past and Future," *Financial Analysts Journal*, vol. 22, no. 6 (November–December 1966), pp. 73–76.

200. ———. "Return, Payout and Growth," *Financial Analysts Journal*, vol. 23, no. 3 (May–June 1967), pp. 91–96.

201. Nerlove, Marc. "Factors Affecting Differences among Rates of Return on Individual Common Stocks," *Review of Economics and Statistics*, vol. 50, no. 8 (August 1968), pp. 312–31.

202. Newell, Gale E. "Revisions of Reported Quarterly Earnings," *Journal of Business*, vol. 44, no. 3 (July 1971), pp. 282–85.

203. Niederhoffer, Victor. "Clustering of Stock Prices," *Operations Research*, vol. 13, no. 2 (March–April 1965), pp. 258–65.

204. ———. "A New Look at Clustering of Stock Prices," *Journal of Business*, vol. 39, no. 2 (April 1966), pp. 309–13.

205. ———. "The Predictive Content of First Quarter Earnings Reports," *Journal of Business*, vol. 43, no. 1 (January 1970), pp. 60–62.

206. Niederhoffer, Victor, and M. F. M. Osborne. "Market Making and Reversal on the Stock Exchange," *Journal of the American Statistical Association*, vol. 61, no. 316 (December 1966), pp. 887–916.

207. Niederhoffer, Victor, and Patrick Regan. "Earnings Changes, Analysts' Forecasts, and Stock Prices," *Financial Analysts Journal*, vol. 28, no. 3 (May–June 1972), pp. 65–71. Reprinted in James Lorie and Richard Brealey, ed., *Modern Developments in Investment Management: A Book of Readings*. 2d ed. Hinsdale, Ill.: Dryden Press, 1978, pp. 548–58.

208. O'Brien, John W. "How Market Theory Can Help Investors Set Goals, Select Investment Managers and Appraise Investment Performance," *Financial Analysts Journal*, vol. 26, no. 4 (July–August 1970), pp. 91–103.

209. Osborne, M. F. M. "Brownian Motion in the Stock Market," *Operations Research*, vol. 7, no. 2 (March–April 1959), pp. 145–73. Re-

printed in Paul H. Cootner, ed., *The Random Character of Stock Market Prices*. Cambridge, Mass.: M.I.T. Press, 1964, pp. 100–28.

210. ———. "Periodic Structure of Brownian Motion of Stock Prices," *Operations Research*, vol. 10, no. 3 (May–June 1962), pp. 345–79. Reprinted in Paul H. Cootner, ed., *The Random Character of Stock Market Prices*, Cambridge, Mass.: M.I.T. Press, 1964, pp. 262–96.

211. ———. "Reply to 'Comments on Brownian Motion in the Stock Market,'" *Operations Research*, vol. 7, no. 2 (March–April 1959); pp. 807–11.

212. Pettit, Richardson R. "Dividend Announcements and Security Performance," Preliminary Working Paper, Rodney L. White Center for Financial Research, Wharton School of Finance and Commerce, University of Pennsylvania, February 19, 1971.

213. Praetz, Peter D. "The Distribution of Share Price Changes," *Journal of Business*, vol. 45, no. 1 (January 1972), pp. 49–55.

214. Pratt, Shannon P. "Relationship between Risk and Rate of Return for Common Stocks." Unpublished D.B.A. dissertation, Indiana University, 1966.

215. Pratt, Shannon P., and C. W. DeVere. "Relationship between Insider Trading and Rates of Return for NYSE Common Stocks, 1960–1966." Unpublished paper prepared for the Seminar on the Analysis of Security Prices, University of Chicago, (May 1968).

216. ———. "Relationship between Insider Trading and Rate of Return for NYSE Common Stocks, 1960–66." Unpublished paper prepared for the Seminar on the Analysis of Security Prices, University of Chicago (May 1968). Reprinted in James Lorie and Richard Brealey, ed., *Modern Developments in Investment Management: A Book of Readings*. 2d ed. Hinsdale, Ill.: Dryden Press, 1978, pp. 259–70.

217. Press, S. James. "A Compound Events Model for Security Prices," *Journal of Business*, vol. 40, no. 7 (July 1967), pp. 317–35.

218. Reilly, F. K. "Price Changes in NYSE, AMEX, and OTC Stocks Compared," *Financial Analysts Journal*, vol. 27, no. 2 (March–April 1971), p. 54.

219. Reilly, F. K., and K. Hatfield. "Experience with New Stock Issues," *Financial Analysis Journal*, vol. 25, no. 5 (September–October 1969), pp. 73–82.

220. Roberts, Harry V. "Stock Market 'Patterns' and Financial Analysis," *Journal of Finance*, vol. 14, no. 1 (March 1959), pp. 1–10. Reprinted in Paul H. Cootner, ed., *The Random Character of Stock Market Prices*. Cambridge, Mass.: M.I.T. Press, 1964, pp. 7–16. Reprinted in Richard E. Ball, ed., *Readings in Investments*, Boston: Allyn and Bacon, Inc., 1965, pp. 369–79. Also reprinted in James Lorie and Richard Brealey, ed., *Modern Developments in Investment Management: A Book of Readings*. 2d ed. Hinsdale, Ill.: Dryden Press, 1978, pp. 154–63.

221. Rogoff, Donald L. "The Forecasting Properties of Insiders' Transactions." Unpublished Ph.D. dissertation, Michigan State University, 1964.

222. Rose, Stanford. "The Stock Market Should Be Twice as High as It Is." *Fortune*, vol. 99, no. 5 (March 12, 1979), pp. 138–44.

223. Rosenberg, Barr. "The Behavior of Random Variables with Nonstationary Variance and the Distribution of Security Prices." Research Program in Finance, Working Paper No. 11. Berkeley: Institute of Business and Economic Research, University of California, 1972.

224. _____. "Extra Market Components of Covariance among Security Prices," *Journal of Financial and Quantitative Analysis*, vol. 9, no. 2 (March 1974), pp. 263–94.

225. _____. "Security Appraisal and Unsystematic Risk in Institutional Investment." *Proceedings of the Seminar on the Analysis of Security Prices*, University of Chicago, vol. 21, no. 2 (November 1976), pp. 171–237.

226. _____. "Institutional Investment with Multiple Portfolio Managers." *Proceedings of the Seminar on the Analysis of Security Prices*, University of Chicago, vol. 22, no. 2 (November 1977), pp. 55–160.

227. _____. "Performance Measurement and Performance Attribution." *Proceedings of the Seminar on the Analysis of Security Prices*, University of Chicago, vol. 23, no. 1 (May 1978), pp. 69–119.

228. Rosenberg, Barr, and James Guy. "Prediction of Systematic Risk from Investment Fundamentals," *Financial Analysts Journal*, vol. 32, no. 3 (May–June 1976), pp. 60–72, and vol. 32, no. 4 (July–August 1976), pp. 62–70.

229. Rosenberg, Barr, and Michel Houglet. "Error Rates in CRISP and COMPUSTAT Data Bases and Their Implications." *Journal of Finance*, vol. 29, no. 9 (September 1974), pp. 1303–10.

230. Rosenberg, Barr, and Vinay Marathe. "Prediction of Investment Risk: Systematic and Residual Risk." *Proceedings of the Seminar on the Analysis of Security Prices*, University of Chicago, vol. 20, no. 1 (November 1975), pp. 85–225.

231. _____. "Common Factors in Security Returns: Microeconomic Determinants and Macroeconomic Correlates." *Proceedings of the Seminar on the Analysis of Security Prices*, University of Chicago, vol. 21, no. 2 (May 1976), pp. 61–115.

232. Rosenberg, Barr, and Walt McKibben. "The Prediction of Systematic Risk in Common Stocks," *Journal of Financial and Quantitative Analysis*, vol. 8, no. 3 (March 1973), pp. 317–33.

233. Rosenberg, Barr, and Andrew Rudd. "The Yield/Beta/Residual Risk Tradeoff." Research Program in Finance Working Paper No. 66. Berkeley: Institute of Business and Economic Research, University of California, November 1977.

234. Rosenberg, Barr, Michel Houglet, Vinay Marathe, and Walt McKibben. "Components of Covariance in Security Returns." Research Program in Finance Working Paper No. 13. Berkeley: Institute of Business and Economic Research, University of California, 1973 (rev. 1975).

235. Ruff, R. T. "The Effect of Selection and Recommendation of a Stock of the Month," *Financial Analysts Journal*, vol. 19, no. 2 (March–April 1965), pp. 41–43.

236. Samuelson, Paul A. "Proof That Properly Anticipated Prices Fluctuate Randomly," *Industrial Management Review*, vol. 6, no. 2
(Spring, 1965), pp. 41–49.

237. Scholes, Myron S. "A Test of the Competitive Hypothesis: The Market for New Issues and Secondary Offerings." Unpublished Ph.D. dissertation, Graduate School of Business, University of Chicago, 1969.

238. _____. "The Market for Securities: Substitution versus Price
Pressure and the Effects of Information on Share Prices," *Journal of
Business*, vol. 45, no. 2 (April 1972), pp. 172–211. Reprinted in James
Lorie and Richard Brealey, ed., *Modern Developments in Investment
Management: A Book of Readings*. 2d ed. Hinsdale, Ill.: Dryden Press,
1978, pp. 198–230.

239. Seneca, Joseph J. "Short Interest: Bearish or Bullish?" *Journal of
Finance*, vol. 22, no. 3 (March 1967), pp. 67–70.

240. _____. "Short Interest: Bullish or Bearish?—Reply," *Journal of Finance*, vol. 23, no. 3 (March 1967), pp. 524–27.

241. Sharpe, William F. "A Simplified Model for Portfolio Analysis,"
Management Science, vol. 9, no. 2 (January 1963), pp. 277–93. Reprinted in James Lorie and Richard Brealey, ed., *Modern Developments in Investment Management: A Book of Readings*. 2d ed.
Hinsdale, Ill.: Dryden Press, 1978, pp. 325–41.

242. _____. "Capital Asset Prices: A Theory of Market Equilibrium under
Conditions of Risk," *Journal of Finance*, vol. 19, no. 3 (September
1964), pp. 425–42. Reprinted in James Lorie and Richard Brealey, ed.,
*Modern Developments in Investment Management: A Book of Read-
ings*. 2d ed. Hinsdale, Ill.: Dryden Press, 1978, pp. 366–83.

243. _____. "Risk Aversion in the Stock Market," *Journal of Finance*, vol.
20, no. 9 (September 1965), pp. 416–22.

244. _____. "Mutual Fund Performance," *Journal of Business*, vol. 39,
no. 1, pt. 2 (January 1966), pp. 119–38.

245. _____. "Linear Programming Algorithms for Mutual Fund Portfolio
Selection," *Management Science*, vol. 13, no 7 (March 1967), pp.
449–510.

246. _____. *Portfolio Theory and Capital Markets*. New York: McGraw-
Hill Book Company, 1970.

247. _____. "Risk, Market Sensitivity and Diversification," *Financial
Analysts Journal*, vol. 28, no. 1 (January–February, 1972), pp. 74–79.
Repr'ted in James Lorie and Richard Brealey, ed., *Modern Develop-
ments in Investment Management: A Book of Readings*. 2d ed.
Hinsdale, Ill.: Dryden Press, 1978, pp. 342–47.

248. _____. "Bonds versus Stocks: Some Lessons from Capital Market
Theory," *Financial Analysts Journal*, vol. 29, no. 6 (November–
December 1973), pp. 74–80.

249. _____. "Imputing Expected Security Returns from Portfolio Composition," *Journal of Financial and Quantitative Analysis*, vol. 9, no.
3 (June 1974), pp. 463–72.

250. _____. "Likely Gains from Market Timing," *Financial Analysts Journal*, vol. 31, no. 2 (March–April 1975), pp. 60–69.

251. _____. "Adjusting for Risk in Portfolio Performance Measurement," *Journal of Portfolio Management*, vol. 1, no. 2, (Winter 1975), pp. 29–34. Reprinted in James Lorie and Richard Brealey, ed., *Modern Developments in Investment Management: A Book of Readings.* 2d ed. Hinsdale, Ill.: Dryden Press, 1978, pp. 442–47.

252. _____. *Investments.* Englewood Cliffs, N.J.: Prentice-Hall, Inc., 1978.

253. Sharpe, William F., and Guy M. Cooper. "Risk-Return Classes of New York Stock Exchange Common Stocks," *Financial Analysts Journal*, vol. 28, no. 2 (March–April 1972), pp. 46–56. Reprinted in James Lorie and Richard Brealey, ed., *Modern Developments in Investment Management: A Book of Readings.* 2d ed. Hinsdale, Ill.: Dryden Press, 1978, pp. 384–94.

254. Sharpe, William F., and Howard B. Sosin. "Risk, Return and Yield: New York Stock Exchange Common Stocks, 1928–1969," *Financial Analysts Journal*, vol. 30, no. 2 (March–April 1976), pp. 33–42.

255. Shelton, John P. "The Value Line Contest: A Test of the Predictability of Stock Price Changes," *Journal of Business*, vol. 40, no. 3 (July 1967), pp. 251–69.

256. Shenker, Israel. "Professors Top Wall Street's Stock Advice," *The New York Times*, Saturday, March 11, 1972, p. 37.

257. Shiskin, Julius. "Systematic Aspects of Stock Price Fluctuation." Unpublished paper prepared for the Seminar on the Analysis of Security Prices, University of Chicago (May 1967). Reprinted in James Lorie and Richard Brealey, ed., *Modern Developments in Investment Management: A Book of Readings.* 2d ed. Hinsdale, Ill.: Dryden Press, 1978, pp. 640–58.

258. Slutsky, Eugene. "The Summation of Random Causes as the Source of Cyclic Processes," *Econometrica*, vol. 5, no. 2 (April 1937), pp. 105–46.

259. Smith, Adam. *An Inquiry into the Nature and Causes of the Wealth of Nations.* 2d ed. vol. 1, bk 2. London: Methuen and Company, Ltd., 1904.

260. Smith, Randall D. "Short Interest and Stock Market Prices," *Financial Analysts Journal*, vol. 24, no. 6 (November–December 1968), pp. 151–54.

261. Solnik, Bruno H. "The International Pricing of Risk: An Empirical Investigation of the World Capital Market Structure," *Journal of Finance*, vol. 29, no. 2 (May 1974), pp. 364–78.

262. _____. "Why Not Diversify Internationally Rather Than Domestically?" *Financial Analysts Journal*, vol. 30, no. 4 (July–August 1974), pp. 48–54.

263. Stigler, George J. "Public Regulation of the Securities Markets," *Journal of Business*, vol. 37, no. 2 (April 1964), pp. 117–42.

264. Stoffels, J. D. "Stock Recommendations by Investment Advisory Services: Immediate Effects on Market Pricing, ' *Financial Analysts Journal,* vol. 22, no. 3 (March 1966), pp. 77–86.

265. Taussig, F. W. "Is Market Price Determinate," *Quarterly Journal of Economics,* vol. 35, no. 5 (May 1921), pp. 394–411.

266. Telser, L. G. "A Critique of Some Recent Empirical Research on the Explanation of the Term Structure of Interest Rates," *Journal of Political Economy,* vol. 75, no. 4 (August 1967), pp. 546–61. Reprinted in James Lorie and Richard Brealey, ed., *Modern Developments in Investment Management: A Book of Readings.* 2d ed. Hinsdale, Ill.: Dryden Press, 1978, pp. 711–726.

267. Tobias, Andrew. *The Only Investment Guide You'll Ever Need.* New York: Harcourt Brace Jovanovich, 1978.

268. Tobin, James. "Liquidity Preference as Behavior Towards Risk," *Review of Economic Studies,* vol. 25, no. 2 (February 1958), pp. 65–85.

269. _____. "The Theory of Portfolio Selection," in F. H. Hahn and F. P. R. Brechling, eds., *The Theory of Interest Rates.* London: Macmillan Company, 1965, pp. 3–51.

270. Treynor, Jack L. "Toward a Theory of Market Value of Risky Assets." Unpublished manuscript, 1961.

271. _____. "How to Rate Management of Investment Funds," *Harvard Business Review,* vol. 43, no. 1 (January–February 1965), pp. 63–76. Reprinted in David A. West, ed., *Readings in Investment Analysis,* Scranton, Pa.: International Textbook Co., pp. 137–58.

272. _____. "The Trouble with Earnings," *Financial Analysts Journal,* vol. 28, no. 5 (September–October 1972), pp. 41–43. Reprinted in James Lorie and Richard Brealey, ed., *Modern Developments in Investment Management: A Book of Readings.* 2d ed. Hinsdale, Ill.: Dryden Press, 1978, pp. 612–16.

273. _____. "The Coming Revolution in Investment Management," in James L. Becksler, *Methodology in Finance–Investments.* Lexington, Mass.: Lexington Books, P. C. Heath and Company, 1972. Reprinted in James Lorie and Richard Brealey, ed., *Modern Developments in Investment Management: A Book of Readings.* 2d ed. Hinsdale, Ill.: Dryden Press, 1978, pp. 424–41.

274. Treynor, Jack L., and Fischer Black. "How to Use Security Analysis to Improve Portfolio Selection," *Journal of Business,* vol. 46, no. 1 (January 1974), pp. 66–86.

275. Valentine, Jerome L. "Investment Analysis and Capital Market Theory." Occasional Paper No. 1. Financial Analysts Research Foundation, 1975.

276. Van Horne, James C. "New Listings and Their Price Behavior." *Journal of Finance,* vol. 25, no. 9 (September 1970), pp. 783–94.

277. Van Horne, James C., and George G. C. Parker. "Technical Trading

Rules: A Comment," *Financial Analysts Journal*, vol. 24, no. 4 (July–August 1968), pp. 128–32.

278. Vasicek, Oldrick A. "A Note on Using Cross-Sectioned Information in Bayesian Estimation of Security Betas," *Journal of Finance*, vol. 28, no. 5 (December 1973), pp. 1233–39.

279. von Neumann, John, and Oskar Morgenstern. *The Theory of Games and Economic Behavior*. New York: John Wiley & Sons, Inc., 1940.

280. Wagner, W. H., and S. C. Lau. "The Effect of Diversification on Risk," *Financial Analysts Journal*, vol. 27, no. 6 (November–December 1971), pp. 48–57.

281. Wallich, Henry C. "What Does the Random-Walk Hypothesis Mean to Security Analysis?" *Financial Analysts Journal*, vol. 24, no. 2 (March–April 1968), pp. 159–62.

282. Walter, James. "Dividend Policies and Common Stock Prices," *Journal of Finance*, vol. 11, no. 1 (March 1956), pp. 29–41.

283. Watts, Ross. "The Information Content of Dividends," *Journal of Business*, vol. 46, no. 2 (April 1973), pp. 191–211.

284. West, Richard R. "Mutual Fund Performance and the Theory of Capital Asset Pricing: Some Comments," *Journal of Business*, vol. 41, no. 4 (April 1968), pp. 230–34.

285. Whitbeck, Volkert S., and Manown Kisor, Jr. "A New Tool in Investment Decision Making," *Financial Analysts Journal*, vol. 19, no. 3 (May–June 1963), pp. 55–62. Reprinted in E. Bruce Fredrikson, ed., *Frontiers of Investment Analysis*, Scranton, Pa.: International Textbook Co., 1965, pp. 335–50. Reprinted in James Lorie and Richard Brealey, ed., *Modern Developments in Investment Management: A Book of Readings*. 2d ed. Hinsdale, Ill.: Dryden Press, 1978, pp. 531–47.

286. Williams, John Burr. *The Theory of Investment Value*. Cambridge, Mass.: Harvard University Press, 1938. Reprinted (in part) in James Lorie and Richard Brealey, ed., *Modern Developments in Investment Management: A Book of Readings*. 2d ed., Hinsdale, Ill.: Dryden Press, 1978, pp. 471–91.

287. Williamson, J. Peter. *Investments: New Analytic Techniques*. New York: Praeger Publishers, 1970.

288. Working, Holbrook. "A Random-Difference Series for Use in the Analysis of Time Series," *Journal of the American Statistical Association*, vol. 29, no. 185 (March 1934), pp. 11–24.

289. _____. "New Ideas and Methods for Price Research," *Journal of Farm Economics*, vol. 38, no. 5 (December 1956), pp. 1427–36.

290. _____. "Note on the Correlation of First Differences of Averages in a Random Chain," *Econometrica*, vol. 28, no. 4 (October 1960), pp. 916–18. Reprinted in Paul H. Cootner, ed., *The Random Character of Stock Market Prices*, Cambridge, Mass.: M.I.T. Press, 1964, pp. 129–31.

291. Wu, Hsiu-Kwang. "Corporate Insider Trading, Profitability and Stock Price Movement." Unpublished Ph.D. dissertation, University of Pennsylvania, 1963.

Periodical references

292. *Financial Analysts Journal*, vol. 32, no. 5 (September–October 1976).

293. *Fortune*, vol. 74, no. 1 (July 1, 1966).

Glossary

Accruals. Expenses charged against current operations but not requiring cash payment until some future date. Thus bond interest may be accrued on the corporation's books each month, although it usually is paid only at six-month intervals.

Accrued interest. Interest accrued on a bond since the last interest payment was made. The buyer of the bond pays the market price plus accrued interest.*

Acid test ratio. A measure of financial liquidity (also known as the quick assets ratio): quick assets (current assets less inventories) divided by current liabilities.

Across-the-market samples. Stock market data can be collected in two ways: "sequentially" or "across-the-market." A sequential sample is data on a particular stock collected over time. An across-the-market sample records data on a group of stocks during a single time period. Thus, an across-the-market sample can be drawn from one financial page of a newspaper.

Active management. A style of investment management which seeks to attain above-average risk-adjusted performance.

Alpha. The nonmarket-related component of a security's return in the equation relating the risk premium on an asset to the risk premium on the market. Its expected value is zero, but its actual value may differ from zero. It is this possibility that explains investors' efforts to identify under-valued or over-valued securities, i.e., those with nonzero alphas.

AMEX. An abbreviation for the American Stock Exchange.

Amortization. Accounting for expenses or charges as applicable rather than as paid. Includes such practices as depreciation, depletion, write-off of intangibles, prepaid expenses, and deferred charges.*

Entries marked with an asterisk (*) are included with the permission of the New York Stock Exchange from the *Glossary: The Language of Investing*, New York: New York Stock Exchange, Inc., 1978.

Annual report. The formal financial statement issued yearly by a corporation. The annual report shows assets, liabilities, earnings—how the company stood at the close of the business year, how it fared profit-wise during the year, and other information of interest to sharehowners.*

Arbitrage. A technique employed to take advantage of differences in price. If, for example, ABC stock can be bought in New York for $10 a share and sold in London at $10.50, an arbitrageur may simultaneously purchase ABC stock in New York and sell the same amount in London, making a profit of $0.50 a share, less expenses. Arbitrage may also involve the purchase of rights to subscribe to a security, or the purchase of a convertible security—and the sale at or about the same time of the security obtainable through exercise of the rights or of the security obtainable through conversion.*

Asset allocation models. The MPT application area that addresses the problem of the amount of assets to be allocated among various investment alternatives.

Asset turnover (sometimes called operating leverage). The ratio of sales per dollar of assets employed during the year. It is calculated by dividing net sales by the average assets. As such, it provides a comparative link between a key balance sheet item (assets) and a key item on the income statement (sales).

Assets. Everything a corporation owns or due to it: cash, investments, money due it, materials and inventories, which are called current assets; buildings and machinery, which are known as fixed assets; and patents and goodwill, called intangible assets.*

Auction market. The system of trading securities through brokers or agents on an exchange such as the New York Stock Exchange. Buyers compete with other buyers while sellers compete with other sellers for the most advantageous price.*

Averages (market). Market averages measure changes in the aggregate value of a group of securities which serve as a "proxy" for the price changes of the market. (See Dow Jones Industrial Average, NYSE Common Stock Index, and S&P 500.)

Balance sheet. A condensed financial statement showing the nature and amount of a company's assets, liabilities, and capital on a given date. In dollar amounts the balance sheet shows what the company owned, what it owed, and the ownership interest in the company of its stockholders.

Basis point. One hundred basis points equal 1 percent. Thus, a basis point is $1/100$ of 1 percent. Accordingly, 50 basis points is the same as $1/2$ of 1 percent, 10 basis points is the same as $1/10$ of 1 percent, 200 basis points is the same as 2 percent, etc.

Bear. Someone who believes the market will decline.

Bear market. A declining market.

Bearer bond. A bond which does not have the owner's name registered on the books of the insurer and which is payable to the holder.

Beta coefficient. The beta coefficient measures sensitivity of rates of return on a portfolio, or on a particular security, to general market movements. If the beta is 1.0, a 1 percent increase in the return on the market will result, on average, in a 1 percent increase in the return on the particular portfolio or asset. If beta is less than 1.0, the portfolio or asset is considered to be less risky than the market. Beta is the regression coefficient of the rate of return on the market in the market model.

Bid and asked. Often referred to as a quotation, or quote, the "bid" is the highest price anyone is willing to pay for a security at a given time, the "asked" is the lowest price anyone will take at the same time.*

Block. A large holding or transaction of stock—popularly considered to be 10,000 shares or more.*

Blue chip. A company known for the quality and wide acceptance of its products or services, and for its ability to make money and pay dividends.*

Blue sky laws. A popular name for laws enacted to protect the public against securities frauds. The term is believed to have originated when a judge ruled that a particular stock had about the same value as a patch of blue sky.*

Board room. A room in a broker's office where prices of leading stocks used to be posted on a board throughout the market day. Today such price displays are normally electronically controlled, although most board rooms have replaced the board with the ticker and/or individual quotation machines.*

Bond. Basically an IOU or promissory note of a corporation usually issued in multiples of $1,000. A bond is evidence of a debt on which the issuing company usually promises to pay the bondholders a specified amount of interest for a specified length of time, and to repay the loan on the expiration date. In every case a bond represents debt—its holder is a creditor of the corporation and not a part owner as is a shareholder.*

Bond interest coverage. A measure of bond safety: total income divided by annual interest on bonds (or earnings before interest and taxes divided by annual interest on bonds).

Bond ratio. A measure of long-term financial risk and leverage: long-term debt divided by total capitalization.

Book value. An accounting term determined from adding all of a company's assets then deducting all debts and other liabilities, plus the liquidation price of any preferred issues. The sum arrived at is divided by the number of common shares outstanding and the result is book value per common share. Book value of the assets of a company or a security may have little or no significant relationship to market value.*

Broker. An agent who handles orders to buy and sell securities. commodities, or other property for a commission.*

Brokers' loans. Money borrowed by brokers from banks or other brokers for a variety of uses. The money may be used by specialists and to help finance inventories of stock they deal in; by brokerage firms to finance the underwriting of new issues of corporate and municipal securities; to help finance a firm's own investments; and to help finance the purchase of securities for customers who prefer to use the broker's credit when they buy securities.*

Bull. One who believes the market will rise.*

Bull market. An advancing market.*

Call. See Option.

Callable. A bond issue, all or part of which may be redeemed by the issuing corporation under definite conditions before maturity. The term also applies to preferred shares which may be redeemed by the issuing corporation.*

The capital asset pricing model. (CAPM). Describes the way prices of individual assets are determined in markets where information is freely available and reflected instantaneously in asset prices—that is, efficient markets. According to this model prices are determined in such a way that risk premiums are proportional to systematic risk, which is measured by the beta coefficient. As such, the CAPM provides an explicit expression of the expected returns for all assets. Basically, the CAPM holds that if investors are risk averse, high-risk stocks must have higher expected returns than low-risk stocks.

Capital gain or capital loss. Profit or loss from the sale of a capital asset. A capital gain, under current federal income tax laws, may be either short-term (12 months or less) or long-term (more than 12 months). A short-term capital gain is taxed at the reporting individual's full income tax rate. A long-term capital gain is subject to a lower tax.*

Capital market line. A graphic portrayal of the average rate of return provided by the marketplace for various levels of risk. The capital market line in the Sharpe model is the line from the risk-free rate of return that is tangent to the efficient frontier of risky assets. It describes the relationship between expected rates of return on efficient portfolios and risk. All efficient portfolios lie on this line if lending and borrowing are permissible at the (same) risk-free rate.

Capital stock. All shares representing ownership of a business, including preferred and common.

Capital structure. The division of the capitalization between bonds, preferred stocks, and common stock. Where common stock represents all, or nearly all the capitalization, the structure may be called "conservative." Where common stock represents a small percentage of the total, the structure is called "leveraged".

Capitalization. Total amount of the various securities issued by a corporation. Capitalization may include bonds, debentures, preferred and common stock, and surplus. Bonds and debentures are usually carried on the books of the issuing company in terms of their par or face value. Preferred and common shares may be carried in terms of par or stated value. Stated value may be an arbitrary figure decided upon by the directors or may represent the amount received by the company from the sale of the securities at the time of issuance.*

Cash flow. Reported net income of a corporation plus amounts charged off for depreciation, depletion, amortization, and extraordinary charges to reserves, which are bookkeeping deductions and not paid out in actual dollars and cents.*

Characteristic lines. The market model describes the relationship between the return on a security and the overall market (represented by a single market index). This relationship can be summarized, for either a security or a portfolio, with a characteristic line. The slope of the line indicates the security's (or the portfolio's) sensitivity to the market's return. The intercept indicates the nonmarket (residual) component of return. In specific technical terms the equation for a security characteristic line is:

$$\tilde{R}_i - \rho = \alpha_i + \beta_{im} (\tilde{R}_m - \rho) + \tilde{r}_i$$

where

$\sim$ = Variable not known in advance.
R_i = Holding period return on security i.
ρ = Riskless rate of return.
α_i = Expected nonmarket excess return on security i.
r_i = Actual deviation from the expected value.
β_{im} = Sensitivity of security i's excess return to the market's excess return.
R_m = Holding period return on the market.
$\tilde{R}_i - \rho$ = Total expected excess return on security i.
$\tilde{R}_m - \rho$ = Excess return on the market portfolio.

Classical security analysis. Security analysis based on the valuation techniques popularized by the late Benjamin Graham. The major shortcoming of this approach is that it does not quantify risk.

Closed-end investment company. (See investment company.)

Cluster analysis. A statistical procedure that is used to discern groups (or "clusters") of stocks within which price movements are highly correlated but between which price movements show little correlation.

Coefficient of determination. See correlation coefficient and r-squared.

Coefficient of variation. The coefficient of variation is the standard deviation divided by the mean, or

$$\sqrt{\frac{\Sigma(x_i - \bar{x})^2}{N}} \Big/ \bar{x}.$$

It is a measure of the *relative* spread of a distribution about its mean. Coefficients of variation can be compared, since they are relative measures. For example, if the standard deviation of a distribution of rates of return were 2 percent, and the mean were 5 percent, the coefficient of variation would be 0.02/0.05 or 0.4 percent.

Collateral. Securities or other property pledged by a borrower to secure repayment of a loan.*

Commission. The broker's fee for purchasing or selling securities or property as an agent.*

Common stock. Securities which represent an ownership interest in a corporation. If the company has also issued preferred stock, both common and preferred have ownership rights. The preferred normally is limited to a fixed dividend but has prior claim on dividends and, in the event of liquidation, assets. Claims of both common and preferred stockholders are junior to claims of bondholders or other creditors of the company. Common stockholders assume the greater risk, but generally exercise the greater control and may gain the greater reward in the form of dividends and capital appreciation. The terms common stock and capital stock are often used interchangeably when the company has no preferred stock.*

Compounding. The arithmetic process of finding the final value of an investment or series of investments when compound interest is applied. That is, interest is earned on the interest as well as on the initial principal.

Conglomerate. A corporation that has diversified its operations, usually by acquiring enterprises in widely varied industries.*

Consolidated balance sheet. A balance sheet showing the financial condition of a corporation and its subsidiaries.*

Consumer price index (CPI). Measures the average change in the prices of a fixed market basket of goods and services over time. At the end of 1978 the expenditure categories that comprised the CPI were: food and beverages 19.2 percent, housing 44.3 percent, apparel and upkeep 5.5 percent, transportation 17.8 percent, medical care 5.0 percent, entertainment 4.0 percent, and other goods and services 4.2 percent.

Continuous compounding. The annual rate of return compounded continuously is the natural logarithm ($\log_e$) of the ratio of the value of the investment at the end of the year to the value at the beginning. For example, if the wealth ratio were 1.1, its natural logarithm would be 0.09531. The annual rate of return compounded continuously would be 9.531 percent. This is easily converted to an annual rate of return compounded annually using the formula $e^x - 1$, where x is the annual rate compounded continuously. If the period is other than one year, the annual rate compounded continuously can be found by dividing the logarithm of the wealth ratio by the number of years in the period.

Convertible. A bond, debenture, or preferred share which may be exchanged by the owner for common stock or another security, usually of the same company, in accordance with the terms of the issue.*

Correlation coefficient. A measure of the relationship between two variables where the "relationship" is the degree to which the two variables move together. If the relationship can be thought to hold in the future, the correlation coefficient can be interpreted as a measure of the degree to which knowing the value of one variable can be used to predict the value of the other. The correlation coefficient is the square of 1 minus the unexplained variance of one variable (i.e., given its relationships to the other) divided by its total variance. Symbolically, for the variables, x_i and x_j

$$\rho_{ij} = \sqrt{1 - \frac{s_{i\cdot j}^2}{s_i^2}}.$$

The square of the correlation coefficient is the coefficient of determination. It measures the percentage of the total variance of i explained by its relationship to j.

Coupon bond. Bond with interest coupons attached. The coupons are clipped as they come due and are presented by the holder for payment of interest.*

Covariance. A measure of the degree to which two variables move together. A positive value means that on average, they move in the same direction. The covariance is related to, but not the same as, the correlation coefficient. It is difficult to attach any significance to the absolute magnitude of the covariance. Symbolically, the covariance between two variables, x_i and x_j, is

$$\frac{\Sigma(x_i - \bar{x}_i)(x_j - \bar{x}_j)}{N}.$$

The covariance is also equal to $\rho_{ij}\sigma_i\sigma_j$, so its magnitude depends not only on the correlation, but also the standard deviations of the two variables. Stated alternatively, the correlation coefficient is the covariance standardized by dividing it by the product of σ_i and σ_j.

Covering. Buying a security previously sold short.*

Cumulative preferred stock. Stock having a provision that if one or more dividends are omitted, the omitted dividends must be paid before dividends may be paid on the company's common stock.*

Curb exchange. Former name of the American Stock Exchange. The term comes from the market's origin on a street in downtown New York.*

Current assets. Those assets of a company which are reasonably expected to be realized in cash, or sold, or consumed during the normal operating cycle of the business. These include cash, U.S. Government bonds, receivables and money due usually within one year, and inventories.*

Current liabilities. Money owed and payable by a company, usually within one year.*

Current ratio (also known as the working capital ratio). Measure of financial liquidity: current assets divided by current liabilities.

Current yield. Annual bond interest divided by market price per bond.

Day order. An order to buy or sell securities which, if not executed, expires at the end of the trading day on which it was entered.*

Dealer. An individual or firm in the securities business acting as a principal rather than as an agent. Typically, dealers buy for their own account and sell to a customer from this inventory. The dealer's profit or loss is the difference between the price paid and the price they received for the same security. The dealers' confirmation must disclose to the customer that they acted as principal. The same individual or firm may function, at different times, either as broker or dealer.*

Debenture. A promissory note backed by the general credit of the issuing company.*

Depletion accounting. Natural resources, such as metals, oil, gas and timber, which conceivably can be reduced to zero over the years, present a special accounting problem. Depletion is an accounting practice consisting of charges against earnings based upon the amount of the asset taken out of the total reserves in the period for which accounting is made. A bookkeeping entry, it does not represent any cash outlay nor are any funds earmarked for the purpose.*

Depreciation. Normally, charges against earnings to write off the cost, less salvage value, of an asset over its estimated useful life. It is a bookkeeping entry and does not represent any cash outlay nor are any funds earmarked for the purpose.*

Diagonal model. See Single-index model.

Differencing interval. An important factor in tests of the weak form of the efficient market hypothesis. This form of the hypothesis holds that the direction of future price changes cannot be predicted from the pattern of "historical" price changes. The differencing interval defines "historical" (such as "day-to-day", or "after a volume surge") in the empirical tests of this form of the hypothesis.

Dilution. An increase in the number of common shares without a corresponding increase in the company's assets. Most convertible issues are protected against this contingency by an "antidilution clause," which reduces the conversion price in the event of dilution.

Diminishing marginal utility of wealth. Marginal utility is the amount of additional satisfaction associated with an additional amount of something such as money or wealth. If successive increments in satisfaction decline as the level of wealth increases, there is diminishing marginal utility. This implies risk aversion, because, at a given level of wealth, the gain in utility associated with some increment in wealth is less than the loss in utility associated with a decrement of the same amount of wealth.

Director. Person elected by shareholders to establish company policies. The directors appoint the president, vice presidents, and all other operating officers. Directors decide, among other matters, if and when dividends shall be paid.*

Discount. The amount by which a preferred stock or bond may sell below its par value. Also used as a verb to mean "takes into account" as the price of the stock has discounted the expected dividend cut.*

Disequilibrium. See Equilibrium.

Dispersion. The spread of a distribution about its average, or mean value. The greater the spread, the greater the variability. It can be measured either absolutely or relatively. Common absolute measures are the standard deviation and the variance. The most common measure of relative dispersion is the coefficient of variation (the standard deviation divided by the mean).

Diversification. The spreading of investments over more than one company or industry to reduce the uncertainty of future returns caused by unsystematic risk.

Dividend. Broadly defined, any distribution of cash or property to corporate shareholders.

Dividend growth models. An analytical framework for determining the value of a share of stock from estimated growth rates in the components of value—earnings and dividend payout ratios.

Dividend payout ratio. The earnings reinvestment rate is the percentage of return that is retained by a company for reinvestment. Typically, the amount that is not reinvested (or used to purchase outstanding shares of the company's common stock) is paid out in dividends. This amount (dividends per share divided by earnings per share) is referred to as the dividend payout ratio.

Dividend yield. Annual dividends per share divided by market price per share.

Double taxation. Short for "double taxation of dividends." The federal government taxes corporate profits once as corporate income; any part of the remaining profits distributed as dividends to stockholders may be taxed again as income to the recipient stockholders.*

Dow Jones Industrial Average (DJIA). A popular price-weighted market index of 30 large industrial companies. Price-weighted means that an increase of 10 percent in the price of a $10 stock has twice the effect of a 10 percent increase of a $5 stock.

Dow theory. A theory of market analysis based upon the performance of the Dow-Jones industrial and transportation stock price averages. The theory says that the market is in a basic upward trend if one of these averages advances above a previous important high, accompanied or followed by a similar advance in the other. When the averages both dip below previous important lows, this is regarded as confirmation of a basic downward trend. The theory does not attempt to predict how long either trend will continue.*

Down tick. See Up tick.

Drunkard's walk. See Random-walk model.

Earnings capitalization rate. The return (earnings) demanded by the marketplace for equity capital. It is easily calculated by inverting the company's price-earnings ratio. For example, a company with an earnings multiple of 5 has an earnings capitalization rate of $1/5$, or 20 percent.

Earnings per share. Net income less preferred dividends divided by shares of common outstanding.

Earnings report. A statement—also called an income statement— issued by a company showing its earnings or losses over a given period. The earnings report lists the income earned, expenses and the net result.*

Efficient. The term used to describe both the speed and accuracy of the process whereby the market, through its participants, translates new information on the economy an industry, or an enterprise, into security prices. An "efficient" market is one in which new information is quickly and accurately reflected in the price of the stock. Conversely, an "inefficient" market is one in which information is not quickly and accurately translated into security prices.

Efficient frontier. The efficient frontier is the locus of all efficient portfolios. If neither lending nor borrowing is allowed, it is that part of the boundary of the feasible set that includes only efficient portfolios of risky assets. If lending and borrowing are permissible, the efficient frontier is the line drawn from the risk-free rate to the point of tangency on the efficient frontier of risky assets. This line is called the capital market line.

Efficient market. See Efficient.

Efficient market hypothesis. The assertion that in a market with numerous investors who prefer high returns over low returns, and low risk over high risk, "information" is of no value. In such a market, an investor can attain no more, nor less, than a fair return for the risks undertaken. The three forms of the efficient market hypothesis are: (1) weak form: a market in which historical price data cannot be used to predict future price changes (see Technical analysis); (2) semistrong form: a market in which all publicly available information is efficiently (i.e., quickly and accurately) impounded on the price of a stock and, hence, a market in which no amount or item of publicly available information can be used to predict future price changes (see Fundamental analysis); and (3) strong form: a market in which even those with privileged (non-public) information cannot obtain superior investment results.

Efficient portfolio. An efficient portfolio is one that is fully diversified. For any given rate of return, no other portfolio has less risk, and for a given level of risk, no other portfolio provides superior returns. All efficient portfolios are perfectly correlated with a general market index, except portfolios with beta coefficients above 1.0 and which do not achieve that relatively high risk by levering an efficient portfolio. Such portfolios lie on the curved frontier of portfolios consisting exclusively of risky assets.

Empirical tests. Tests based on studies of actual data.

Equilibrium. A market condition in which there is no pressure for change. In disequilibrium, investors are dissatisfied with either the securities they hold or the prices of these securities and, as a result, there is pressure for change. At any moment, however, the market is in equilibrium, reflecting the combined influence of all investors' wealth, preferences, and predictions.

Equity. The ownership interest of common and preferred stockholders in a company.

Equity risk premium. The difference between the rate of return available from risk-free assets (such as U.S. Treasury bills) and that available from assuming the risk inherent in common stocks.

ERISA (Employee Retirement Income Security Act of 1974). This law requires that persons engaged in the administration, supervision, and management of pension monies have a *fiduciary responsibility* to ensure that all investment-related decisions are made: (1) with the care, skill, prudence and diligence . . . that a prudent man . . . *familiar with such matters* (italics added) *would use*. . . . , (2) *by diversifying the investments . . . so as to minimize risk.* (italics added) . . . This wording mandates two significant changes in traditional investment practice: (1) the age-old "prudent man" rule has been replaced by the notion of a prudent "expert," (2) the notion of a prudent investment has been replaced by the concept of a prudent *portfolio*.

Ex ante. The term is used to distinguish forward-looking, or predicted, variables.

Ex post. The term is used to distinguish backward-looking, or historical, variables.

Excess return. The return derived from a security (during a specified holding period) less the return from holding a riskless security (such as a short-term government obligation) during the same period.

Exchange acquisition. A method of filling an order to buy a large block of stock on the floor of the Exchange. Under certain circumstances, a member-broker can facilitate the purchase of a block by soliciting orders to sell. All orders to sell the security are lumped together and crossed with the buy order in the regular auction market. The price to the buyer may be on a net basis or on a commission basis.*

Exchange distribution. A method of selling large blocks of stock on the floor of the Exchange. Under certain circumstances, a member-broker can facilitate the sale of a block of stock by soliciting and getting other member-brokers to solicit orders to buy. Individual buy orders are lumped together and crossed with the sell order in the regular auction market. A special commission is usually paid by the seller; ordinarily the buyer pays no commission.*

Ex-dividend. A synonym for "without dividend." The buyer of a stock selling ex-dividend does not receive the recently declared dividend. Every dividend is payable on a fixed date to all shareholders recorded on the books of the company as of a previous date of record. For example, a dividend may be declared as payable to holders of record on the books of the company on a given Friday. Since five business days are allowed for delivery of stock in a "regular way" transaction on the New York Stock Exchange, the Exchange would declare the stock "ex-dividend" as of the opening of the market on the preceding Monday. That means anyone who bought it on and after Monday would not be entitled to that dividend.*

Expected rate of return. The expected rate of return on an asset or portfolio is the weighted arithmetic average of all possible outcomes, where the weights are the probabilities that each outcome will occur. It is the expected value or mean of a probability distribution.

Ex-rights. Without the rights. Corporations raising additional money may do so by offering their stockholders the right to subscribe to new or additional stock, usually at a discount from the prevailing market price. The buyer of a stock selling ex-rights is not entitled to the rights.*

Extra. The short form of "extra dividend." A dividend in the form of stock or cash in addition to the regular or usual dividend the company has been paying.*

Extramarket covariance. The tendency for homogeneous groups of stocks to move together but in a way that is independent of the market as a whole.

Extramarket risk. Risk arising from comovements of homogeneous groups of stocks whose movements are independent of those of the market as a whole.

Face value. The value of a bond that appears on the face of the bond, unless the value is otherwise specified by the issuing company. Face value is ordinarily the amount the issuing company promises to pay at maturity. Face value is not an indication of market value. Sometimes referred to as par value.*

Feasible set. The feasible or attainable set includes all individual securities and all combinations (portfolios) of two or more of these securities available to the investor within the limits of the available capital.

Filter rules. Rules based on the assumption that trends exist in stock prices but that these patterns are obscured by insignificant fluctuations, or market "noise". The filter precept is utilized to justify a procedure whereby all price changes smaller than a specified size are ignored. The remaining data are then examined. A typical filter rule might be: if the stock price advances 5 percent (signaling a breakout), buy and hold the stock until it declines by 5 percent (signaling the start of a reversal). At that time, sell the stock held and sell short an equal amount until the stock again moves up 5 percent. Under such a rule, all moves of less than 5 percent are ignored. Filter techniques seek to discover "significant moves" by studying price changes of a given magnitude, irrespective of the length of time between them.

Financial leverage. The measure of how many dollars of assets are held in relation to each dollar of stockholders' equity—in other words, how much of a company's asset base is financed with stockholders' equity and how much with borrowed funds. It is calculated by dividing average assets by average stockholders' equity. As such, it provides a comparative link between two key balance sheet items, assets and equity.

Fiscal year. A corporation's accounting year. Due to the nature of their particular business, some companies do not use the calendar year for their bookkeeping. A typical example is the department store which finds December 31 too early a date to close its books after the Christmas rush. For that reason many stores wind up their accounting year January 31. Their fiscal year, therefore, runs from February 1 of one year through January 31 of the next. The fiscal year of other companies may run from July 1 through the following June 30. Most companies, though, operate on a calendar year basis.*

Fixed assets. See Assets.

Fixed charges. A company's fixed expenses, such as bond interest, which it has agreed to pay whether or not earned, and which are deducted from income before earnings on equity capital are computed.*

Flat income bond. This term means that the price at which a bond is traded includes consideration for all unpaid accruals of interest. Bonds which are in default of interest or principal are traded flat. Income bonds, which pay interest only to the extent earned are usually traded flat. All other bonds are usually dealt in "and interest," which means that the buyer pays to the seller the market price plus interest accrued since the last payment date.*

Floor. The trading area where stocks and bonds are bought and sold on an exchange.

Forward interest rate. The prevailing interest rate for a contract in a specific future, or "forward," time period.

Full covariance model. See Markowitz model.

Fundamental analysis. Analysis based on factors such as sales, earnings, and assets that are "fundamental" to enterprise. The usefulness of fundamental analysis is challenged by the semistrong form of the efficient market hypothesis which holds that the analysis of publicly available fundamental information cannot improve an investor's rate of return.

Funded debt. Usually interest-bearing bonds or debentures of a company. Could include long-term bank loans. Does not include short-term loans, preferred or common stock.*

General mortgage bond. A bond which is secured by a blanket mortgage on the company's property, but which may be outranked by one or more other mortgages.*

Geometric mean. The geometric mean is the nth root of the product of n observations. It is the correct measure to use when averaging annual rates of return, compounded annually, over time. In calculating the average of rates of return, it is necessary to take the geometric mean of wealth ratios in order to allow for negative rates. The average rate of return is then the geometric mean minus one. For example, if the annual rates of return for two years were 10 percent and 8 percent, the average annual rate of return would be

$$\sqrt[v]{1.1 \times 1.08} - 1$$

or .0899. If the annual rates for two years were 100 percent and −50 percent, the average annual rate of return would be

$$\sqrt[v]{2.0 \times 0.5} - 1 = 0.0.$$

Growth stock. Stock of a company with a record of growth in earnings at a relatively rapid rate.

Holding company. A corporation which owns the securities of another, in most cases with voting control.

Implied return. See Implicit discount rate.

Implicit discount rate. Basically, the implicit discount rate (or implied return) for a stock is the same as the yield to maturity for a bond. It is the expected average annualized rate of return that equates the current price with the forecasted dividend stream.

Inactive stock. An issue traded on an exchange or in the over-the-counter market in which there is a relatively low volume of transactions. Volume may be no more than a few hundred shares a week or even less.*

Indenture. A written agreement under which bonds and debentures are issued, setting forth maturity date, interest rate, and other terms.*

Independence (statistical). If two variables are statistically independent, changes in the two variables are unrelated. Knowledge of the changes in one is of no value in predicting the other. (The weak form of the efficient market hypothesis asserts the statistical independence of successive price changes.)

Index. A statistical yardstick expressed in terms of percentages of a base year or years. For instance, the Federal Reserve Board's index of industrial production is based on 1967 as 100. An index is not an average.*

Indifference curve. An indifference curve represents combinations of, say, risk and return, that are equally valued. For risk averters, indifference curves are convex from below when return is measured on the vertical axis and risk on the horizontal axis. The shape varies with the risk-return preferences of the individual.

Information coefficients (IC's). The term used to describe the correlation coefficients derived from tabulations of ex ante predictions of performance and ex post results.

Institutional investor. An organization whose primary purpose is to invest its own assets or those held in trust by it for others. Includes pension funds, investment companies, insurance companies, universities, and banks.*

Intangible assets. See Assets.

Interest. Payments a borrower pays a lender for the use of the lender's money. A corporation pays interest on its bonds to its bondholders.*

Interest coverage. The number of times that interest charges are earned, found by dividing the (total) fixed charges into the earnings available for such charges (either before or after deducting income taxes).

Interest-rate risk. When interest rates rise the market value of fixed-income contracts (such as bonds) declines. Similarly, when interest rates decline the market value of fixed-income contracts increases. Interest-rate risk is the risk associated with these fluctuations.

Internal rate of return. Term analogous to the familiar yield to maturity on a bond. The internal rate of return is the rate of discount which makes the net present value of an investment equal to zero. In the case of a bond,

$$P_o - \sum_{t=1}^{N} \frac{I_t}{(1 + i)^t} + \frac{P_N}{(1 + i)^N} = 0,$$

where P_o is the initial price, P_N is the terminal price, I_t is the interest in year t, i is the internal rate of return.

Intrinsic value. The value that asset "ought" to have as judged by an investor. Discrepancies between current market value and intrinsic value are often the basis of decisions to buy or sell the asset.

Inventories. Current assets representing the present stock of finished merchandise, goods in process of manufacture, raw materials used in manufacture, and sometimes miscellaneous supplies such as packing and shipping material. These are usually stated at cost or market value, whichever is lower.

Investing. To forego present spending in exchange for expected future benefits. Since today's price is known, investing entails a certain sacrifice in hopes of attaining an uncertain future benefit.

Investment bankers. Also known as underwriters they stand between the corporation issuing new securities and the public. The usual practice is for one or more investment bankers to buy outright from a corporation a new issue of stocks or bonds. The group forms a syndicate to sell the securities to individuals and institutions.*

Investment company. A company or trust which uses its capital to invest in other companies. There are two principal types: the closed-end and the open-end, or mutual fund. Shares in closed-end investment companies are readily transferable in the open market and are bought and sold like other shares. Capitalization of these companies remains the same unless action is taken to change, which is seldom. Open-end funds sell their own new shares to investors, stand ready to buy back their old shares, and are not listed. Open-end funds are so called because their capitalization is not fixed; they issue more shares as people want them.*

Issue. Any of a company's securities, or the act of distributing such securities.*

Least-square regression line. Minimizes the sum of the squares of the vertical deviations of observations from a line drawn through them. For example, if a regression line is fitted to points representing pairs of values of x_i and x_j, the equation is

$$x_i = a + bx_j.$$

The squared vertical distances of the actual values of x_i from the theoretical values, given its relationship to x_j are minimized. The mean values of x_i and x_j will always be a point on the regression line.

Leverage. The effect on the per-share earnings of the common stock of a company when large sums must be paid for bond interest or preferred stock dividends, or both, before the common stock is entitled to share in earnings. Leverage may be advantageous for the common stock when earnings are good but may work against the common when earnings decline. Example: Company A has 1,000,000 shares of common stock outstanding, no other securities. Earnings drop from $1,000,000 to $800,000 or from $1 to 80 cents a share, a decline of 20 per cent. Company B also has 1,000,000 shares of common but must pay $500,000 annually in bond interest. If earnings amount to $1,000,000, there is $500,000 available for the common or 50 cents a share. But earnings drop to $800,000 so there is only $300,000 available for the common, or 30 cents a share—a drop of 40 per cent. Or suppose earnings of the company with only common stock increased from $1,000,000 to $1,500,000—earnings per share would go from $1 to $1.50, or an increase of 50 per cent. But if earnings of the company which had to pay $500,000 in bond interest increased that much—earnings per common share would jump from 50 cents to $1 a share, or 100 per cent. When a company has common stock only, no leverage exists because all earnings are available for the common, although relatively large fixed charges payable for lease of substantial plant assets may have an effect similar to that of a bond issue.*

Liabilities. All the claims against a corporation. Liabilities include accounts and wages and salaries payable, dividends declared payable, accrued taxes payable, fixed or long-term liabilities such as mortgage bonds, debentures, and bank loans.*

Lien. A claim against property. A bond is usually secured by a lien against specified property of a company.*

Limit order. An order to buy or sell a stated amount of a security at a specified price, or at a better price.

Liquidation. The process of converting securities or other property into cash. The dissolution of a company, with cash remaining after sale of its assets and payment of all indebtedness being distributed to the shareholders.*

Liquidity. The ability of the market in a particular security to absorb a reasonable amount of buying or selling at reasonable price changes.

Liquidity is one of the most important characteristics of a good market.*

Liquidity market line. A security market line for a group of stocks with approximately the same market liquidity.

Liquidity ratio. A measure of financial liquidity: cash plus marketable securities divided by current liabilities.

Liquidity risk. The possibility of sustaining a loss from current market value by the process of liquidation, or converting the investment into cash.

Logarithmic change. The use of absolute and percentage price changes can be confusing. Clearly, a $1 price change for a $10 stock is 10 percent while a $1 price change for a $100 stock is only 1 percent. Also, if a stock rises from $50 to $100 it appreciates 100 percent. However, if the stock then falls from $100 back to the original $50 the decline is only 50 percent. Since the difference between two logarithms measures the rate of change (instead of the magnitude of change) logarithms eliminate the confusion that arises when dealing with absolute price changes. By definition, a logarithm of a number is the power to which the base (say 10) must be raised to yield that number. Thus, the base 10 logarithms for 10, 100 and 1000 are 1, 2 and 3 respectively. If the price of one stock appreciated from $10 to $100 its absolute appreciation would be $90. If another holding appreciated from $100 to $1000 its absolute appreciate would be $900. In each case, however, the difference between the logarithms is 1—indicating that the rate for change from $10 to $100 is the same as from $100 to $1000.

Long. Signifies ownership of securities: "I am long 100 U.S. Steel" means the speaker owns 100 shares.*

Margin. The amount paid by the customer when using credit to buy a security. Under Federal Reserve regulations, the initial margin required in the past years has ranged from 50 percent of the purchase price all the way to 100 percent.*

Market model. Describes the relationship between the returns on individual securities (or portfolios) and the returns on the market portfolios. Specifically, the market model holds that returns on an individual security (or portfolio) are linearly related to an index of market returns. As such, the market model provides the conceptual foundation for the single-index portfolio selection model. (See Characteristic lines.)

Market order. An order to buy or sell a stated amount of a security at the most advantageous price.*

Market portfolio. Includes all risky assets in proportion to their market value. In the capital asset pricing model, it is the optimum portfolio of risky assets for all investors. Graphically, it is located at the point of tangency of a line drawn from the risk-free rate of return to the efficient frontier of risky assets.

Market price. In the case of a security, market price is usually considered the last reported price at which the stock or bond sold.*

Markowitz model. Delineates the decisions that will be made by a population of normal investors—each exercising his or her personal preferences.

Maturity. The date on which a loan or a bond or debenture comes due and is to be paid off.*

Mean absolute deviation. The mean absolute deviation is the average of the absolute values (the signs are disregarded) of the deviations of a group of observations from their expected value. Symbolically it is

$$\frac{\Sigma |x_i - \bar{x}|}{N}.$$

Median. The median of a distribution is the value that divides the number of observations in half. If the distribution is normal, the mean and the median will coincide. If the distribution is not normal and has positive skewness, the mean will exceed the median. If the skewness is negative, the mean will be below the median.

Member corporation. A securities brokerage firm, organized as a corporation with at least one member of the New York Stock Exchange, Inc. who is an officer and a holder of voting stock in the corporation.*

Member firm. A securities brokerage firm organized as a partnership and having at least one general partner who is a member of the New York Stock Exchange, Inc.*

Member organization. This term includes New York Stock Exchange Member Firm and Member Corporation.*

Modern investment theory (MIT). See Modern portfolio theory.

Modern portfolio theory (MPT). The theoretical constructs that enable investment managers to classify, estimate, and control the sources of risk and return. In popular usage, the term is not limited to "portfolio" theory. Instead, the term encompasses all notions of modern investment, as well as portfolio, theory. Accordingly, MPT is synonymous with such terms as new investment technology (NIT) and modern investment theory (MIT).

Modigliani-Cohn thesis. The hypothesis that inflation has an advantageous impact on a corporate debt that (with other inflation-related factors) has been systematically overlooked by investment analysts.

Modigliani-Miller (M-M hypothesis). The hypothesis that the market pricing mechanism will adjust a firm's cost of capital so as to minimize the importance of the firm's internal decisions regarding capital structure.

Multi-index model. A portfolio selection model that is based on the relationship between each security's rate of return and the rate of return of homogeneous groups of securities that move together as groups but whose group movements are unrelated.

Multiple correlation. A measure of the relationship between one variable (the dependent variable) and two or more other variables (the independent variables) simultaneously. It is an extension of simple correlation to include more than one independent variable.

Municipal bond. A bond issued by a state or a political subdivision, such as county, city, town, or village. The term also designates bonds issued by state agencies and authorities. In general, interest paid on municipal bonds is exempt from federal income taxes and state and local income taxes within the state of issue.

Mutual fund. See Investment company.

NASD. The National Association of Securities Dealers, Inc. An association of brokers and dealers in the over-the-counter securities business organized to "adopt, administer and enforce rules of fair practice and rules to prevent fradulent and manipulative acts and practices, and in general to promote just and equitable principles of trade for the protection of investors."*

NASDAQ. An automated information network which provides brokers and dealers with price quotations on securities traded over-the-counter. NASDAQ is an acronym for National Association of Securities Dealers Automated Quotations.*

Negotiable. Refers to a security, title to which is transferable by delivery.*

Net asset value. A term usually used in connection with investment companies, meaning net asset value per share. It is common practice for an investment company to compute its assets daily, or even twice daily, by totaling the market value of all securities owned. All liabilities are deducted, and the balance divided by the number of shares outstanding. The resulting figure is the net asset value per share.*

Net change. The change in the price of a security from the closing price on one day and the closing price on the following day on which the stock is traded. The net change is ordinarily the last figure on the stock price list. The mark $+1\frac{1}{8}$ means up $1.125 a share from the last sale on the previous day the stock traded.*

Net quick assets. A measure of financial liquidity: quick assets (current assets minus inventories) minus current liabilities.

New investment technology (NIT). See Modern portfolio theory.

New issue. A stock or bond sold by a corporation for the first time. Proceeds may be used to retire outstanding securities of the company, for new plant or equipment, or for additional working capital.*

New York Stock Exchange composite index. See New York Stock Exchange common stock index.

Nominal return. The nominal return on an asset is the rate of return in monetary terms, i.e., unadjusted for any change in the price level. The nominal return is contrasted with the real return which is adjusted for changes in the price level.

Noncumulative. A preferred stock on which unpaid dividends do not accrue. Omitted dividends are, as a rule, gone forever.*

Nonmarket risk. See Residual risk.

"Normalized" earnings. The earnings one would expect in a "normal" or mid-cyclical year. There is no general agreement about the best way to normalize earnings, but it is not uncommon to use a moving average for three, four, or five or more years. Normalized earnings are sometimes called "steady-state" earnings.

Normative theories. Normative means "normal" or "standard". In economics, a normative theory refers to the way investors "normally" behave. In this context, portfolio theory is a normative theory—it specifies how normal risk-averse investors will behave.

NYSE. An abbreviation for the New York Stock Exchange.

NYSE Common Stock Index. A value-weighted index (one where the weight given each stock corresponds to the market value of the company's outstanding shares) of all common stocks listed on the New York Stock Exchange.

Odd lot. An amount of stock less than the established 100-share unit or 10-share unit of trading: from 1 to 99 shares for the great majority of issues, 1 to 9 for so-called inactive stocks.*

Off-board. This term may refer to transactions over-the-counter in unlisted securities, or to a transaction involving listed shares which was not executed on a national securities exchange.*

Offer. The price at which a person is ready to sell. Opposed to bid, the price at which one is ready to buy.

One-factor model. See Single-index model.

Open-end investment company. See Investment company.

Operating leverage. See Asset turnover.

Optimizers. See Portfolio optimization.

Option. A right to buy (call) or sell (put) a fixed amount of a given stock at a specified price within a limited period of time. The purchasers of options hope that the stock's price will go up (if they bought a call) or down (if they bought a put) by an amount sufficient to provide a profit greater than the cost of the contract and the commission and other fees required to exercise the contract. If the stock price moves in the opposite direction, the price paid for the option is lost entirely. Individuals who write (sell) options are obliged to deliver or buy the stock at the specified price.*

Over-the-counter. A market for securities made up of securities dealers who may or may not be members of a securities exchange. Over-the-counter is mainly a market made over the telephone. Thousands of companies have insufficient shares outstanding, stockholders, or earnings to warrant application for listing on the New York Stock Exchange, Inc. Securities of these companies are traded in the over-the-counter market between dealers who act either as principals or as brokers for customers. The over-the-counter market is the principal market for U.S. Government and municipal bonds.*

Owners' equity. Capital invested by stockholders.

Paper profit. An unrealized profit on a security still held. Paper profits become realized profits only when the security is sold.*

Par. In the case of a common share, par means a dollar amount assigned to the share by the company's charter. Par value may also be used to compute the dollar amount of the common shares on the balance sheet. Par value has little significance so far as market value of common stock is concerned. Many companies today issue no-par stock but give a stated per share value on the balance sheet. In the case of preferred shares and bonds, however, par is important. It often signifies the dollar value upon which dividends on preferred stocks, and interest on bonds, are figured. The issuer of a 6 percent bond promises to pay that percentage of the bond's par value annually.*

Participating preferred. A preferred stock which is entitled to its stated dividend and, also, to additional dividends on a specified basis upon payment of dividends on the common stock.*

Passive management. A style of investment management that seeks to attain average risk-adjusted performance.

Performance index. A "total return" index of investment performance. A performance index differs from the popular market indexes, or so-called averages (such as the Dow Jones Industrial Average) in that the popular measures do not include the return derived from dividends and other distributions to shareholders.

Performance measurement. The MPT application area involved with the measurement of risk-adjusted performance.

Point. In the case of shares of stock, a point means $1. If ABC shares rises 3 points, each share has risen $3. In the case of bonds a point means $10, since a bond is quoted as a percentage of $1,000. A bond which rises 3 points gains 3 percent of $1,000, or $30 in value. An advance from 87 to 90 would mean an advance in dollar value from $870 to $900 for each $1,000 bond. In the case of market averages, the word point means merely that and no more. If, for example, the Dow-Jones Industrial average rises from 870.25 to 871.25, it has risen a point. A point in this average, however, is not equivalent to $1.*

Portfolio. Holdings of securities by an individual or institution. A portfolio may contain bonds, preferred stocks and common stocks of various types of enterprises.*

Portfolio characteristic line. See Characteristic line.

Portfolio optimization. Starting with a universe of securities that has been valued in terms of (a) expected return, (b) variances of expected return, and (c) covariance of return with every other security under consideration, the process of portfolio optimization involves selecting the portfolio that minimizes risk for a given level of risk. In practice, the computerized optimization programs can impose manifold constraints on the characteristics of the resultant portfolio. Typical constraints would be that the resultant portfolio have no more than 5 percent of the portfolio's value in a single stock, that the average current yield be at least 4 percent per annum, etc.

Positive theories. A positive theory is best described by an analogy to a machine. In a "positive" machine, the outcomes are determined by the mechanism. In a similar sense, a positive theory describes a mechanism that can be used for prediction. Portfolio theory is a positive theory. Basically, portfolio theory holds that if investors are risk averse and act as portfolio theory suggests, the price-setting mechanism relating risk and expected return will be consistent and can be predicted.

Preferred stock. A class of stock with a claim on the company's earnings before payment may be made on the common stock and usually entitled to priority over common stock if the company liquidates. Usually entitled to dividends at a specified rate—when declared by the Board of Directors and before payment of a dividend on the common stock—depending upon the terms of the issue.*

Premium. The amount by which a preferred stock, bond or option may sell above its par value. In the case of a new issue of bonds or stocks, premium is the amount the market price rises over the original selling price. Also refers to a charge sometimes made when a stock is borrowed to make delivery on a short sale. May refer, also, to redemption price of a bond or preferred stock if it is higher than face value.*

Present value. The actual value discounted at an appropriate rate of interest. The discounting reflects the productivity of capital and the risk premium. For example, the present value of a share of stock, V_o, is the stream of future payments discounted to perpetuity, or,

$$\sum_{t=1}^{\infty} \frac{P_t}{(1 + i)^t}$$

where P_t are the payments in period t and i is the rate of discount.

Price-earnings ratio. The price or a share of stock divided by earnings per share for a 12-month period. For example, a stock selling at $50 a share and earning $5 a share has a price earnings ratio, or P/E, of 10.

Primary distribution. Also called primary offering. The original sale of a company's securities.*

Principal. The person for whom a broker executes an order, or a dealer buying or selling for his own account. The term "principal" may also refer to a person's capital or to the face amount of a bond.

Probability distribution. A distribution of possible outcomes with an indication of the subjective or objective probability of each occurrence.

Prospectus. The official selling circular that must be given to purchasers of new securities registered with the Securities and Exchange Commission so investors can evaluate those securities before or at the time of purchase. It highlights the much longer Registration Statement filed with the Commission. It warns the issue has not been approved (or disapproved) by the Commission and discloses such material information as the issuer's property and business, the nature of the security offered, use of proceeds, issuer's competition and prospects, management's experience, history, and remuneration and certified financial statements. A preliminary version of the prospectus, used by brokers to obtain buying indications from investors, is called a red herring. This is because of a front-page notice containing a large red legend warning that the document is preliminary and "subject to completion or amendment".*

Proxy. Written authorization given by a shareholder to someone else to vote at a shareholders meeting.*

Proxy statement. Information required by SEC to be given stockholders as a prerequisite to solicitation of proxies for a security subject to the requirements of Securities Exchange Act.*

Quick assets. Measure of financial liquidity: current assets minus inventories.

Quotation. Often shortened to "quote." The highest bid to buy and the lowest offer to sell a security in a given market at a given time.*

Rally. A brisk rise following a decline in the general price level of the market or in an individual stock.*

Random selection. Random selection is similar to picking stocks by throwing darts at a stock listing. Technically, random selection means that each element in the relevant population has a known and positive probability of selection.

Random-walk model. The name historically given to the weak form of the efficient market hypothesis. A random walk implies that there is no discernible pattern of travel. The size and direction of the next step cannot be predicted from the size and direction of the last or even from all the previous steps. Random walk is a term used in mathematics and statistics to describe a process in which successive changes are statistically independent. The serial correlation is zero.

Real return. An inflation-adjusted return. (See Nominal return.)

Record date. The date on which one must be registered as a shareholder on a stock book of a company in order to receive a declared dividend or, among other things, to vote on company affairs.*

Red herring. See Prospectus.

Redemption price. The price at which a bond may be redeemed before maturity, at the option of the issuing company. Redemption value also applies to the price the company must pay to call in certain types of preferred stock.

Refinancing. Same as refunding. New securities are sold by a company and the money is used to retire existing securities. Object may be to save interest costs, extend the maturity of the loan, or both.*

Reflection. A situation in which stock prices are believed to reverse as if they are "reflected" away from certain "resistance" or "support" levels.

Registered bond. A bond which is registered on the books of the issuing company in the name of the owner. It can be transferred only when endorsed by the registered owner.

Registered representative. In a New York Stock Exchange Member Organization, an employee who has met the requirements of the Exchange as to background and knowledge of the securities business. Also known as an account executive*.

Registration. Before a public offering may be made of new securities by a company, or of outstanding securities by controlling stockholders—through the mails or in interstate commerce—the securities must be registered under the Securities Act of 1933. Registration statement is filed with the SEC by the issuer. It must disclose pertinent information relating to the company's operations, securities, management and purpose of the public offering. Securities of railroads under jurisdiction of the Interstate Commerce Commission, and certain other types of securities, are exempted. On security offerings involving less than $300,000, less information is required. Before a security may be admitted to dealings on a national securities exchange, it must be registered under the Securities Exchange Act of 1934. The application for registration must be filed with the exchange and the SEC by the company issuing the securities. It must disclose pertinent information relating to the company's operations, securities and management.*

Regression analysis. Regression or correlation analysis is a statistical technique for estimating the relationship between one variable (dependent variable) and one or more other variables (independent variables). The relationship estimated, usually a least-squares regression equation, is often used to predict the value of the dependent variable, given the values of the independent variable, or variables.

Regression coefficient. A regression coefficient indicates the responsiveness of one variable to changes in another. If the relationship between two variables is described by a straight line, the regression coefficient is the slope of the line. The regression coefficient between rates of return on an asset and rates of return on the market is called the beta coefficient.

Regular way delivery. Unless otherwise specified, securities sold on the New York Stock Exchange are to be delivered to the buying broker by the selling broker and payment made to the selling broker by the buying broker on the fifth business day after the transaction. Regular way delivery for bonds is the following business day.*

Regulation T. The federal regulation governing the amount of credit which may be advanced by brokers and dealers to customers for the purchase of securities.*

Regulation U. The federal regulation governing the amount of credit which may be advanced by a bank to its customers for the purchase of listed stocks.*

Reinvestment rate. The percentage of a company's earnings that are retained for investment.

REIT. Real Estate Investment Trust, an organization similar to an investment company but concentrating its holdings in real estate investments. Generally REIT's are required to distribute as much as 90 percent of their income.*

Relative response coefficients. Used in the calculation of the so-called "fundamental" betas, a relative response coefficient is the ratio of the expected response of a security to the expected response of the market if both the security and the market are impacted by the same event.

Relative strength continuation. Generally referred to as merely "relative strength," this is the occasionally observed tendency for stocks that have either above-average or below-average performance in one period to continue that performance in the "next" period.

Replacement cost accounting. Balance sheets tend to be misleading because they typically value assets at cost plus installation. To overcome this problem assets can be valued at replacement cost. For fiscal years ending on or after December 25, 1979 the Financial Accounting Standards Board requires approximately 1,350 of the largest U.S. corporations to report supplementary information based on constant (inflation-adjusted) dollars and current (replacement) costs.

Residual risk. The aggregate of specific risk and the risk arising from extramarket covariance.

Residual standard deviation. A summary measure of the distances from the plotted points to a "least squares" regression line. The residual standard deviation is an ex post measure of a security's specific, or non-market, risk.

Resistance level. A price level that is believed to pose a barrier to upward price movements.

Return. See Yield.

Return on assets (sometimes abbreviated ROA). The percentage of new profit earned on total assets. As such it provides a comparative link between a key item on the balance sheet (assets) and a key item on the income statement (income).

Return on equity (sometimes abbreviated ROE). A key measure of the profitability of an equity investment—is the net income earned by a company expressed as a percentage return on the stockholders' investment. Its relationship to return on assets and financial leverage is as follows:

Return on assets × Financial leverage = Return on equity

$$\frac{\text{Earnings}}{\text{Assets}} \times \frac{\text{Assets}}{\text{Equity}} = \frac{\text{Earnings}}{\text{Equity}}$$

As such it provides a comparative link between a key balance sheet item (equity) and a key income statement item (income).

Return on sales. Return on sales (sometimes abbreviated ROS and sometimes called the operating margin, or net profit margin) is the percentage of profit earned on sales. It is calculated by dividing net income, or earnings, by net sales. As such it provides a comparative link between two key items on the income statement—earnings and sales.

Reward to variability ratio. The reward-to-variability ratio is the risk premium on an asset per unit of risk as measured by the variability or standard deviation.

Rights. When a company wants to raise more funds by issuing additional securities, it may give its stockholders the opportunity, ahead of others, to buy the new securities in proportion to the number of shares each owns. The piece of paper evidencing this privilege is called a right. Because the additional stock is usually offered to stockholders below the current market price, rights ordinarily have a market value of their own and are actively traded. In most cases they must be exercised within a relatively short period. Failure to exercise or sell rights may result in actual loss to the holder.*

Risk aversion. All rational investors can be characterized as being "risk averse." This means that for any level of return a rational investor will prefer the lowest level of available risk. Similarly, for any given level of risk a rational investor will prefer the highest level of available return. Basically risk aversion means riskiness matters and is disliked. A risk averter will hold a portfolio of more than one stock in order to reduce risk for a given expected return. Technically, the utility function of a risk averter will depend on rate of return and risk and will not be linear. This implies diminishing marginal utility of wealth. This implies that a risk-averse investor will incur additional risk only in exchange for an expected higher rate of return.

Risk-free asset. Typically a noncallable, default-free bond such as a short-term government security. While such an asset is not risk-free in an inflation sense, it is (under the rationale that the government can always print money) risk-free in a dollar sense.

Risk-free rate of return. The risk-free rate of return is the return on an asset that is virtually riskless. For example, Treasury bills maturing in one year have a precisely predictable nominal rate of return for one year. The risk premium on an asset is the rate of return in excess of the risk-free rate. The risk-free rate is normally used in portfolio theory to represent the rate for lending or borrowing.

Risk neutrality. Risk neutrality means risk does not matter. A risk-neutral investor cares only about rate of return and would hold a portfolio of one asset—the one with the highest expected rate of return. Risk neutrality implies constant marginal utility of wealth. The utility function for such an investor is linear.

Risk premium. On an asset, the actual return minus the risk-free rate of return. In the capital asset pricing model, the risk premium for any asset is proportional to its beta—the measure of sensitivity to general market movements. If R_i is the rate of return on an asset, and ρ is the riskless rate, $R_i - \rho$ is the risk premium.

Risk-reward spectrum. A construct used to illustrate that (in a rational market place) higher and higher anticipated rewards are always accompanied by incremental increases in risk (measured as the deviations between expected and actual results). The left end of the spectrum represents the lowest risk investment—typically short-term government obligations. Moving to the right on the spectrum—through a continuum of common stock investments—each incremental increase in expected return is accompanied by an incremental increase in risk.

R-squared (R^2). The proportion of a security's (or a portfolio's) total risk that is market related. Technically, R-squared is the coefficient of determination.

Round lot. A unit of trading or a multiple thereof. On the NYSE the unit the trading is generally 100 shares in stocks and $1,000 par value in the case of bonds. In some inactive stocks, the unit of trading is 10 shares.*

Rule of "72". A convenient technique for either mental or pencil-and-paper *estimation* of compound interest rates—derived from the fact that a 7.2 percent return per year is the interest rate that will double the value of an investment in ten years. Hence, "years to double" an investment with a given annual rate of return can be estimated by dividing the "rate of return" into 72. For example, if an investment's annual return is 6 percent, its value will double in *approximately* 12 years (72 ÷ 6). If an investment's annual return is 9 percent, its value will double in *approximately* eight (72 ÷ 9) years. Similarly, the "rate of return" that will double the value of an investment in a given number of years can be estimated by dividing the number of "years to double" into 72. For example, the value of an investment will double in six years if the annual rate of return is *approximately* 12 percent (72 ÷ 6).

Rule of halves. The benchmark for a "typical" balance sheet. That is, on the left side half the assets are current and half are fixed. On the right side, half is in the liability category and half is in the owner's equity category. Further, the rule of halves can be applied to the liability category where "typically" half are current and half are long-term.

Runs. A sequence of price changes in the same direction. The number of runs in a sequence of price changes is the number of reversals in sign plus one. Thus, if a series of price changes is described as zero, positive and negative, the sequence $+ + + - + + + + - - 0 - -$ would have six runs.

Sampling. Sampling is the process of selecting a subset of a population. It may or may not be random. The usefulness of a sample depends upon its representativeness, or the degree to which one can make inferences about the excluded population on the basis of the sample.

S&P 425. An index of the 425 industrial stocks that comprise the S&P 500.

S&P 500. A composite index of 500 stocks—425 industrials with the remainder railroads and utilities. In contrast to the Dow Jones Industrial Average (DJIA) the weighting of the relative importance of the component stocks in the S&P 500 corresponds to the market value of the company's outstanding shares.

Seat. A traditional figure-of-speech for a membership on an exchange.*

SEC. The Securities and Exchange Commission, established by Congress to help protect investors. The SEC administers the Securities

Act of 1933, the Securities Exchange Act of 1934, the Securities Act Amendments of 1975, the Trust Indenture Act, the Investment Company Act, the Investment Advisers Act, and the Public Utility Holding Company Act.*

Secondary distribution. Also known as a secondary offering. The redistribution of a block of stock some time after it has been sold by the issuing company. The sale is handled by a securities firm or group of firms and the shares are usually offered at a fixed price which is related to the current market price of the stock.*

Security characteristic line. See Characteristic lines.

Security market line. A construct used to portray the relationship between risk and return. In equilibrium, every security will plot on this line.

Security market plane. A three dimensional diagram that incorporates the security market line and the security yield line.

Security valuation models. Typically based on the precept that the value of a share of common stock is the sum of the discounted present value of the estimated future stream of dividends.

Selection risk. See Residual risk.

Semistandard deviation. The semistandard deviation is analogous to the standard deviation, but only the observations below the mean are taken into account. The deviations, $(x_i - \bar{x})$, are all negative. The measure is relevant if one is interested only in downside or adverse risk.

Separation theorem. States that the choice of an optimum portfolio is independent of, or separate from, the optimal combination of risky assets. The latter is the same for all investors if lending and borrowing are allowed. Individual needs determine only the amount of borrowing or lending.

Serial correlation. Measures the degree to which what happens "next" in a series of events (such as price changes) is related to what happened previously. Since the weak form of the efficient market hypothesis (also known as the random-walk model) holds that a stock's "next" price change cannot be predicted from its previous price changes, the serial correlation of period-to-period price changes (such as day-to-day or week-to-week) is frequently used to test this hypothesis.

Settlement. Conclusion of a securities transactions in which a customer pays a debit balance owed to a broker or receives from the broker the proceeds from a sale.*

Short covering. Buying stock to return stock previously borrowed to make delivery on a short sale.*

Short position. Stocks sold short and not covered as of a particular date. On the NYSE, a tabulation is issued once a month listing all issues on the Exchange in which there was a short position of 5,000 or more shares and issues in which the short position had changed by 2,000 or more shares in the preceding month.*

Short sale. Short sales are made by people who expect the market to go down. In a regular securities transaction, shares are bought first and sold later. In a short transaction, the sale comes first, the purchase later. A short sale is effected by borrowing stock through a broker and selling it at the current market price. The proceeds of the sale are then held as collateral for the loan of the stock. To close out the short position the borrowed stock must be replaced. This is done by buying an equivalent number of shares at the then current market price. If a short sale is made at $100 and the short can later be closed by buying the stock at $90, there will be a $10 per share profit (before any intervening interest on the loan and repayment of any individual income).

Single-index model. A portfolio selection model which uses the relationship between each security's rate of return and the rate of return on a market index as a substitute for explicit data on the covariance of each pair of securities under study.

Sinking fund. Money regularly set aside by a company to redeem its bonds, debentures, or preferred stock from time to time as specified in the indenture or charter.*

SIPC. Securities Investor Protection Corporation which provides funds for use, if necessary, to protect customers' cash and securities which may be on deposit with a SIPC member firm in the event the firm fails and is liquidated under the provisions of the SIPC Act. SIPC is not a Government Agency. It is a non-profit membership corporation created, however, by an Act of Congress.*

Skewness. Skewness is a measure of the asymmetry of a distribution. A normal distribution is symmetrical and has no skewness. If there are more observations to the left of the mean, the skewness is positive; if more to the right, negative.

Specialist. A member of the New York Stock Exchange, Inc. who has two functions. First, to maintain an orderly market insofar as reasonably practicable, in the stocks in which he or she is registered as a specialist. In order to maintain an orderly market, the Exchange expects the specialist to buy or sell for his or her own account, to a reasonable degree, when there is a temporary disparity between supply and demand. Second, the specialist acts as a broker's broker. When a commission broker on the Exchange floor receives a limit order, say, to buy at $50 a stock then selling at $60—it is not practical to wait at the post where the stock is traded to see if the price reaches the specified level. In such cases the order can be left with the specialist, who will try to execute it in the market if and when the stock declines to the specified price. There are about 400 specialists on the NYSE.*

Speculator. One who is willing to assume a relatively large risk in the hope of gain.*

Split. The division of the outstanding shares of a corporation into a larger number of shares. A 3-for-1 split by a company with 1 million shares outstanding results in 3 million shares outstanding. Each holder of 100 shares before the 3-for-1 stock split would have 300 shares, although the proportionate equity in the company would remain the same: 100 parts of 1 million are the equivalent of 300 parts of 3 million.*

Stable Paretian distribution. There is considerable evidence that stock price changes are not "normally" distributed but rather approximate what is known as a "stable Paretian" distribution. Basically, this distribution is used to accommodate the abnormally large number of "large" price changes.

Standard deviation. The standard deviation is a commonly used measure of dispersion. It is the square root of the variance. It is based on deviations of observations from the mean and is therefore in the same units as the observations. A measure of relative dispersion is the standard deviation divided by the mean (the coefficient of variation). This is often useful in comparing distributions that differ substantially in the magnitude of the numbers. The formula for the standard deviation, σ, is

$$\sqrt{\frac{\Sigma(x_i - \bar{x})^2}{N}}.$$

Standard error (of estimate). Provides a probabilistic measure of the differences between "true" and "sample estimated" values (of alpha and beta).

Standard and Poor's Index. See S&P 425 and S&P 500.

Stock ahead. Sometimes an investor who has entered an order to buy or sell a stock at a certain price will see transactions at that price reported on the ticker tape while his or her own order has not been executed. The reason is that other buy and sell orders at the same price came in to the specialist ahead of this order and had priority.*

Stock dividend. A dividend paid in securities rather than cash. The dividend may be additional shares of the issuing company, or in shares of another company (usually a subsidiary) held by the company.*

Stockholder of record. A stockholder whose name is registered on the books of the issuing corporation.*

Stop limit order. A stop order which becomes a limit order after the specified stop price has been reached.*

Stop order. An order to buy at a price above or sell at a price below the current market. Stop buy orders are generally used to limit loss or protect unrealized profits on a short sale. Stop sell orders are generally used to protect unrealized profits or limit loss on a holding. A stop order becomes a market order when the stock sells at or beyond the specified price and, thus, may not necessarily be executed at that price.*

Street. The New York financial community in the Wall Street area.*

Street name. Securities held in the name of a broker instead of the customer's name are said to be carried in a "street name." This occurs when the securities have been bought on margin or when the customer wishes the security to be held by the broker.*

Support level. A price level that is believed to pose a barrier to downward price movements.

Sustainable dividend growth rate. The theoretical rate at which dividends can grow (derived from the product of the company's return on equity and earnings reinvestment rate).

Syndicate. A group of investment bankers who together underwrite and distribute a new issue of securities or a large block of an outstanding issue.

Systematic risk. Risk that is related to market covariance—the tendency for an individual security's or a portfolio's return to fluctuate with the return on the market portfolio. It can be estimated statistically from the market model. The percentage of total variability that is systematic is given by the coefficient of determination and the degree of responsiveness to market movements is measured by beta.

Take-over. The acquiring of one corporation by another—usually in a friendly merger but sometimes marked by a "proxy fight". In "unfriendly" take-over attempts, the potential buying company may offer a price well above current market values, new securities, and other inducements to stockholders. The management of the subject company might ask for a better price or fight the take-over or merger with another company.*

Technical analysis. Analysis based on the study of historical price and volume data. The usefulness of technical analysis is challenged by the weak form of the efficient market hypothesis which holds that the analysis of historical price and volume information is a useless endeavor.

Tender offer. A public offer to buy shares from existing stockholders of one public corporation by another company or other organization under specified terms good for a certain time period. Stockholders are asked to "tender" (surrender) their holdings for stated value, usually at a premium above current market price, subject to the tendering of a minimum and maximum number of shares.*

Thin market. A market in which there are comparatively few bids to buy or offers to sell or both. The phrase may apply to a single security or to the entire stock market. In a thin market, price fluctuations between transactions are usually larger than when the market is liquid. A thin market in a particular stock may reflect lack of interest in that issue or a limited supply of or demand for stock in the market.*

Third market. Trading of stock exchange listed securities in the over-the-counter market by non-exchange member brokers and all types of investors.*

Tick. The term used to describe price changes between successive securities transactions. An "up" tick (also called a plus tick) designates a transaction at a higher price than the preceding trade. A "zero-plus" tick is a term used for a transaction at the same price as the preceding trade but higher than the preceding different price. A stock may be sold short only on an up tick, or on a "zero-plus" tick. A down tick, or "minus" tick, is a term used to designate a transaction made at a price lower than the preceding trade. A "zero-minus" tick is a transaction made at the same price as the preceding sale but lower than the preceding different price.

Tick (cumulative). The most sensitive indicator of intraday market activity. Tick measures the net difference of the total number of stocks that have traded up in price from their previous trade and the total number of stocks that have traded down in price from their previous trade.

Ticker. The instruments which display prices and volume of securities transactions within minutes after each trade.

Time-weighted return. Pursuant to the recommendations set forth in the 1968 report by the Bank Administration Institute entitled "Measuring the Investment Performance of Pension Funds" most performance figures are "time weighted." "Time weighting" eliminates the effect of periodic additions and withdrawals that are beyond the control of the investment manager. The time-weighted rate of return is a weighted average of the internal rates of return for subperiods dated by the contribution or withdrawal of funds from a portfolio at the time of each cash inflow or outflow and the dates on which these occur. Rates of return on mutual fund shares are time-weighted rates of return.

Tipees. Persons who come into possession of confidential information. The law holds that a tipee receiving "material inside information" becomes a de facto insider and must either disclose the information publicly or refrain from trading on it. Since it is illegal to enter into securities transactions on the basis of information that is not publicly available, all parties to securities transactions are guaranteed equal access to the same material facts.

Tips. Supposedly "inside" information on corporation affairs.*

Total return. Total return means that all dividends and income are added, and fees, such as brokerage commissions, are subtracted from the aggregate value of a portfolio to arrive at the true measure of "total" performance.

Trader. One who buys and sells for short-term profit.*

Transfer. This term may refer to two different operations. For one, the delivery of a stock certificate from the seller's broker to the buyer's broker and legal change of ownership, normally accomplished within a few days. For another, to record the change of ownership on the books of the corporation by the transfer agent. When the purchaser's name is recorded on the books of the company, dividends, notices of meetings, proxies, financial reports and all pertinent literature sent by the issuer to its securities holders are mailed direct to the new owner.*

Transfer agent. A transfer agent keeps a record of the name of each registered shareowner, his or her address, the number of shares owned, and sees that certificates presented for transfer are properly cancelled and new certificates issued in the name of the transferee.*

Treasury stock. Stock issued by a company but later reacquired. It may be held in the company's treasury indefinitely, reissued to the public, or retired. Treasury stock receives no dividends and has no vote while held by the company.*

Treynor index. The Treynor index of performance is the reward per unit of risk as measured by volatility or beta. It indicates the rate of return on the market index required to make the expected rate of return on a portfolio equal to the risk-free rate.

Turnover rate. The volume of shares traded in a year as a percentage of total shares listed on an Exchange, outstanding for an individual issue or held in an institutional portfolio. In 1975, the turnover rate on the New York Stock Exchange was 21%.*

Underwriter. See Investment banker.

Unlisted. A security not listed on a stock exchange. (See Over-the-counter).

Unsystematic risk. The variability not explained by general market movements. It is avoidable through diversification. Only inefficient portfolios have unsystematic risk. (See Residual risk).

Utility function. It describes the relationship for an individual between various amounts of something such as wealth and the satisfaction it provides. If one's preferences are known, the utility functions can often be approximated by precise mathematical equations. The signs and values of its derivatives indicate the direction and magnitude of changes in utility associated with changes in the amount of the good possessed.

Valuation models. See Security valuation models.

Variance. The variance of a distribution is a measure of variability based on squared deviations of individual observations from the mean value of the distribution. Its square root, the standard deviation, is a commonly used measure of dispersion. The formula for the variance is,

$$\sigma^2 = \frac{\Sigma(x_i - \bar{x})^2}{N}.$$

If the distribution is of future outcomes that are now known with certainty, the variance is a weighted average of the squared deviations and the weights are the probabilities of occurrence. That is,

$$\sigma^2 = \Sigma P_i [x_i - E(x)]^2.$$

Volatility. That part of total variability due to sensitivity to changes in the market. It is systematic and unavoidable risk. It is measured by the beta coefficient. Efficient portfolios have no additional risk, and volatility is the only source of variability in rates of return.

Volume. The number of shares traded in a security or an entire market during a given period. Volume is usually considered on a daily basis and a daily average is computed for longer periods. Record daily volume on the New York Stock Exchange is 81,620,000 shares on October 10, 1979. Average daily volume during 1977 was 20,928,000 shares.*

Voting right. The stockholder's right to vote his or her stock in the affairs of the company. Most common shares have one vote each. Preferred stock usually has the right to vote when preferred dividends are in default for a specified period. The right to vote may be delegated by the stockholder to another person.*

Warrant. A certificate giving the holder the right to purchase securities at a stipulated price within a specified time limit or perpetually. Sometimes a warrant is offered with securities as an inducement to buy.*

Wealth ratio. A wealth ratio is the terminal value of an investment divided by its initial value. It is used in calculating rates of return. The wealth ratio is expressed as W_t/W_o where W_t refers to the terminal value and W_o to the initial value. The annual rate of return compounded continuously is

$$\log_e \frac{\left(\dfrac{W_t}{W_o}\right)}{n},$$

where n is the number of years in the period. The annual rate of return compounded annually is $e^x - 1$, where x is the annual rate compounded continuously.

Weighting. The specification of the relative importance of each of a group of items that are combined. For example, stocks included in indexes may be equally weighted or weighted according to value.

When issued. A short form of "when, as and if issued." The term indicates a conditional transaction in a security authorized for issuance but not as yet actually issued. All "when issued" transactions are on an "if" basis, to be settled if and when the actual security is issued and the Exchange or National Association of Securities Dealers rules the transactions are to be settled.*

Wire house. A member firm of an exchange maintaining a communications network linking either its own branch offices, offices of correspondent firms, or a combination of such offices.*

Working capital. Measure of financial liquidity: current assets minus current liabilities.

Yield. Also known as return. The dividends or interest paid by a company expressed as a percentage of the current price. A stock with a current market value of $40 a share paying dividends at the rate of $2.00 is said to return 5 percent ($2.00 ÷ $40.00). The current return on a bond is figured the same way. A 6 percent $1,000 bond selling at $600 offers a current yield return of 10 percent ($60 ÷ $600).*

Yield curve. A visual representation of the term structure of interest rates.

Yield tilt fund. An alternative to a pure index fund, a yield tilt fund diversifies its holdings among a universe of stocks that is "tilted" in the direction of higher yield—such as the high-yield stocks that comprise the S&P 500. Yield tilt funds are based on the assertion that, since dividend income is taxed at higher rates, the market must compensate for this taxation by providing higher returns for the high-yield segment of the market. If this assertion is true, tax-exempt investors could benefit from this market inefficiency by investing in high-yield stocks.

Yield-to-maturity. The average annualized rate of return that will prevail over the entire multi-period duration of an investment.

Index